Language Endangerment

Up to 90 per cent of humanity's traditional languages and cultures are at risk and may disappear this century. While language endangerment has not achieved the publicity surrounding environmental change and biodiversity loss, it is just as serious, disastrously reducing the variety of human knowledge and thought. This book shows why it matters, why and how it happens, and what communities and scholars can do about it.

David and Maya Bradley provide a new framework for investigating and documenting linguistic, social and other factors which contribute to languages shifting away from their cultural heritage. Illustrated with practical in-depth case studies and examples from the authors' own work in Asia and elsewhere, the book encourages communities to maintain or reclaim their traditional languages and cultures.

DAVID BRADLEY is Professor of Linguistics at La Trobe University and President of the UNESCO Comité International Permanent des Linguistes (International Permanent Committee of Linguists). He has authored or contributed to many books, including the UNESCO *Atlas of Languages in Danger* (1996; 2001; 2010).

MAYA BRADLEY established the Department of Linguistics at La Trobe University after teaching at other universities on three continents. She has co-authored or co-edited several books, including *Language Endangerment and Language Maintenance* (2002).

KEY TOPICS IN LINGUISTIC ANTHROPOLOGY

'Key Topics in Linguistic Anthropology' focuses on the main topics of study and research in linguistic anthropology today. It consists of accessible yet challenging accounts of the most important concepts, phenomena and questions to consider when examining the relationship between language and culture. Some topics have been the subject of study for many years, and are re-examined in the light of new developments in the field; others are issues of growing importance that have not so far been given a sustained treatment. Written by leading experts, and designed to bridge the gap between textbooks and primary literature, the books in the series can either be used on courses and seminars, or as succinct one-stop guides to a particular topic for individual students and researchers.

Published titles:

Speech Communities by Marcyliena Morgan

Language Endangerment by David Bradley and Maya Bradley

Language Endangerment

DAVID BRADLEY
La Trobe University

MAYA BRADLEY
La Trobe University

CAMBRIDGE
UNIVERSITY PRESS

CAMBRIDGE
UNIVERSITY PRESS

University Printing House, Cambridge CB2 8BS, United Kingdom

One Liberty Plaza, 20th Floor, New York, NY 10006, USA

477 Williamstown Road, Port Melbourne, VIC 3207, Australia

314–321, 3rd Floor, Plot 3, Splendor Forum, Jasola District Centre, New Delhi – 110025, India

79 Anson Road, #06–04/06, Singapore 079906

Cambridge University Press is part of the University of Cambridge.

It furthers the University's mission by disseminating knowledge in the pursuit of education, learning, and research at the highest international levels of excellence.

www.cambridge.org
Information on this title: www.cambridge.org/9781107041134
DOI: 10.1017/9781139644570

First published 2019

Printed in the United Kingdom by TJ International Ltd. Padstow Cornwall

A catalogue record for this publication is available from the British Library.

Library of Congress Cataloging-in-Publication Data
Names: Bradley, David, 1947– author. | Bradley, Maya, author.
Title: Language endangerment / David Bradley, Maya Bradley.
Description: New York, NY : Cambridge University Press, [2019] | Series: Key topics in linguistic anthropology | Includes bibliographical references and index.
Identifiers: LCCN 2019013154 | ISBN 9781107041134 (hardback : alk. paper) | ISBN 9781107641709 (pbk. : alk. paper)
Subjects: LCSH: Endangered languages. | Endangered languages–Case studies. | Language obsolescence. | Language obsolescence–Case studies. | Linguistic change. | Linguistic change–Case studies.
Classification: LCC P40.5.E53 B73 2019 | DDC 306.44–dc23
LC record available at https://lccn.loc.gov/2019013154

ISBN 978-1-107-04113-4 Hardback
ISBN 978-1-107-64170-9 Paperback

Contents

Tables

Acknowledgements

We are very grateful to friends and colleagues in many communities in Asia, including the Lisu, Gong, Lahu, Bisu and many others, for their intelligence, patience and thoughtful assistance over many years. We also thank our partner universities and organizations and colleagues there for their co-operation and practical and intellectual help: Mahidol, Chulalaongkorn and Payap universities in Thailand; Yunnan Minzu University, the Chinese Academy of Social Sciences, the Yunnan Academy of Social Sciences and Southwest University of Nationalities in China; and our own university, La Trobe University in Melbourne, Australia and colleagues and students here.

We also acknowledge and thank the following funding organizations: the Australian Research Council (A59701122, A59803475, A00001357, DP0772046), the Intangible Cultural Heritage Section of UNESCO, the Comité International Permanent des Linguistes (CIPL), the Leverhulme Foundation, the Centre National de la Recherche Scientifique (CNRS) in France, the Thailand Research Fund and various universities around the world, most notably La Trobe University since 1982.

To the students who helped us to develop our ideas while teaching them courses on this topic, and contributed their own fascinating and valuable experiences, many thanks! This includes students at La Trobe University over many years as well as 3LSS (London/Leiden/Lyons Summer School), the School of Oriental and African Studies (SOAS), 2009; the Linguistic Society of America (LSA) Summer Institute, the University of Colorado, 2011; the Workshop on Language Contact in Asia and the Pacific, University of Macao, 2012 and Chulalongkorn University hundredth anniversary Linguistics Summer School, Thailand, 2017.

Many research students have worked with us on topics in this area; their theses and other publications are frequently referred to in this volume. Some have also contributed information for case studies in the communities where they work: Edrinnie Kayambazinthu on Malawi and Temmy Thamrin on Minangkabau.

We also acknowledge input from colleagues at our Workshops on the Sociolinguistics of Language Endangerment, supported by CIPL: the first at SOAS in 2009, the second at the LSA Summer Institute in 2011, the third at Yunnan Minzu University in China in 2014, the fourth at Payap University in Thailand in 2015 and the fifth at Cape Town during the twentieth International Congress of Linguists in 2018. We also acknowledge valuable discussions with many colleagues at conferences of the Australian Linguistic Society, the Southeast Asian Linguistics Society, the International Conference on Sino-Tibetan Languages and Linguistics, the eighteenth, nineteenth and twentieth International Congresses of Linguists in Seoul, Geneva and Cape Town, respectively, at the Academia Sinica in Taiwan, the Trace Foundation in New York and the CNRS in Paris, and during seminars and courses given at Dartmouth, Yale, Uppsala, Chulalongkorn, Mahidol, Lisbon, Macao and other universities, also CIPL international workshops on endangered languages at Bogazici University in Turkey, Ivane Javakhishvili Tbilisi State University in Georgia and Vytautas Magnus University in Lithuania.

For comments and suggestions on draft chapters and information for case studies, we thank Rob Amery and his colleagues at Kaurna Warra Karrpanthi, Steve Anderson, Alan N. Baxter, David Brookshaw, Nancy Dorian, Stefan Georg, Juha Janhunen, Edrinnie Kayambazinthu, M. Paul Lewis, Yaron Matras, Andrey Nefedov, Mario Pinharanda Nunes, Daniel Telli, Brett Todd, Edward Vajda, Akira Yamamoto and an anonymous Cambridge University Press reviewer. Matthias Brenzinger and Sheena Shah are the authors of the case study on N‖ng in Chapter 3. There are many others whose comments and help over the years have been of great assistance; we hope they will not be too upset if we cannot name them all, and we thank them too!

For permission to use quotations, we thank Rob Amery and Kaurna Warra Karrpanthi, the Burke Museum of Natural History and Culture, the late Joshua A. Fishman, Michael Krauss, M. Paul Lewis, Matti Morottaja and Tove Skutnabb-Kangas, Bernie Perley, Kirk Person, Anna Chatrina Brunold-Riatsch for Pro Idioms, Akira Yamamoto and Ofelia Zepeda.

1 Introduction

> Obviously we must do some serious rethinking of our priorities, lest
> linguistics go down in history as the only science that presided
> obliviously over the disappearance of 90% of the very field to which
> it is dedicated.
>
> Krauss (1992: 10)

The above strong and emotive quote poses the key problem which
motivates this book. Krauss indicated that most of the endangered
languages then spoken would stop being spoken during the twenty-
first century. In Krauss (2007a: 3) he increases this further, and indicates that 95 per cent of the world's languages are endangered to some
degree. It is clear that a high proportion of the world's linguistic
diversity is endangered, as Robins and Uhlenbeck (1991), Wurm
(1996, 2001), Brenzinger (2007a), Moseley (2007), UNESCO (2009) and
recent editions of the *Ethnologue* since Lewis and Simons (2014), among
many other sources, also indicate.

The current loss of human linguistic diversity is at a higher rate of
biodiversity loss than we are seeing in biological and ecological systems.
It is now normal around the world to be concerned about climate change
and its effects such as bleaching of coral and weather changes; pollution
and other kinds of environmental problems; endangerment and extinction of animal and plant species through habitat loss; overexploitation of
resources and other damage to the ecosystem. Human linguistic diversity has not yet reached the same level of public awareness and concern,
sometimes even among the actual communities whose languages are at
risk. Yet, language is the very thing which makes us human and allows
our societies to function, and a massive reduction in the diversity and
variety of human languages is also a catastrophe with profound consequences for our cultural and intellectual future.

It is very often the case that a language shift takes place while a
community has other urgent concerns such as economic progress,

education for their children, health, integration into wider society and other practical needs. At the same time, people are often not completely aware of the progress of language shift, and may feel that their language is OK, even when it is not. This delayed recognition of language shift (Schmidt, 1990) may lead to a situation where it becomes very difficult to reclaim the language and begin to use it more widely again. Sometimes, there has been a shameful history of minority language suppression, as, for example, in much of North America, Australia and elsewhere, and language reclamation efforts have only become possible once communities have become aware of the problem and policies have changed in recent years.

Linguists and others have long been concerned about language endangerment, starting in antiquity. The Roman Emperor Claudius produced an Etruscan dictionary, which unfortunately has not survived. Various anthropologists and linguists including Franz Boas from the late nineteenth century and Edward Sapir, John Harrington, Morris Swadesh, Mary Haas and many others in the first half of the twentieth century worked extensively on endangered languages of the Americas, as did various linguists on other continents. Swadesh (1948) provides a number of case studies of language loss, mainly in North American settings. Descriptive work continued and accelerated in the second half of the twentieth century. In addition, dialectologists have done a great deal of work on endangered regional dialects of many languages since the mid-nineteenth century, continuing with recent studies by linguists such as Denison (1971) on Walser German as spoken in Italy and many others, most notably Nancy Dorian on East Sutherland Gaelic (Dorian, 1978, 1981). Thus, research on endangered languages is not new, but the concerns about how to respond to it are new.

The issue of a responsible response by linguists and linguistics to this problem was raised by Ken Hale and became the topic of a Linguistic Society of America (LSA) symposium in January 1991, which led to the publication of a collection of seven short papers in *Language*, vol. 68, no. 1, March 1992, including Krauss (1992) quoted earlier, initiated by Hale (1992). This focus has continued to be a strong component of linguistic research ever since.

Another approach to the same issue was presented in Robins and Uhlenbeck (1991) as a prelude to a major discussion held at the 'International Congress of Linguists' in Québec in August 1992, one of the two key themes of that congress. The Comité International Permanent des Linguistes (CIPL), the organizer of that congress, has been a leader in raising the profile of language endangerment within the discipline and more widely through the work of Stephen Wurm and others, and in organizing a very large number of conferences and workshops on this topic, such as workshops on the sociolinguistics of language endangerment, running regularly since 2000; see the CIPL website: www.ciplnet.com for more information.

Fortunately, much of the effort of workers within the discipline over the last twenty-five years has been redirected into responses to calls to action by CIPL, Krauss and others. This includes a greatly increased emphasis on the documentation of languages, most notably endangered ones, using data-based and theoretically neutral analytic models and bringing together expertise from other disciplines to document other aspects of the societies where the languages are spoken. Also, many more fieldworkers have started to work together with the communities who are the source of their data, and thus their livelihoods, in a more co-operative way, as discussed in Chapter 3 – this is our ethical duty. A great deal of thought and work has been put into methods for improving the future prospects for many languages, both through more effective deployment of linguistic resources and political advocacy, as discussed in Chapter 8, educational improvements and direct efforts to expand the use of a large number of endangered languages, as discussed in Chapter 9, and in general moving to improve the status and self-esteem of the communities and their pride in themselves and their languages, as discussed in Chapter 4.

Few people now believe that the problem is as extreme as Krauss suggested; we can also hope that community efforts and the work of insider and outsider fieldworkers are helping to reduce the severity of the eventual outcome, and, in many cases, to reverse the process of language shift. One of the purposes of this book is to understand language endangerment better, show how it happens and suggest how it can be reversed.

1.1 HOW MUCH ENDANGERMENT IS THERE?

Just as it is very difficult to give an exact figure about how many languages there are in the world, it is difficult to quantify exactly how many of them are endangered, and to what degree. There are some parts of the world where related similar and sometimes even unrelated ethnic groups and languages are lumped together, and others where extremely similar speech varieties are divided into separate ethnic and linguistic categories, which may then be viewed as distinct languages. Also, although Chapter 2 outlines various attempts to systematize the categorization of degrees of endangerment, these are often not applied consistently, even by different researchers within the same collective research projects nominally based on the same criteria. We should also bear in mind that 'enumeration is rooted in Western civilization's hegemony over indigenous groups' (Hinton, 2002: 150).

Simons and Fennig (2018) suggest that 370 languages have become extinct since 1950, an average rate of nearly six languages per year; there are probably others that we do not know about. Other estimates are much higher: Anderson (2010: 129) suggests that a language is disappearing every two weeks; like the estimate of Krauss, this appears to be an emotive exaggeration.

There are certain areas of the world where many languages from a variety of genetic families are endangered, known as language hot-spots, where more research is particularly urgent; Anderson (2010: 132) cites seventeen examples. Such areas are also interesting due to the complex language contact phenomena which occur there.

General surveys of endangerment around the world have been undertaken by a number of bodies. The first was CIPL, with the results published in Robins and Uhlenbeck (1991). UNESCO Paris supported a series of three editions of an atlas of languages in danger, with a gradually increasing scope (Wurm, 1996, 2001; UNESCO, 2009); this is now primarily web-based and periodically updated. The LSA initiated the survey reported in Yamamoto (1996). A 2000 conference supported by Volkswagenstiftung eventually led to the survey published in Brenzinger (2007a). A very wide-ranging survey based on a standard questionnaire was initiated by UNESCO Barcelona, as reported in Martí et al. (2005). Various scholars, including many of those involved in other earlier attempts, co-operated to produce the information in Moseley (2007). The most comprehensive effort to document the level of endangerment in languages around the world, supported by SIL International, is embodied in successive editions of the *Ethnologue* (www.ethnologue .com), starting from Lewis and Simons (2014) and continuing up to the current edition, Simons and Fennig (2018), using their Extended Graded Intergenerational Transmission Scale framework discussed in Chapter 2. The National Science Foundation and the Henry Luce Foundation supported the Catalogue of Endangered Languages (ELCat) project based at the University of Hawaii, which launched the survey website (www.endangeredlanguages.com) in 2012, partly in response to issues with problems in the data and methodology of the *Ethnologue*; this website was regularly updated and improved up to 2016 and continues to exist, although updates are not currently being added.

Improved versions of several surveys are in planning or preparation, including UNESCO (2009), Moseley (2007) and ELCat; the *Ethnologue* also has annual updates. The first author of this book has worked closely with CIPL and UNESCO and contributed to nearly all of these attempts, including Wurm (1996, 2001), the UNESCO Barcelona survey, Brenzinger (2007a), Moseley (2007), UNESCO (2009) and ELCat, and anonymously provided information for all recent editions of the *Ethnologue*.

There are various gatekeepers and funders who have supported and, in some cases, organized linguistic work on endangered languages in the last couple of decades: CIPL since 1991; UNESCO, the Endangered Language Fund and the Foundation for Endangered Languages all separately since 1996; Arcadia Fund supporting the Hans Rausing Endangered Language Project and its ongoing Endangered Languages Documentation Programme since 2002, among others. At the regional level, the Japanese Endangered Languages of the Pacific Rim project (1999–2003) supported a very wide range of research based mainly in Japan but also elsewhere around the Pacific rim, and produced an enormous series of published volumes containing a wealth of valuable data. At the national level, in Germany the Volkswagenstiftung had a funding area Dokumentation bedrohte Sprachen (documentation of endangered languages) from 1999 to 2013. The Netherlands Nederlanse Vereiniging van Pedagogen en Onderwijskundigen (Association of Educationalists in the Netherlands; NVO) also developed a similar focus area. In the United States, the National Science Foundation and the National Endowment for the Humanities have an ongoing joint Documenting Endangered Languages programme since 2005. In Thailand, the Thailand Research Fund has extensively supported documentary work on the endangered languages of Thailand and work with communities to maintain these languages. China has moved through a series of initiatives, most recently, from May 2015 the China Language Resource Protection Project of the Ministry of Education and its State Language Commission, currently targeting work on 900 local varieties of Chinese and 300 indigenous minority languages, most of them endangered to some degree. Many similar initiatives are underway at the national level around the world.

1.2 WHY DOES IT MATTER?

The rhetoric about why loss of languages matters has followed a number of paths. Starting from Hale (1992: 1), the general reason is that it leads to loss of cultural and intellectual diversity. Crystal (2000: 27–67) reifies this into five categories:

(1) Diversity
(2) Identity
(3) History
(4) Human Knowledge
(5) Linguistic Interest

By diversity, Crystal means both ecological knowledge and the flexibility to adapt that it confers. Identity and History are often related, and are psychologically and socially important. Human Knowledge relates to the information contained in a language and culture. Linguistic Interest relates to structural factors of typological diversity and to historical linguistic factors concerning the relationships of languages, both phylogenetic and related to contact.

Krauss (2007b) subsumes the reasons under three arguments: Ethical, scientific and biological. The Ethical argument relates to the human rights of communities; the scientific argument is divided into linguistic, informational and abstract; the biological argument includes a human linguistic biodiversity component, which Krauss calls the logosphere, and an aesthetic component.

Bird (2017) proposes a six-way functional division:

1) Language-as-species   to be captured and preserved
2) Language-as-resource   to be exploited
3) Language-as-tool   to be used for various purposes
4) Language-as-lens   shaping view of the world
5) Language-as-connection   identity, belonging, relationships
6) Language-as-expression   art, etc.

These three systems align, as shown in Table 1.1; in some cases there is overlap or incommensurability. For example, language arts such as

Table 1.1 *Why language loss matters*

Crystal (2000)	Krauss (2007b)	Bird (2017)
Diversity	Biological/logosphere	Language-as-resource
Identity	Ethical	Language-as-connection
History		
Human Knowledge	Scientific/abstract	Language-as-lens
	Scientific/informational	Language-as-tool
	Biological/aesthetic	Language-as-expression
Linguistic Interest	Scientific/linguistic	Language-as-species

songs, poetry, stories and proverbs are part of Crystal's Human Knowledge, Linguistic Interest and Diversity; of Krauss's Biological/aesthetic, Biological/logosphere and Scientific/linguistic, and of Bird's Language-as-expression, Language-as-species and Language-as-resource; although the only categories which directly mention language arts are Krauss's Scientific/aesthetic and Bird's Language-as-expression.

For more specific examples of the kinds of cultural and linguistic diversity which may disappear with a language, see the discussion in Chapters 6 and 7. Basically, the Diversity, Biological/logosphere or Language-as-resource argument is at least as strong as any other biodiversity argument about plants, animals and ecosystems: loss of a language decreases the riches of humanity and eliminates one version of humanity's unique communicative resource – language. If 95 per cent, or even half, of the world's animal, plant or ecosystem diversity was in danger of disappearing this century, there would be extreme concern and radical remedial action. It is thus sad that there has only been limited public concern; we do not see large demonstrations in favour of linguistic biodiversity and protection of endangered languages and the linguistic ecosystem, as we do concerning global warming or whales. There are many green political parties around the world, promoting the protection of biodiversity and the environment; most mainstream political parties now also have similar concerns. However, mainstream parties, even green parties, do not support the right to maintain linguistic diversity. While most parties support human rights, very few consider maintenance of language diversity as a core human right, even where the national language policy is nominally supportive. There are many small political parties based on group identity and solidarity; some of the more successful ones, such as the Scottish Nationalists, are regional parties for whom language is not a key issue. It is only those parties of minority groups where the language is a key local symbol and component of identity, as discussed in Chapter 4, who have direct concerns about the local endangered minority language persisting and expanding. Even in such cases, it may take a long time for such parties to make an impact, and language is usually not their sole or main concern. For example, Plaid Cymru in Wales was established in 1925; it has Welsh language revival as the fourth of its current five goals. However, it took until 1966 to succeed in an election, and is still a relatively small party, although it has a substantial minority in the Welsh Assembly; and it has helped to raise the profile of Welsh language and greatly expand its maintenance and use.

A key reason for maintaining a language is to preserve the group's identity and maintain positive attitudes about the group and its language and culture, as discussed in Chapter 4. This is Crystal's Identity and Bird's Language-as-connection; it could also be seen as a component of Krauss's ethics argument. Tsunoda (2006: 134–43) has a long list of identity-related reasons for keeping a traditional language. These include identity, pride and self-esteem; group solidarity; connection of language and land and sovereignty; language as a gift from the ancestors and for future generations. Note the concern with continuing transmission of language and culture from ancestors through the present to descendants, a process discussed in Chapter 5.

Krauss puts the ethics argument first: that the right to maintain a language is a human right. This is a powerful and widespread argument, and, as we will see in Chapter 8, it is a key component of the Universal Declaration of Linguistic Rights (World Conference on Linguistic Rights, 1996) supported by UNESCO as a matter of international language policy. Krauss's ethics argument does not correspond exactly to Crystal's Identity nor to Bird's Language-as-connection, although it is related. Similarly, Crystal's History is not a separate argument for Krauss nor a function for Bird; it could be included in Bird's Language-as-connection, but does not fit so well in Krauss's ethics argument; for Krauss it would be a combination of the Biological/logosphere and Scientific/informational arguments.

One aspect of language loss which is frequently remarked on is the arrangement and packaging of real-world and cultural knowledge into linguistic forms and systems. This is the Whorfian argument: every language encapsulates a different worldview and classification of reality, using different categories (Whorf, 1956). This is what Bird (2017) means by Language-as-lens: language as a lens through which the world is viewed. One often sees expressions of regret among groups whose language is being lost about the disappearance of important and emotive sociocultural categories with the words which express them in the language. This also includes a wide range of cultural knowledge – how to act and not to act in various situations, concepts of beauty, humour and similar distinctive ways of categorizing and viewing the world.

Another related area of loss is in the area of artistic expression: verbal art of all kinds including literature, both oral and written; humour; song; nonverbal art and artistic cultural artefacts, music, dance, ritual; and combinations: for example, dance accompanied by music and song while using artistic cultural artefacts and wearing special clothing in a ritual setting. These are the Biological/aesthetic, Language-as-expression and part of the Diversity arguments for the preservation of a language. They also extend into and relate to the arguments connected to the Whorfian Language-as-lens.

In many cases, there will be irretrievable loss of valuable linguistic information if the disappearing language has unusual typological characteristics such as unique or unusual sounds or structures. Crystal, Krauss and Bird each have a category for this: Linguistic Knowledge, Scientific linguistic and Language-as-species; some examples are given in Chapter 7. The same is true for cultural practices: if something unique disappears, anthropology will not be aware of the full range of possibilities found in human societies; some examples are found in Chapter 6. In all cases, there will be less information available to reconstruct the linguistic and cultural history of humanity, as the language will no longer be available to comparative and historical linguists. In some cases, the endangerment, if it proceeds to the loss of the language, will result in the complete loss of a genetic family of languages, thus permanently reducing the historical linguistic diversity of humanity. For one such instance, see the case study in Chapter 6 on Ket, the sole remaining Yeniseian language.

Crystal's Linguistic Interest, Krauss's Scientific/linguistic, and Bird's Language-as-resource could be seen as a self-serving justification for academic linguistic research, not directly relevant to community needs and desires or other factors. However, once a language is documented, should the community change its views, a reclamation process is feasible, as discussed in Chapter 9. Also, some aspects of the documentation of a language, such as the collection of traditional text, vocabulary and cultural materials of the many types discussed in Chapter 6 and the creation or improvement of an orthography and a dictionary, as discussed in Chapter 8, are valuable and useful in themselves for the heritage of the community and for humanity and are an essential precursor to any reclamation process. Furthermore, the linguist can and should develop connections and skills which can be deployed to help the community with their language and in other ways, as discussed in Chapter 3.

One further important reason for research in communities whose languages and other traditional knowledge are endangered has not always been emphasized. There may be unique ecological information lost, such as knowledge of the medicinal properties of plants and other natural products which is valuable for humanity as a whole. This includes a wide range of wild and cultivated plants with commercial potential, and in some cases valuable medicinal uses. The treatment of malaria would be problematic without quinine, a Central American traditional herbal medicine, and the latest and most effective antimalarial, artemisinol, an extract from wormwood traditionally used in upland areas of south-western China but only brought into the modern

pharmacopoeia in the last twenty years. Many other important medicines come from similar sources: heart medications such as digitalis
and skin medications such as *Aloe vera*. Another example is local
knowledge: how to adapt to a particular ecological environment, what
crops can resist local pests, what natural products can be collected,
how they should be prepared and used. These and similar types of
unique local knowledge could be seen as part of Crystal's Human
Knowledge and/or Diversity, Krauss's Scientific/informational and
Bird's Language-as-resource, but are not explicitly discussed by any
of them.

Many economists, even ecologically and socially aware ones such as
Sachs (2008), have claimed that loss of language diversity does not
matter, and some even suggest that it will be more efficient if linguistic
diversity decreases, so that international communication can be facilitated. Sachs (2008) places this in the moral context of poverty reduction.
Linguists such as Ladefoged (1992) have also expressed a similar view,
which is also widespread among majority groups around the world, and
even among some minorities whose languages are endangered; in fact,
such wrong-headed views are part of the cause of language endangerment. Crystal (2000: 26–32) also summarizes this view, only to rebut it
thoroughly. Similarly, Romaine (2009) comprehensively demolishes the
arguments of Sachs, outlining many of the reasons already discussed
why linguistic diversity is both normal and valuable.

The world already has a number of languages of wider communication (LWCs), foremost among which over the last couple of centuries
is English, and increasing bilingualism and multilingualism including
an appropriate LWC such as English is highly positive for poverty
reduction, social and economic development and international communication. The economists simply reflect the incorrect community
view that bilingualism is abnormal and subtractive; but, as we will see
in Chapter 5, neither of these assumptions is correct: bilingualism is
normal and extremely widespread, has almost certainly been widespread throughout human history, and provides both social and cognitive advantages.

Thus, maintaining a society's cohesion through the continuation of
its chief means of expression, its language, is both a cognitive and
social positive; it is in no way a disadvantage, provided that appropriate
and necessary levels of bilingualism develop. That so many communities around the world have not been encouraged to maintain their
own languages is partly a result of incorrect community views about
bilingualism and traumas due to majority-group and majority-
language hegemony, and partly a reflection of the nation-building

processes focused on a national language which have spread around the world over the last few centuries. Similar situations also arose during various earlier periods of major imperial expansion, leading to earlier waves of language extinction, for example multiple waves of invasions of Anatolia starting nearly four millennia ago and continuing intermittently up to 1453; ancient north India during the Aryan conquest from over three millennia ago; south-western Europe during the Roman Empire starting over two millennia ago; or south-eastern China during the southward expansion of the Han Chinese during the last two millennia.

Much of the rhetoric from linguists on why language endangerment matters has been couched in rather self-serving and overdramatic terms. How this is framed on a variety of websites is summarized by Bird (2017). We need to step back and think about what language loss means to a community, return to the basic arguments put forward already, and move ahead with action rather than hand-wringing.

1.3 WHAT IS TO BE DONE?

The preliminary question here is: who needs to do what? One type of role is as an outsider expert or team of experts working with the community to document its language and culture. An outsider expert may through time develop into what Dorian (2001) has called a **sojourner**, a long-term worker with ongoing close links within the community who can contribute to its progress. Another type of role is the insider who works as a consultant with the outsider, under the direction of the outsider, to provide in-group data and information. Such insider roles can develop into a two-way learning process, and the insiders may also acquire skills and become expert researchers; this is the ideal situation, as they provide a bridge into the community and have an ongoing commitment and personal involvement. The outsider expert can help the insider colleagues to obtain additional training, and to obtain resources for implementing language-related programmes within the community. The community as a whole, or some substantial component of it, must also be participant; the leaders of the community are often the key to mobilizing community efforts. Majority group leaders and nearby local majority people may also need reassurance that the goals are unthreatening. Local government, education and other authorities should ideally be well disposed or at least not actively resist any proposed activity. Thus the answer to the 'who' question is ideally multiplex, although it may start with one outsider as a catalyst. In some cases, a community may desire, request and recruit outsiders to provide technical linguistic expertise; in others, local or national governments or bodies associated with them may initiate such contacts and provide links with the relevant community.

Lenin (1961) discusses in depth how to start a revolution. Many of the steps he advocates are also applicable to how an outsider linguist can become a catalyst for change: recruiting, leading, motivating and training others, working within existing structures, advocacy with elites on behalf of the group concerned, helping to set an agenda, doing basic preparation using established expertise, carrying our effective publicity and outreach, implementing new strategies and using new tools and technologies. Not all of the steps advocated by Lenin are appropriate; in particular, outsiders should not be involved in removing and replacing local elites, nor in instigating and implementing major political, social and economic changes.

The outsider alone cannot achieve much beyond simple documentation. For a lasting impact on the community and better prospects for the persistence of its language, insiders must be involved, and, where possible, take the lead. This includes those insider colleagues who work with the outsiders, existing insider leadership elites, new innovating outsider elites such as teachers and government administrators, and the youth of the community.

1.4 SUMMARY AND OUTLINE

Chapter 2 outlines some of the ways in which language endangerment has been approached and classified within linguistics. The topics of Chapter 3 include the ethical and practical issues arising during work in a community. Chapter 4 outlines issues relating to identity and attitudes about languages and other aspects of human societies, and how to change them where possible. In Chapter 5, we discuss the process of language learning, the positive nature of multilingualism and the ways and places where languages are used. Chapter 6 considers a wide range of nonlinguistic factors and how they may influence the persistence of a traditional language. The linguistic side of language endangerment and its effects on language structure are the topic of Chapter 7. Chapter 8 summarizes issues related to government and other policies on language and the various planning activities which need to be applied to any language, including the development or improvement of a writing system where necessary, among other measures. Chapter 9 provides a typology of language maintenance and revitalization, also strategies for reclaiming any endangered language according to community desires and needs. These must have realistic goals and feasible implementation strategies. Chapter 10 is concerned with a wide range of practical, methodological and technological techniques used in fieldwork; as linguistic, pedagogical and other technology improves in the future, there are certain to be many new developments in this area. Chapter 11 is a brief conclusion outlining prospects for work to maintain humanity's linguistic heritage in the future. Chapters 2–10 each end with a detailed case study on an endangered language or community, illustrating the issues raised in that chapter; in addition, many other relevant examples are discussed in the text. When more advanced linguistic or anthropological terminology is introduced, each new term is presented in **bold** and explained in a glossary found at the back.

DISCUSSION QUESTIONS

Trace the history of language knowledge within your family. How far back you need to go to find bilingual or multilingual relatives, and when and why did they stop speaking some of their languages?

If you are bilingual or multilingual, discuss your relative ability in each of your languages. Which of them you feel to be your mother tongue, and why?

Find out what language was traditionally spoken where you currently live. Is this language still spoken in the area or somewhere else? If not, when did it stop being spoken, and why?

SUGGESTIONS FOR FURTHER READING

Crystal (2000) is a delightful and positive introduction to the field with a maximum of erudition and a minimum of technical jargon.
Abley (2003) uses a well-organized and compelling journalistic approach to a number of case studies of language endangerment around the world.

2 Stages of Language Endangerment

Our Bisu village has been established for many years
Our grandmothers and grandfathers have carried on
Our Bisu village is the place of all people
The old people and children know everything
Now, the three Bisu villages
Our children, do not forget
These three villages, we're all brothers and sisters
And let's not forget our language
Help to speak the language and preserve it
So that our language does not die out completely
All our people and our children
If we do not continue speaking Bisu, who will?

Moon Tacaan (1998), cited in Person (2005: 131)

Scholars have proposed a number of different ways of categorizing and scaling language endangerment; in this chapter we will look at the main approaches.

In the early days of work on language endangerment, many negative terms were used to refer to this field: language death, language contraction, obsolescence (Dorian, 1989); perilinguistics (peril + linguistics), thanatoglossia and necroglossia (Matisoff, 1991: 201, 224). Endangered languages used to be called dying languages or, less negatively, threatened languages, and languages no longer spoken were said to be dead languages. In the last twenty years, we have moved away from these morbid metaphors and the terminology has become more stable, but the situation has continued to deteriorate, even though public awareness of language endangerment and scholarly attention to it have greatly increased.

2.1 SCALES OF ENDANGERMENT

The critical factor in language survival is transmission of the language to children in the family. Most attempts to rank degrees of language

14

endangerment rely on this as the sole or main factor; this includes the Wurm (1998) scale, also the Krauss (2000, 2007a), UNESCO (2003a) and Grenoble and Whaley (2006) scales which derive from the Wurm scale; it is also the strongest factor in the Catalogue of Endangered Languages (ELCat) scale (Lee & Van Way, 2016). Transmission is also a major factor in parts of the Fishman (1991) Graded Intergenerational Disruption Scale (GIDS) and the Lewis and Simons (2010) Extended GIDS (EGIDS). The various scales of endangerment are discussed in chronological order of development in this chapter. Several have been used in wide-ranging attempts to create an inventory of the world's endangered languages; all greatly oversimplify the situation, which requires detailed sociolinguistic investigation, as outlined in Chapters 4–8.

The main language transmission distinction made in all scales of endangerment is the age of the youngest people in the community who learned the language in the family as children: typically children, adults of childbearing age, adults of grandparent age or adults of great-grandparent age. Another is what proportion of each generation actually learns the language: all, many, some or a few; the finest-graded studies attempt to categorize this in terms of percentage use in each generation in different locations; this is not made explicit or quantified in most scales. A further issue, given its current name by Dorian (1977), is whether younger speakers use a different version of the language from earlier generations; those whose language knowledge is incomplete and whose language system differs substantially from that of their elders but who can still function in the language are usually called **semispeakers**. As we will see in the Bisu case study, and in Chapters 4 and 5, the attitude of older speakers to the speech of semispeakers may be crucial for the ongoing transmission of the language. A further widespread possibility is passive speakers or understanders: people with the ability to understand but with little or no speaking ability. In most cases, the breakdown of language transmission is gradual, but it can be abrupt and is then called *tip* or abrupt transmission breakdown.

2.2 FISHMAN GIDS

The Fishman GIDS (Fishman, 1991: 87–111), devised by the American sociologist of language Joshua A. Fishman, was the first formal attempt to create a hierarchy of levels of endangerment. It is an eight-point scale, shown in Table 2.1.

Table 2.1 *Fishman GIDS*

Level	Description
Level 1	The language is used in education, work, mass media and government at the nationwide level
Level 2	The language is used for local and regional mass media and governmental services
Level 3	The language is used for local and regional work by both insiders and outsiders
Level 4	Literacy in the language is transmitted through education
Level 5	The language is used orally by all generations and is effectively used in written form throughout the community
Level 6	The language is used orally by all generations and is being learned by children as their first language
Level 7	The childbearing generation knows the language well enough to use it with their elders but is not transmitting it to their children
Level 8	The only remaining speakers of the language are members of the grandparent generation

This model is a composite based on language status and wider domains of language use (Levels 1–4), existence and use of a written form of the language (Levels 4 and 5) and generational distribution of speakers and in-group oral domains of use (Levels 5–8). Fishman sees the crucial factors as (1) intergenerational transmission within the family and (2) range of domains in which a language is used. It is presupposed that, if a language is used at a particular numerical level, it must also be used at all the numerically higher levels: Level 4 implies also Levels 5–8. This is clearly an oversimplification; for example, there are many languages which have a written form transmitted through education in all or part of a community (Level 4), but this is not effectively used throughout the community (Level 5) and such a language is sometimes not transmitted to all or most children orally in the family (Level 7). There are languages not normally used in writing (Level 6 or higher) which nevertheless are used by outsiders, in media and by local, regional or national governments (Levels 1–3). Unlike the UNESCO and related scales, GIDS is thus not really linear and does not reflect a progression away from oral language transmission other than in Levels 6–8. Levels 1–4 are actually incommensurable with Levels 5–8.

As we will see in Section 2.5, Lewis and Simons (2010) propose an extended version of GIDS; this has the same inherent problems as the original GIDS: nonlinearity due to combining incommensurable status, domain and transmission characteristics.

2.3 THE WURM SCALE

One of the early leaders in work on language endangerment was the Hungarian-Australian linguist Stephen A. Wurm, who worked extensively to document languages of Papua New Guinea, the Pacific and Australia. Through his efforts, UNESCO became involved in fostering work on language endangerment. He developed the five-point scale of endangerment shown in Table 2.2, which remains the basis of the standard modern scale, and edited the first two editions of a UNESCO *Atlas of the World's Languages in Danger of Disappearing*, Wurm (1996, 2001), which apply the scale outlined in Wurm (1998: 192) to a wide range of endangered languages, and also is used in Moseley (2007), among other places.

UNESCO was unhappy with the term 'endangered language', and required a change to 'language in danger of disappearing' for the atlases which they published. By the time of the third edition of Wurm's atlas (UNESCO, 2009), this was shortened to 'language in danger'.

2.4 KRAUSS AND OTHER SCALES DERIVED FROM THE WURM SCALE

One of the leaders in bringing awareness about language endangerment to North America is the American linguist Michael Krauss (1934–), who works on a range of endangered Na-Dené languages, notably recently extinct Eyak. His 1991 keynote lecture to the

Table 2.2 *Wurm endangerment scale*

Term	Description
Potentially endangered	Not all children learn the language
Endangered	No children learn the language
Seriously endangered	The youngest speakers are in the parent generation
Moribund	The youngest speakers are in the grandparent generation
Extinct	No speakers of the language remain

Linguistic Society of America annual meeting, a strongly worded state-ment supporting work on endangered languages and assistance to their communities around the world, is published in its journal, *Language* (Krauss, 1992) and quoted in part as an epigraph to Chapter 1.

Some terminological changes and additions to the Wurm scale were proposed by Krauss in 2000. The first version of the seven-point Krauss scale was developed co-operatively in a workshop convened by Matthias Brenzinger and held at Bad Godesberg, Germany on 12–17 February 2000 and then circulated to participants (Krauss, 2000), who included Wurm, the authors of this book and other leading scholars working in the area of language endangerment in a variety of areas around the world. It uses letters *a* to *e*, including *a+* and *a–* as well as descriptive coding, and adds two additional terms to the Wurm scale at the least endangered level, 'safe' and 'stable'; the distinction here is between languages which expand into new domains of use (*a+*, safe) versus those which do not, but remain in use in existing domains (*a*, stable). Krauss (2007a: 5–8) also proposes further ± distinctions within the letter categories other than *a* and *e*, maximally *b+*, *b–*, *c+*, *c–*, *d+* and *d–* or a further six subcategories for a total of 13 points on this scale; but he does not propose descriptive terms for these additional six subcategories.

In addition to forming the basis for the classification of endangered languages in Brenzinger (2007b), some of the terminology in this scale was also adopted in 2003 by the UNESCO Intangible Cultural Heritage Section (UNESCO, 2003a) as a minor amendment to the Wurm scale, changing from Wurm (1998) to Krauss (2000) terms: 'endangered' to 'definitively endangered', 'seriously endangered' to 'severely endan-gered', and 'moribund' to 'critically endangered'. UNESCO (2009) replaced Wurm's original term 'potentially endangered' with 'vulner-able' and changed 'definitively endangered' to 'definitely endangered', but did not adopt Krauss's alternative terms 'instable' or 'eroded' (which describe two slightly different types of situation), and did not adopt the term or category 'stable'; thus, the 2009 UNESCO scale is a six-point one.

A six-point scale identical to the UNESCO scale but using different terminology was proposed by Grenoble and Whaley (2006: 18). Note that some terms in this scale refer to different categories: 'disappear-ing' for '(definitively) endangered', 'moribund' for 'severely endan-gered', and 'nearly extinct' where Wurm uses 'moribund' and UNESCO and Krauss use 'critically endangered'. Fortunately for the avoidance of confusion, the Grenoble and Whaley hierarchy is not widely used. Table 2.3 compares these classifications.

Table 2.3 *Endangerment scales of UNESCO, Krauss and Grenoble/Whaley*

UNESCO (2003a, 2009)	Krauss (2000, 2007a)	Grenoble and Whaley (2006)
Safe	*a+*, safe *a*, stable	Safe
Potentially endangered (2003) Vulnerable (2009)	*a−*, instable, eroded	At risk
Definitively endangered (2003) Definitely endangered (2009)	*b*, definitively endangered	Disappearing
Severely endangered	*c*, severely endangered	Moribund
Critically endangered	*d*, critically endangered	Nearly extinct
Extinct	*e*, extinct	Extinct

The UNESCO scale is now very widely used, for example in Moseley (2007), UNESCO (2009) and many other recent sources. The UNESCO atlas should soon be available at www.unesco.org and has been regularly updated since it went online in late 2009.

UNESCO (2015) has a much more detailed language vitality index, based on some of the same principles with numerous additions; this is discussed further in Section 2.9. Its explicit link to an endangerment scale is in its Factor 9 generational language use, in which the aforementioned UNESCO scale is repeated, with two modifications: 'potentially endangered' (2003) or 'vulnerable' (2009) is changed to 'unsafe', and 'extinct' is not present.

2.5 EGIDS

Lewis and Simons (2010: 110) propose and discuss a thirteen-point EGIDS, from Levels 0 to 10 including two subcategories of Levels 6 and 8. They also associate a term as well as a numerical value at each level, as seen in Table 2.4. Some of these terms are somewhat misleading; for example, Level 3, 'trade', might suggest use as a language of wider communication (**LWC**), potentially supraregional or even supranational. Also, some labels used in EGIDS are confusing compared with the terms in the widely used Wurm and UNESCO scales.

It is useful to have the additional end categories, EGIDS Levels 0 and 9 and 10, which are a gap in GIDS. Unlike the Krauss scale, but like the

Table 2.4 *Lews & Simons EGIDS language endangerment scale*

Level	Label	Description
0	International	The language is used internationally for a broad range of functions
1	National	Same as Fishman Level 1
2	Regional	Same as Fishman Level 2
3	Trade	Same as Fishman Level 3
4	Educational	Same as Fishman Level 4
5	Written	The language is used orally by all generations and is effectively used in written form in parts of the community
6a	Vigorous	Same as Fishman Level 6
6b	Threatened	The language is used orally by all generations but only some of the childbearing generation are transmitting it to their children
7	Shifting	The childbearing generation knows the language well enough to use it among themselves but none are transmitting it to their children
8a	Moribund	Same as Fishman Level 8
8b	Nearly extinct	The only remaining speakers of the language are members of the grandparent generation or older who have little opportunity to use the language
9	Dormant	The language serves as a reminder of heritage identity for an ethnic community. No one has more than symbolic proficiency
10	Extinct	No one retains a sense of ethnic identity associated with the language, even for symbolic purposes

UNESCO, Grenoble and Whaley scales and GIDS, there is no distinction within EGIDS Level 0 or 'safe' languages. EGIDS Levels 9 and 10 explicitly distinguish 'dormant' languages, which still have symbolic importance to a community, as opposed to 'extinct' languages, which do not. No other proposed scales cater for this important distinction; however, it is implicit in the implementation of the UNESCO atlas, which excludes EGIDS Level 10 languages. Distinction within EGIDS Levels 6 and 8 according to the proportion of child learners and current grandparents who actually speak the language is also useful, but these remain dichotomous and are still an oversimplification of the scalar nature of transmission breakdown discussed in Chapter 5. The decision that all EGIDS Level 6b languages are 'threatened' is somewhat artificial; there can obviously be a continuum in the proportion of children who are learning the traditional language, and where that proportion remains high, even if not all children learn the language in the home, a language is probably not yet truly 'threatened'; other scales deal with this continuum more explicitly, and treat languages where there is still substantial transmission to some children as 'vulnerable' rather than 'threatened'.

Lewis and Simons as the editors of the seventeenth edition of the *Ethnologue* (Lewis & Simons, 2014) have implemented the EGIDS throughout this attempt at an exhaustive inventory of the world's languages, and this has continued and been updated in the eighteenth edition (Lewis & Simons, 2015a) and all later editions. The *Ethnologue* is compiled and maintained by SIL International, a Christian missionary organization which has been very active in documenting endangered and other languages around the world. For each country, there is an SIL International member who is in charge of the entries for languages of that country, and input to the process is mainly from SIL International members, with internal deadlines that are not publicly announced. SIL International also manages the International Organization for Standardization (ISO) standard list of languages of the world, ISO 639-3, in which every language that they recognise and include in the *Ethnologue* has a three-letter code. Available ISO codes for every language cited in this volume are given in the language index. Coverage in both is improving, but of uneven quality: often inconsistent for the same language across national borders, with a tendency to recognise too many independent languages and to perpetuate errors, even where corrections have been provided to them by non-members of SIL International. Nevertheless, this is probably the most widely cited source on linguistic diversity around the world, and the UNESCO (2009) online atlas of endangered languages risks being superseded by it in popular use, now that *Ethnologue* includes an EGIDS endangerment rating for every language.

2.6 OLSI INDEX OF VITALITY

The Osservatorio linguistico della Svizzera italiana (OLSI) has devised an index of vitality primarily designed for evaluating Italian in Switzerland, but it also has the potential to be more widely applicable. This is outlined in Moretti et al. (2011: 20–2). It includes twenty-six components in eleven categories on a scale of 1 (poor, below 10 per cent) to 6 (excellent, above 90 per cent), including a variety of items also present in most other scales and in the various endangerment factors discussed in later chapters: Chapter 4: attitude factors (L1, M5);

Chapter 5: transmission and use factors (B2, A1, C2, C3, D1, E1, E2, F1, G1, H1, H2, H3, I1); Chapter 6: other factors (demographic B1, B3, F2, geographical A2, economic C1, C2, C3, political D2, education I2) and Chapter 7: linguistic factors (M1, M2, M3, M4). It includes some factors not included in most other scales, such as use in companies and in job advertising (C2, C3), use on websites (E2), knowledge and use by others including immigrants (G1, I1) and use at universities, in scientific research and tourism (H2, H3); these may be less relevant for endangered languages in developing nations.

2.7 EULAVIBAR LANGUAGE VITALITY BAROMETER

The European Language Diversity for All (ELDIA) project (www.eldia-project.org), which started in 2011, is intended to investigate the current sociolinguistic situation of Finno-Ugric languages in Europe, and ultimately to assist in their revitalization. This project devised a barometer of language vitality, EuLaViBar, which is based on a questionnaire aimed at quantifying four topics about these languages: opportunities, desire, capacity and available language products. Data is scaled from 0 (maximally negative) to 4 (maximally positive); thus, unlike most other scales, high numbers reflect greater language use, less endangerment and more positive attitudes. Of the thirty-nine questions and sub-questions which form the basis of this barometer, six questions have a five-point scale, twenty-two questions have a three-point scale and eleven questions have a two-point yes/no scale. Many questions investigate reported language use, five look at media, four look at language legislation and two consider language in education. Most questions relate to more than one of the four areas; twenty-nine include opportunity, twenty-two include desire, fourteen include capacity and six relate to available language products. Some of the questions may be less relevant for languages spoken in underdeveloped nations, and, like any questionnaire-based data, EuLaViBar relies entirely on self-report; see further discussion on the issues for this kind of data in Chapter 3.

2.8 ELCAT LANGUAGE ENDANGERMENT INDEX

The ELCat language endangerment index (LEI) is described in Lee and Van Way (2016); see (www.endangeredlanguages.com). The ELCat project, based at the University of Hawaii, is an independent corpus of materials on endangered languages drawing on crowdsourced information from linguists around the world, not just based on previous UNESCO or *Ethnologue* sources. The LEI has four components, of which the first and most heavily weighted is, as usual, intergenerational transmission; this forms 40 per cent of the weight in the scale. The second component is number of speakers, the third is speaker number trends and the fourth is domains of use; each has a weight of 20 per cent. For each scale, there is a hierarchy: 5 (critically endangered), 4 (severely endangered), 3 (endangered), 2 (threatened), 1 (vulnerable) and 0 (safe); these terms correspond exactly to those in recent versions of the UNESCO endangerment scale. The 1–5 transmission score is doubled, and then the four scores are added to reach a score between 0 and 25 which is then multiplied by 4 to give a score from 0 per cent (completely safe) to 100 per cent (most critically endangered); then, the overall LEI endangerment ranking rates languages over 80 per cent as critically endangered, those over 60 per cent as severely endangered, those over 40 per cent as endangered, those over 20 per cent as threatened and those with lower non-zero scores as vulnerable; a language with a score of 0 per cent is rated as safe. The second component of the LEI, number of speakers, is problematic; as we will see in some case studies, some languages with quite large numbers of speakers, such as Minangkabau (case study, Chapter 4), may be endangered, and some languages with relatively few speakers may nevertheless not be endangered.

2.9 OTHER FACTORS IDENTIFIED IN SCALES

In the discussion of the endangerment scales discussed in Sections 2.2–2.7, various additional factors are identified but not integrated into the rankings. These include some of the factors noted in Chapter 1 and discussed in detail in Chapters 4–8.

As we have seen, Fishman (1991, 2001) explicitly uses transmission, domains of use (oral, written, education, work, mass media, government) and government policy among the criteria for GIDS ranking. His discussion elaborates and gives many examples of the physical, demographic, social and cultural factors involved. Fishman (1991: 306–13) makes the important and often neglected observation that the goal for an endangered language is to enter into a diglossic relationship in which it serves various 'low' functions for a bilingual minority population, and thus has a reason to continue in use alongside a national language ('high').

Wurm (1991, 1996, 1998, 2001, 2002) and many other publications by this author discuss economic, cultural and political factors leading to language endangerment; these are elaborated further in Chapters 6 and 8. He also discusses language attitudes and resources, but does not build any of these explicitly into his endangerment scale, which is based solely on transmission – which he views as the overall outcome of decisions made by speakers based on linguistic, sociocultural, political, economic and other factors.

UNESCO (2003a) identified nine core factors for assessing the endangerment status of languages, as reported in Brenzinger (2007b: x–xi):

(1) Intergenerational language transmission
(2) Absolute number of speakers
(3) Proportion of speakers within the total population
(4) Loss of existing language domains
(5) Response to new domains and media
(6) Material for language education and literacy
(7) Governmental and institutional language attitudes and policies, including official language status and use
(8) Community members' attitudes towards their own language
(9) Amount and quality of documentation

The goal of work within the original UNESCO paradigm was to provide information on all nine factors for each language, as implemented in UNESCO (2009). Factor 1 is seen in every scale discussed in this chapter; this area is further investigated in Chapter 5. Factors 2 and 9, also seen in ELCat and in UNESCO (2015), are often used as criteria for setting priorities: work in the smallest communities with the least-documented languages is more likely to receive language endangerment funding support; conversely, government policy is likely to privilege larger groups with better-documented languages. Factor 3 is related to Factor 1; Factors 2 and 3 provide additional demographic information, whose importance is discussed in more detail in Chapter 6. Factor 6 is a practical issue also considered in Chapter 6 in the context of literacy and in Chapter 8 in the context of language policy and the development and use of orthographies. This is also the key factor in GIDS and EGIDS Levels 4 and 5, and implicitly also in EGIDS Levels 0–3. Factors 4 and 5 look at domains of language use, also discussed in Chapter 5. Factor 7 is the main topic of Chapter 8, and Factor 8 and related issues, the key to success or failure in language maintenance, are explored in Chapter 4.

Krauss (2007a) gives general and some specific examples of situations where various types of transmission, demographic, domain, geographic and other factors combine. He explicitly ranks transmission above demography and domains (2007a: 5): a language not learned by anyone by the age of five is already definitionally 'definitively endangered'/*b*+ rather than *a*–, even if everyone in the community above that age can and does speak it. Unlike all others, Krauss explicitly mentions the obvious possibility that a language may be at a range of different degrees of endangerment (2007a: 5–8), either at different locations or on a continuum in the same location. He also notes the possibility of reversal of endangerment, and provides terms to distinguish various subtypes of reversal: 'revitalized' for languages whose endangerment decreases due to language maintenance efforts, like Hawaiian; 'revived' for an 'extinct'/*e* language, like Cornish, which was not used for any purpose for a substantial period but has come back into use; 'renativized' for languages such as Hebrew, which had continuing religious use and then returned to daily spoken and other uses; and 'nativized' for pidgins, which become creoles (2007a: 7–8); this terminology on reclaiming endangered languages is further developed in Chapter 9. One gap in the literature on language endangerment concerns pidgins which never become nativized; as these have not become the first language of any community, they are usually not included, although they are of considerable linguistic interest.

In addition to the age of transmission factor, Grenoble and Whaley (2006: 18) note a decreasing proportion of speakers within a group and by age within a group, decreasing domains of use and lack of official status. Many of the EuLaViBar questions relate to domains of use, and one of four components of the ELCat LEI is domains of use.

Moseley (2007: xii–xiv) cites a wide range of external events which may lead to language endangerment: natural disaster, disease, ecological damage, loss of territory and displacement. He also lists cohesion of the nation-state and the associated language policy in favour of the national language and against others, the consequent exclusion of endangered languages from education, media and religion, and negative majority attitudes as reasons for language endangerment; for more discussion, see Chapters 3, 6 and 8. He also lists some desiderata for successful revitalization: improved prestige, economic prosperity, power and rights, improved education and literacy in the mother tongue for the groups whose languages are endangered; for more discussion, see Chapter 9.

In setting out EGIDS, Lewis and Simons (2010) do not discuss the factors underlying movement along the EGIDS in a particular language community. However, Lewis (2008: 37–47) provides a framework for sociolinguistic metadata on any language that is a clear advance on the

UNESCO (2003a) nine factors. It includes seven parameters, most with two to nine sub-factors: age, demographics, language use, language cultivation/development, status/recognition, language attitudes and documentation. All of these parameters are discussed in much greater detail in Chapters 4–8.

Like Krauss (2007a), Lewis and Simons (2010: 117–18) propose a typology of revitalization and revival, with different criteria and terminology for EGIDS Levels 6b–9 in such cases, as discussed further in Chapter 10. Lewis (2011) introduces a sustainable use model which provides a framework for language maintenance at various levels; minimally, 'sustainable history' (the language is documented but not spoken, the community does not identify with it) at EGIDS Level 10, 'extinct'; 'sustainable identity' (community maintains language identity and some symbolic use but no fully proficient speakers) at EGIDS Level 9, 'dormant'; 'sustainable orality' (strong language identity, vigorous oral use by all, family or local language transmission) at EGIDS Level 6a, 'vigorous' and maximally, 'sustainable literacy' (vigorous oral and widespread written use supported by sustainable institutions) at EGIDS Level 4, 'educational'. To move towards sustainable use at EGIDS Level 6a (orality) or EGIDS Level 4 (literacy), Lewis (2011) proposes five necessary conditions for sustainability: functions, acquisition, motivation, environment and distinct niche, or 'FAMED', discussed further in Chapter 9.

The OLSI index of vitality and the EuLaViBar scale includes various questions about language use in a wide variety of domains (Chapter 5), and the EuLaViBar also includes questions on legislation concerning language, which relates to language policy (Chapter 8). The ELCat LEI scale also includes an explicit domains of use component which is 20 per cent of the weight in the index.

UNESCO (2015) proposes a new set of twenty-two factors in a language vitality index, mainly on a five-point scale. Like the EuLaViBar scale, stronger language maintenance and use is assigned the highest value, 5; and the lowest language use has a value of 1; absence of language use is assigned the value 0 in some scales, increasing them to six-point scales. Factors 1–6 relate to speakers, 7–16 relate to the use of the language, 17 and 18 are status-related and 19–21 concern corpus issues (Chapter 8), and, finally, 22 relates to the degree of internal diversity.

(1) Size of speech community
(2) Total population
(3) Reference community

(4) Geographical distribution
(5) Multilingualism
(6) Language attitude
(7) Socio-geographical scope
(8) Functionality in a linguistic repertoire
(9) Generational language use
(10) Language use in administration
(11) Language use in education
(12) Language use in print media
(13) Language use on the radio
(14) Language use on TV
(15) Language use in cultural production
(16) Language use in new domains
(17) Status of a language
(18) Institutional language attitude
(19) Level of graphization
(20) Quality of documentation
(21) Level of standardization
(22) Language variation

It is not at all clear how these many factors are intended to be combined into a single language vitality index. This index is not just intended for endangered languages; UNESCO proposes to extend it to every language of the world. However, given the political constraints which UNESCO operates under, the very detailed information required, the subjective judgements embedded in most of the factors and the great likelihood that different experts will apply different judgements in such cases, this is highly ambitious. Also, when a language is endangered, many of the factors considered are quite unstable and subject to rapid change, and so, without constant updating by experts with local knowledge that is already the basis of every other attempt to rate levels of endangerment, the outcome may not only be incomplete and inconsistent, but will also very rapidly be out of date.

2.10 HOW WELL CAN ENDANGERMENT BE SCALED?

Endangerment is a continuum with many contributing factors, and any language spoken in more than one location is usually at different points on this continuum in different places. Thus, any attempt to break endangerment into discrete linear categories, whether based primarily on transmission alone or composite, is highly artificial.

The compilers of most of the scales of endangerment recognise and discuss this.

Another wrong assumption is that language shift is a one-way process; that an extinct language cannot be revived and that an endangered language cannot be revitalized. As we will see in Chapter 7 in the case study of Hebrew, complete renativization of a language no longer spoken in everyday life but used mainly for liturgical purposes for two millennia has been achieved. Yiddish, since 1945 virtually gone from its original territory in Central and Eastern Europe, no longer spoken by most of the descendants of this community elsewhere and often reported to be dying (Fishman, 1981), is alive and expanding within some traditional Orthodox Jewish groups, whose population is increasing rapidly worldwide. Other communities are now trying to revive their languages, like Kaurna, as shown in Chapter 9, and many more are attempting revitalization, like Bisu seen in this chapter as well as most of the other languages in other case studies.

Walsh (2009) criticizes composite linear scales of endangerment such as GIDS from the perspective of various revitalization and revival processes now underway in Australia. In such a situation, a language may simultaneously be at a very high level of endangerment from the transmission perspective but also at a much lower level due to the creation, teaching and official use of writing systems in schools and elsewhere; and there is expansion of language use in families and domains through time as well. So languages do move from a greater to a lesser level of endangerment as well as the other way, as Fishman (2001: 466), Krauss (2007a) and Lewis and Simons (2010: 108) also observe.

The move towards more positive terminology continues: recently extinct languages are now often called 'sleeping' or in EGIDS 'dormant', with the implication that they can be reawakened or revived. On the other hand, anthropology has traditionally been a more polemical discipline, and Perley (2012a) strongly, and with justification, criticizes purely linguistic approaches which do not support community aspirations and desires for their endangered languages; he calls much of the work on endangered languages 'zombie linguistics', and the documentary approach outlined in Chapter 11 is derided as 'mortuary linguistics': putting a recording of a language in a digital archive instead of keeping it in the mouths of the community. For more discussion of this issue, see also Chapter 3.

In contrast to the narrow economic rationalist approach advocating the universal spread of English and other LWCs, more and more people around the world are coming to think that their heritage is important and valuable, and that their traditional language is a major part of this. It is important to channel in-group and wider community attitudes in the direction of more positive views about endangered languages: their value, as seen in Chapter 1, their symbolic importance, as seen in Chapter 4, and the feasibility of maintaining, revitalizing or reviving them as seen in case studies throughout this book, using methods discussed in Chapter 9.

2.11 HOW MANY LANGUAGES ARE ENDANGERED?

Any attempt to enumerate languages and their degree of endangerment is inexact and extremely difficult to apply consistently worldwide. Furthermore, levels of endangerment change rapidly. Lewis and Simons (2014) suggest that 373 languages have become extinct since 1950, an average rate of just under six languages per year; in the one year between Lewis and Simons (2015a) and Lewis et al. (2016), the latter reports that nine languages ceased to be spoken, while new information caused them to reinstate four languages previously listed as dormant or extinct. Other estimates are much higher; Anderson (2010: 129) suggests that currently one language is disappearing every two weeks. The exact identification, classification and separation of languages and dialects is very problematic, and there are some areas of the world where detailed surveys of languages and dialects have not yet been completed, and additional languages are still being located. For example, in Burma and parts of south-western China, a great deal of work remains to be done.

Bradley (2011a: 69–75) discusses the problems of rating endangerment levels, with case studies on China, Burma and Thailand. These contrast the in-depth and sophisticated surveys that have been carried out in Thailand since the 1970s; the Procrustean local Chinese surveys, based on the official national minority classification of the 1950s and the rather incomplete data available for Burma. Some cases of revisions to earlier endangerment ratings due to new fieldwork are also discussed. This means that endangerment ratings in a country like Thailand are quite clear and reliable, while those for a country like Burma are much less so. It also suggests why any numerical data on languages and their level of endangerment in China differs markedly depending on whether the language classification is the latest official Chinese line, 126 languages as in Sun and Huang (2005), a standard linguistic and sociolinguistic approach with over 200 languages, as in Bradley (2011a), or a classification breaking groups down even further, such as that embodied in recent editions of the *Ethnologue* which list about 300 spoken languages; many of these are not endangered.

Contributors to Brenzinger (2007a), originally prepared in 2000, list 350 languages as 'unsafe', 376 as 'definitively endangered', 218 as 'severely endangered', 277 as 'critically endangered' and 89 as 'extinct'. However, this does not include languages from Australia or South Asia, and the coverage of extinct languages is restricted as the brief did not request the listing of these languages; they are only included for some parts of the world. A more thorough survey in Moseley (2007) listed 453 languages as 'unsafe', 758 as 'definitively endangered', 435 as 'severely endangered', 285 as 'critically endangered' and 456 as 'extinct' (duration unspecified). UNESCO (2009) contains 573 'unsafe', 585 'definitely endangered', 491 'severely endangered' and 550 'critically endangered' languages, and 222 languages 'extinct' since 1950; this has been augmented slightly in the online edition. The distribution of these languages by regions of the world is shown in Table 2.5. In each cell, the first figure is from Brenzinger (2007a), the second is from Moseley (2007) and the third is from UNESCO (2009). Differences among the figures are due to different judgements about levels of endangerment and about separating dialects versus combining them into languages, different levels of information available to different scholars and different procedures concerning extinct languages; for example, for Australia, none are included in Brenzinger, in Moseley, every known language extinct since 1788 is listed, while, in UNESCO, only languages believed to have become extinct since 1950 are given. These totals also do not include revived languages such as Kaurna (case study, Chapter 8) or renativized languages like Hebrew (case study, Chapter 7). The UNESCO listing also gives different degrees of endangerment for the same language in different locations; in such cases, the figures given here reflect only the least endangered location for that language. An up-to-date list of endangered languages worldwide is currently being compiled by the ELCat project based at the University of Hawaii, and has been in its current form since mid-2016; an update is proposed.

Since the *Ethnologue* seventeenth edition (Lewis & Simons, 2014), each of over 7,000 languages has been given an EGIDS rating; about a third of languages are Level 6b or lower. This is similar to the proportion of languages listed as endangered in UNESCO (2009), 2,199. In addition, nearly 400 further languages extinct since 1950 (EGIDS Level 10) are listed in recent editions of the *Ethnologue*.

As we can see, and as Nettle (1999) among others have also observed, there is a correlation between language endangerment and region.

Table 2.5 *Language endangerment by region*

Region	Unsafe/ vulnerable	Definitively endangered	Severely endangered	Critically endangered	Extinct
Middle East	15/–/5	0/3/32	0/3/20	0/2/9	1/0/10
North America	14/55/33	5/47/38	11/44/43	32/40/97	10/124/58
Latin America	82/171/187	11/164/129	46/140/92	130/53/122	36/67/33
Eurasia[a]	45/–/37	56/93/87	63/43/69	13/28/28	–/10/14
South Asia	–/53/101	–/150/101	–/82/25	–/28/35	–/1/6
East/South East Asia	23/36/40	63/82/87	40/30/51	19/13/49	–/10/18
Africa	43/1/46	131/88/64	14/23/83	40/29/86	41/23/49
Australia	–/16/17	–/26/13	–/30/30	–/48/39	–/166/6
Oceania[b]	128/121/107	110/106/66	44/40/78	43/44/85	1/55/28
TOTAL					
Brenzinger (2007a)	350	376	218	277	89
Moseley (2007)	453	758	435	285	456
UNESCO (2009)	573	585	491	550	222

[a] Without South Asia, East Asia, South East Asia and the Middle East.
[b] Without Australia.

31

There is less linguistic diversity in areas such as the Middle East and elsewhere in Eurasia where migration is easier, advanced civilizations have long been established, and so linguistic diversity has been eroded over many millennia, leaving fewer remaining languages to become endangered there. Conversely, there is greater remaining linguistic diversity closer to the equator where ecological conditions are more favourable, and in areas where access is more difficult due to geographical factors. In areas which underwent intensive settlement from Europe more or less recently, such as the Americas and Australia, earlier residual diversity remains but the pace of endangerment has been very rapid since the arrival of the European settlers.

Harmon and Loh (2010) designed an index of linguistic diversity (ILD) using 1,500 randomly selected languages of the 7,299 languages in the 2005 edition of the *Ethnologue*, just over 20 per cent of the total. They compared speaker populations for these 1,500 languages in all editions of the *Ethnologue* from 1970 to 2005. The sample represented languages of the genetic language families of the world in approximate proportion to their representation among the world's languages; it was also roughly representative of languages with different speaker populations and geographical distribution. A total of 157 languages which showed extreme fluctuation in speaker population between editions were excluded; some other languages were also excluded for various other reasons. Overall, the ILD shows that smaller languages have decreasing numbers of speakers. The ILD shows a 20 per cent decrease over the thirty-five years, starting slowly and speeding up since 1988. This suggests that the proportion of speakers of smaller languages has decreased; thus, an increasing proportion of humanity is speaking 'large' languages.

Case studies on nine endangered languages at the ends of chapters in this volume are based on our work in Asia and elsewhere. For every language referred to, the standard ISO 639-3 reference code is given in the index. These case studies illustrate some of the difficulties which arise in attempting to apply one set of endangerment criteria worldwide; a language may be more or less endangered in different places, and languages may show changes in endangerment through time – not just becoming more endangered, but also sometimes becoming more vital.

CASE STUDY: BISU

Bisu is a Tibeto-Burman language spoken in three villages in Northern Thailand (Doi Chomphu and Doi Pui Kham in Chiang Rai province and

Phadaeng in Phayao province), two villages in north-eastern Burma (Yaw Tan and Namt Theun in Mong Yang Township) and one in south-western China (Laopinzhai in Menghai county); within living memory it was spoken in one additional village in Thailand, Takaw (also known as Din Daeng) near Mae Sruai, and in the nineteenth century in several other villages in Thailand and Burma; all are within about 200 km. The villages in Thailand came from Burma in the 1850s; the villages in China and Burma are about 50 km apart. In the early 1970s, the Bisu in these three countries did not know about each other, although there was a vague memory among the Bisu in Thailand that they had come from Burma, and one Bisu monk from Burma (the Bisu are Theravada Buddhist) visited the Bisu in Thailand some time in the 1940s. Officially, they used to be classified as part of the Lawa group or more recently as Bisu in Thailand, are the Pyin ethnic group in Burma (also spelled Pyen in some sources) and are unclassified for ethnic group in China, where they are locally known as Laopin in Chinese. The Thai ethnic category Lawa is a large composite group which formerly included a variety of small groups with Mon-Khmer languages as well as two other endangered Tibeto-Burman languages, Mpi of Phrae province and Gong of Suphanburi and Uthai Thani province in Thailand. Pyin and Laopin are related exonyms; the autonym of Bisu everywhere is Bisu, also pronounced [mbisu] and [misu] in some locations.

The first report of the Bisu in Thailand, under the name Lawa, is from 1876 (Hallett, 1890: 220) when they lived in a number of villages in the Takaw area; the first report of the Bisu under the name Pyin or Pyen in Burma is from surveys done in the late nineteenth century (Scott & Hardiman, 1900) who stated that the language was then disappearing, and indeed it has disappeared from the locations where the British colonial administrators found it, which were near Keng-tung, between the current Bisu villages in Burma and those in Thailand; however, it is still spoken in two villages in Burma, and still listed as one of the 135 ethnic groups of Burma.

According to Maung Maung Tun (2014), there are 615 Bisu in the two villages in Burma; Xu (2005) indicates a Bisu population in the one village in China of 240. The three Bisu villages in Thailand have a combined population of approximately 750, so the total ethnic group is just over 1,600 people, with about 1,000 speakers. The younger people in some villages are not acquiring the language. In Thailand, this shift is furthest advanced in Phadaeng, somewhat less advanced in Doi Chomphu and has started in Doi Pui Kham, which used to be a stronghold of the language. Maung Maung Tun (2014) carried out an in-depth recent survey of language attitudes and use in the Bisu and Laomian villages in

Burma and China; the shift is less advanced there. The Laomian, unlike the Bisu, are officially classified as Lahu nationality in China; some Laomian live mingled in Lahu villages, others live in separate Laomian villages, and most speak Lahu. Some Laomian moved to Burma from China after 1958, but they are not recognised as an ethnic group of Burma; in Burma, they live in an extremely remote area long controlled by the Burma Communist Party and more recently by the Wa.

When one of the authors (David) first came to the Bisu community in Thailand in 1977, the language was still remembered but not used by old people in Takaw, and was rapidly disappearing even from Phadaeng (Bradley, 1983, 1988). With Moon Tacaan and others, we worked out a Bisu orthography using Thai letters, and he started revitalization work in his own village, Phadaeng. This orthography was revised and accepted by the entire community in 1998, and has recently received Thai government approval. In 1977, David played them recordings of texts in a related language, the main variety of Phunoi, spoken in north-eastern Laos, in which they found similar words but which they could not understand. From 1996, an American linguist, Kirk Person, started to work with the community in Doi Chomphu; other Chinese and American linguists have since joined in. In 1997, David sent recordings of Laomian to the Bisu in Thailand; that language has since been further documented by Chinese linguists (Xu, 2001, 2005). In 2002, a group of Bisu from Thailand went to the Bisu village in China with Chinese linguists and two American linguists working on Bisu and Phunoi, and found it to be very similar to Thailand Bisu; they also went to a Laomian village and found many similar words in that language, as in Phunoi, but it was not intelligible to them (Person, 2005). Full-scale revitalization started in 1998 in a joint effort among people from the three villages in Thailand, as described in Person (2018). The Bisu from Thailand also went and found the Bisu in Burma and brought some of them to Thailand for linguistic work. Some of the Phunoi from Laos have also started to visit the Bisu in Thailand. The Bisu in China have started to intermarry with the Bisu from Burma, and now the network of contact is complete, although intermittent and difficult across national borders. Person (2018) attributes the breakdown of transmission of Bisu in Doi Chomphu since 1997 to the economic crisis which sent parents and grandparents to work in fields for longer hours, leaving their children in a childcare centre in a nearby Northern Thai village; he suggests that an unsupportive village headman in Doi Pui Kham from 2006 to 2014 was a similar trigger. In reality, many factors have been contributing to the language's decline since the mid-nineteenth century.

Bisu is 'extinct' in some locations in Burma and Thailand which were Bisu in the 1880s but no longer identify as such, has recently ceased to be spoken and so 'dormant' in Takaw, 'critically endangered' but undergoing revitalization in Phadaeng, 'severely endangered' in Doi Chomphu, recently became 'endangered' in Doi Pui Kham and is at least 'vulnerable' in the villages in Burma and China, although the trend there is also not positive. The current *Ethnologue* lists Bisu in Thailand as EGIDS Level 6b ('threatened'), separately lists Pyen (the Bisu in Burma) as EGIDS Level 5 ('developing') and does not include the Bisu in China; this reflects the lack of co-ordination across countries in the *Ethnologue* and preference for SIL materials, even when contradicted by other materials which have been provided to them. Bisu is officially classified under different names in three countries. There are no monolingual Bisu, but in some locations the language is still learned by children in the family; in others, some children now learn it in revitalization classes. In Thailand, it is written with a Thai-based script not suitable for use in Burma or China; in Burma, a script has been developed following the principles of **Romanized** Lahu, a related language which the Bisu in Namt Theun village also speak; they were converted to Christianity by Lahu evangelists and currently use the Lahu Bible. In the other Bisu village in Burma, Yaw Tan, Shan rather than Lahu is the lingua franca.

Some practical issues which arose when devising the Bisu orthography using Thai letters are discussed in Chapter 8; these illustrate both general principles and show how community input can lead to novel solutions to problems. A couple of years ago, a Thai linguist tried to impose a minor spelling reform to make the Thai-based Bisu script conform to the patterns used in other minority languages in Thailand; this has not been accepted by the community. In late 2017, the Royal Society, Thailand's language policy body, approved the final version of the Thai-based Bisu script; the American linguist Kirk Person has been the key outsider in this process.

Bisu is full of Shan, Northern Thai and Thai loanwords; in Namt Hteun, there are also some Lahu loanwords. Some of these loanwords have been in the language so long that they have undergone sound changes within Bisu; for example, 'count' is /dàp/, from Shan /nàp/. This change from **nasals** to **voiced stops** distinguishes Bisu, Laomian, Phunoi and Sangkong from all other related Tibeto-Burman languages. The change was gradual, starting with a shift to a pre-nasalized voiced stop; so earlier [m] became [mb] and only later became [b], as in the name of the Bisu. It also was only partial; the Phadaeng dialect retains nasals before **front** vowels. For example, 'fire' is [mì] in Phadaeng, [mbì] in more conservative speech and [bì] in the speech of younger people; compare this with Burmese [mî], Lahu [mi] and Laomian, Phunoi and Sangkong [bì].

Before 1977, each local subgroup of Bisu thought that they were the only Bisu, and had relatively negative attitudes about their language. Now there are local and cross-border initiatives to preserve and document it, based largely on local initiative from the Bisu in Thailand assisted by outside experts, and quite a few community members are enthusiastic language promoters. The creation and use of not one but two scripts has moved Bisu much higher on the GIDS and EGIDS, which, as we have seen, are partly based on literacy and its uses. The new attitude is reflected in Moon's poem at the beginning of this chapter, originally written in Thailand Bisu. A classification of degree of endangerment based on information available prior to 1977 would have said that Bisu was an unwritten 'severely endangered' language spoken in Thailand, which corresponds to Level 7 on the GIDS; but, from new information and changes in community attitudes and resources, it is now known to be spoken in three countries where it is 'vulnerable' to 'extinct' or Level 5–10 on the EGIDS in different locations; thus, covering a spectacularly wide range.

The Bisu have learned to compromise to help maintain their language. Moon's name is actually [hmun] with a **voiceless** nasal initial, but the voiceless nasals are not written as younger people do not use them and would have difficulty learning which words to write them in; so he writes his own name in a way he knows to be innovative and which does not reflect the way he usually pronounces it. His own Phadaeng village dialect uses [m] in many words that have [b] before front vowels in other villages, but he has no problem in accepting that these and other similar words should be written with [b]. Similarly, the Bisu from Burma and China and some older people in Thailand use [mb] in the same words; the autonym can also be pronounced [mbisu] in China and Burma, and sometimes by older people in Doi Chomphu and Doi Pui Kham, and usually as [misu] in Phadaeng, but everyone agrees to write this with [b]. This attitude of avoiding purism, making compromises about dialect differences and accepting the speech forms of younger people makes language maintenance much easier.

DISCUSSION QUESTIONS

Consider the situation of a language in a migrant community. How different is it from the language in its original location and how does its endangerment differ? If it stops being spoken in a migrant community, does this make a difference in the original community?

How will transmission of a language differ if it is primarily learned through education rather than in the home? Is school learning alone a viable long-term language maintenance or revitalization strategy?

Consider the level of endangerment of a language with only one extended family of fluent speakers of all ages including children. Who uses the language within the home and family settings and feel positive about their identity? What alternative future scenarios can you predict for this language?

SUGGESTIONS FOR FURTHER READING

For an overview of language endangerment processes and comparison of Krauss endangerment scale and the six-point scale proposed by Grenoble and Whaley (2006: 18), see Grenoble (2011).

For a description of the Krauss (2007a) seven-point endangerment scale implemented in a wide-ranging survey of endangered languages around the world, see Brenzinger (2007a).

For a summary of the EGIDS scale and how to implement it, see Lewis and Simons (2010).

3 Working in a Community

An Indian View of Linguists

We've had 10 linguists
Just about ten
They came and went
But we don't know when

They watched our lips
And sculpted our words
Fully convincing us
That they are nerds

Not all fall into the
Nerd category
For each one carries
Their own special story

Always saying, 'Just
say it once more.'
We say it and say it
'til our tongues get sore

Some of them women
Some of them men
We're so thankful
They're not our kin

We've had 10 linguists
Just about ten
They came and went
But we don't know when

Margaret Mauldin, Teri Billy, Marie Strickland and
Linda Harjo (1993), cited in Yamamoto (1994)

Ethical research is not just a moral obligation, inappropriate behaviour is unacceptable. It can have bad consequences for a community and for later researchers; no one welcomes the eleventh nerd. Communities and individuals within them have priorities, and they usually do not include spending time with an outsider whose future intentions and use of the material collected are unknown. They often suspect that researchers wish to benefit financially from what is collected; and in truth nearly all researchers do wish to benefit, at least in terms of advancing their academic discipline and their own career. It is wise to have a truthful and understandable reason why you want to do your research in a particular place which you can explain to people.

This chapter outlines the ethical requirements for doing field research; it should be read in conjunction with the guidelines of professional organizations, universities, governments and others who control research access. It also discusses some possibilities for working together with a community towards shared goals, and the kinds of people inside and outside a community who may be able to assist.

3.1 ETHICS OF RESEARCH IN A COMMUNITY

There are various standard codes for ethical behaviour in field research. These include the American Anthropological Association (2012), Linguistic Society of America (2009), Australian Linguistic Society (1990) and many others. All recent fieldwork manuals contain a chapter which discusses ethical obligations; see, for example, Bowern (2008: 148–69) and Dobrin (2008). There have been decades of controversy and confrontation within anthropology about the ethics of fieldwork, for example concerning Chagnon's work with the Yanomami (Tierney, 2000; Chagnon, 2013). This is an area which requires serious and careful attention; it is *not* just a matter of filling in forms and compliance.

Dwyer (2006: 38–40) suggests five basic principles for research in a community:

(1) do no harm
(2) reciprocity
(3) do some good
(4) informed consent
(5) archive and disseminate results

Principle 1 is self-evident, and normally not difficult to fulfil. Harm includes causing people to lose privacy, lose face, feel insufficiently acknowledged or reimbursed for their work, be viewed negatively as complicit in the researcher's activities and disclosing community secrets, or feel discontented for any other reason (Dobrin 2008: 38), as well as more obvious types of physical harm that are unlikely in social science research. Principle 3 is discussed in Section 3.2 and Principle 2 is discussed in Section 3.3.

Principle 4 is one of the chief concerns of ethics committees, alongside issues related to Principle 1 and privacy issues; cynics may feel that their concern is mainly to protect the institution from legal difficulties and place the onus on the researcher. The difficulty with informed consent is how to help people from within a community to understand what you want and agree to it, before you have actually started to work with them and therefore before they know you or what you are doing. Ethics committees usually expect you to explain what you want in a written information sheet and obtain signed consent on a written consent form, which is normally required to include a series of specific and rather confronting statements about giving and withdrawing consent and various unrealistic contact procedures – how is a person from a remote village, without Internet and with no knowledge of English, supposed to email an ethics committee at an English-medium university in a developed country with a complaint? Or to submit a withdrawal of consent form to a researcher who has returned overseas? Special procedures often apply with children (whose parents' consent is also required; in some countries police checks are also obligatory), for collecting data inside an institution such as a school (where parent, teacher, principal and even government consent may be required), and for work with disadvantaged communities – sometimes including minority communities, such as for all work in an Australian Aboriginal community. Another group requiring special treatment, sometimes highly relevant where a language is endangered, is elderly or frail people; often the last remaining or most fluent speakers are all elderly.

As members of a university ethics committee, we have seen some attempts to avoid the problem of culturally inappropriate written ethics forms by preparing two information sheets, two consent forms and two withdrawal of consent forms: one set in English for the committee conforming to university guidelines, and another set with rather different content in another language. This relies on the members of the ethics committee not having knowledge of the other language, and is in itself unethical unless the content really is functionally identical and has simply been adjusted to conform to a different set of cultural norms.

Ethics committees, which also go under various other names such as 'institutional review board', are usually partly composed of social science researchers and can normally be persuaded to accept an oral consent procedure where it is culturally appropriate; they may require your explanation and the oral consent to be recorded at the beginning of work with each community member. Oral consent can be very appropriate when literacy in a national language is restricted and when written forms in a national language are a form of cultural oppression which minority people find distressing and difficult or impossible to deal with.

Even an oral version of a consent procedure which conforms to ethics committee guidelines may be close to incomprehensible when presented in the first language of the community, containing as it does numerous complex culture-bound concepts. It is also impossible to prepare consent materials in the language before any research on the language has been done, and so a local national language may have to be used, with the attendant problems concerning your and the community's degree of oral knowledge of the national language. Many of the best potential co-workers, older traditional speakers of an endangered language, simply don't know the national language well enough to deal with a complex ethics procedure, even orally. So, work with them can only proceed after this is explained to them in their own language, they understand what is being done and why, and give consent.

Note that recording without prior consent and concealed recording are not acceptable; this means that every participant in a conversation must give consent first, preferably in advance, and be aware when you are recording them. This can be impossible when recording in public situations where there are many participants, some unknown to you. Covert recording by researchers is also illegal in some countries.

Principle 5 is relatively new; it is a reaction to the development of archiving technology that makes it possible to store large quantities of data in systematically described ways (see Chapter 11 for discussion) and make it widely accessible for the long term. This was formerly a major problem, with materials like the Harrington corpus on Native American languages now requiring massive work input to get them into usable form, and a great deal of irreplaceable data collected by earlier generations of fieldworkers disappearing when their closets are cleared after they die. On the other hand, archiving imposes a large burden of additional work on current fieldworkers to put their materials into a form appropriate for an archive, and it means that communities and speakers must understand that some of what they say will be accessible in an archive. This also means that access to archived material needs to be controlled – which may be problematic for some archives, funding bodies and universities in the future.

Access controls need to be in place for culturally sensitive materials. For example, some materials from Australian Aboriginal communities should only be heard or seen by people of a particular gender, or by people of that gender who have been formally initiated into the group as adults. The linguist and anthropologist Ted Strehlow, who lived and worked with the Aranda in Central Australia most of his life, tried to avoid this issue by delaying publication until all the speakers were dead (Strehlow, 1947). Later, there was great controversy about his publication of sensitive sacred songs (Strehlow, 1971) and especially after his death concerning the disposal of sacred artefacts which he collected over his lifetime; most of these objects are now in a dedicated local museum, the Strehlow Research Centre, with proper access controls, or in the hands of traditional Aboriginal owners, the descendants of the deceased elders who gave them to Strehlow long ago.

One concern related to Principle 5 as well as 1 is privacy and confidentiality in materials disseminated outside of the community. Often people will say things that they would prefer not to become common knowledge within the group, let alone outside. This is especially true during long-term fieldwork, where the researcher knows the community members well. Dorian (2010a), who has been working with the same group for forty years, discusses the need to redact private materials before they become more widely accessible. Macri (2010) and Perley (2012a) make similar observations from the perspective of community insiders.

The question of privacy and the use of names in published or archived materials can be a vexed one. If real names are used, anonymity is lost and there is no privacy. Some scholars use pseudonyms instead of personal and place names; but it is not really so difficult to work out which Midwestern US town is Middletown (Lynd & Lynd, 1929) or which Australian town is Bradstow (Wild, 1974). For an endangered language spoken in only one location, concealing place names is pointless, if not counterproductive. In some cases, ethics guidelines and community requests may conflict: an expectation of anonymity versus the desire of a singer to have his name associated with his song or the desire of co-workers to have their name on the dictionary they produce with you. Where kinship and genealogical information is collected, again there may be issues about privacy. These issues should be openly discussed with local people, and they should decide whether they want to be named in connection with various kinds of data that they provide, and which data should remain private or restricted.

Ownership of information, intellectual property and copyright are also a legal issue when materials are being archived and disseminated in accordance with Principle 5. Some communities feel that their language and culture are private property, not to be studied by or known to outsiders, and not for dissemination in research or other publications (Macri, 2010: 38). In such a case, only an insider can do research, and that insider is blocked from using the results outside the community or placing them in an open archive.

Even in the much more usual situation where the group is more open about its language and culture and happy for materials to be disseminated, there may still be some things that are sensitive; and in all cases traditional and legal ownership, intellectual property rights and copyright must be maintained and respected.

Some kinds of traditional knowledge have substantial commercial value – for example, medical applications of ethnomedical knowledge, as we have seen for the anitmalarials quinine and artemisinol. There are many other examples where the original community derived no benefit from their intellectual property, although humanity as a whole did. Drug companies employ botanists to troll through research publications on ethnomedicine and ethnobotany, and the group whose medicine it was usually derives no benefit. This kind of commercial exploitation of minorities' knowledge is not new, and has led to a lack of trust and sometimes even secretiveness and concealment of traditional knowledge. If a researcher does collect commercially sensitive or valuable information, it should only be disseminated with the knowledge and consent of whoever provided the information.

Finally, as part of Principle 5, materials need to be returned to the community in forms that are appropriate, useful and valuable to them; this is discussed further in Section 3.2.

3.1.1 Approvals, Permissions and Access

Depending on where a researcher is based and where they wish to conduct fieldwork, approval may be required from a range of bodies. The home institution of most researchers will have an ethics committee, institutional review board or similar body, with its guidelines; often such guidelines are fairly stringent, as they need to apply also to medical and other kinds of research, which can be intrusive or dangerous, unlike most anthropological and linguistic work. In some cases, an ethics committee can even prevent research from proceeding or continuing (Battin et al., 2014), so the process needs to be treated seriously. If there is a funding body involved, it may have separate ethical and compliance requirements, such as obtaining written consent to work in a community and accounting for disbursement of funds. Such guidelines often include a requirement for medical and liability insurance and a requirement to obey all relevant laws; this should go without saying.

As suggested in Chapter 10, it is highly desirable to have close contacts with colleagues at nearby educational institutions where the fieldwork is being carried out; a local university can also sometimes assist in obtaining government and other kinds of approval, and may be able to provide a base. Even a school can also give some assistance; but note that becoming involved with a local institution can sometimes restrict access to parts of a community, create obligations to carry out work required by that institution, and put you on a particular side in divisions and disputes. The more local your connection is, the more likely such issues are to arise. A university will almost inevitably be dominated by the majority group in a country and use its national language; schools are also usually a vehicle for introducing the national language into minority areas. Thus, they may be regarded negatively by the minority people with whom you wish to work; be careful where you affiliate.

The government of the location where research is to be done may have a national, regional or local organization which controls access to the field, and which has ethical, reporting and other requirements for obtaining a research visa if one is not a citizen of the country – for example, the National Research Council of Thailand. In China, the controlling bodies include the Nationalities Commission of China and its regional offices at provincial/regional, prefectural and county level; the foreign affairs offices in governments of autonomous regions (like Tibet and Xinjiang) or provinces, of autonomous prefectures or prefectures, of autonomous counties or counties and of townships or towns; also the leaders of village clusters and villages. In Australia there are regional land councils who control access for any purpose, not just research, and regional language centres which can be a base for research.

Where minority groups have a corporate existence, as is often the case in North America, there are tribes with bands (local sections of the tribe); the tribal council controls access to and work in the community. This means that there are designated tribal leaders, elected or hereditary; often such leaders have their own agenda and will seek to guide a new researcher into a particular line of work. Some tribes employ anthropologists and/or linguists; in such a case the tribe obviously decides what is done and controls the resulting outputs and whether and how they are disseminated. This can mean that, if the approval for research depends on tribal decisions, the material and outcomes can remain unused and inaccessible, even to the researcher who collected them. If a tribe or similar group feels that its language is private and not for outsiders, as is not uncommon in North America, such difficulties are particularly likely; see for example Hill (2002) concerning the publication of a Hopi dictionary.

There are often various educational institutions such as tribal colleges or other nearby colleges and universities who carry out various kinds of training and research work at the local level. In China, there is an entire network of national, regional and provincial *minzu* (nationalities) universities and institutes whose original mission was to educate members of China's national minorities; now they also have large numbers of Han Chinese majority students. Around the world, there are various religious seminaries, institutes and other educational institutions which work mainly with the groups who have converted to their religion; for example, a large number of Christian institutions in Burma, where the government university system does not deliver the kind of tertiary education that many potential students want. Such colleges, institutes, universities and seminaries often have staff who are specialists in ethnographic and linguistic work, and give training in the local languages and cultures to members of minority groups. Colleagues in these institutions can be very valuable contacts, knowledgeable and experienced local people who themselves do related teaching and research and are often members of minorities. They can often introduce a new fieldworker into a suitable village situation or introduce you to a range of possible field options using their personal networks.

Most traditional societies have an internal political leadership structure, whether aristocratic and hierarchical or based on consensus. There may be hereditary rulers at various levels; sometimes these hierarchies are co-opted into a modern political structure. Thus, the Nosu and Nasu *nzymop* 'kings' in south-western Sichuan, north-eastern Yunnan and north-western Guizhou in south-western China, who ruled substantial areas up to the size of a modern Chinese county or even prefecture, were initially transformed into Chinese *tusi*, literally 'local ruler' many hundreds of years ago, before being replaced by direct Chinese administrators. This process was only finally completed in the late 1950s, when China eliminated all remaining residual local political control in areas such as the Nosu area in Liangshan prefecture, south-western Sichuan. Local leaders are sometimes co-opted into the modern political system – for example, as village headmen in many parts of the world.

Another more democratic pattern is to have a council of elders who meet to discuss and arrive at decisions; this may be formally structured and recognised as part of the government, as in the case of the Indian village *panchayat*, or be simply an informal group of respected older men. Whatever the local political structures are, the incoming outsider needs to be aware of them, respect them and co-operate with them.

Achieving consensus in a less hierarchical society with a village council can be a slow and delicate process, while, in a more hierarchical one, once the leadership accepts the outsider, everything is settled.

There can also be a hierarchy associated with religion. For example, the Akha in far south-western China, northern Laos, north-eastern Burma and far northern Thailand have a village priest in their traditional religion, the *dzoe ma*, who is the real village leader; the Akha term is historically related to the Nosu and Nasu term *nzymop* 'king', mentioned earlier. The second most important ritual leader among the Akha is the blacksmith, *ba ji*. The government-appointed Akha village headman, unless he is also the *dzoe ma*, normally has little traditional authority, despite whatever government responsibilities he may have. In some other societies, traditional religious leaders have little power; the Lisu, who live south-west of the Nosu and whose language is also closely related to Nosu, have a village priest called *meu meu* who has no temporal authority and carries out his religious duties only once a year. Partial conversion to an outside religion may divide some communities and introduce an additional set of religious leaders. Curiously, the main modern meaning of the Lahu term *jaw maw* (related to Nosu *nzymop*, Akha *dzoe ma* and Lisu *meu meu*) is 'white missionary'; its original meaning was 'lord, master' and it was formerly sometimes used to refer to traditional Lahu messianic leaders who led large revitalization movements – for examples, see Walker (2003: 505–47). The first really successful white Christian missionary, Marcus Vincent Young, who converted many Lahu from 1903 onwards, was effectively a Lahu messianic leader, and liked to be called *jaw maw*; since then, other white missionaries and sometimes other white people are also addressed this way. The Lahu live in far south-western China, north-eastern Burma, far northern Thailand and north-western Laos, between the Lisu and the Akha, and all these languages are historically closely related (Bradley, 1979a).

It may be that the home university has students from the country where a fieldworker plans to go. A personal connection with a local family can be helpful in the initial stages of fieldwork, but note that this will almost always be a connection with a member of the majority elite or middle class, not with the target group for research. Conversely, once you are in the field, you may find that there are immigrants from the group you are working with who live near your home; these can sometimes be found prior to fieldwork through immigrant community organizations, and can be a valuable resource.

When you choose a local person to work with, you may also be choosing their family; they can become your family, provide you with hospitality and assistance, expect you to side with them in any disputes and help them in times of crisis. You may even be invited to join the family in a more formal sense: be assigned to their skin group (moiety, clan) in an Australian Aboriginal community, become a classificatory relative for the purpose of addressing you, and get an in-group name. Such a connection carries ongoing responsibilities and should not be entered into lightly.

Some outsiders, missionaries or aid workers may be extremely helpful in gaining access to communities for fieldwork and for local background knowledge. They have long familiarity with the situation, and often substantial spoken language skills. Some missionaries, notably members of SIL International and Wycliffe, also have linguistic training and do substantial linguistic research. Some SIL International members do valuable language development work: testing for dialect intelligibility, developing standard languages, designing orthographies, preparing teaching materials and implementing literacy programmes. Linguists and especially anthropologists have long had an ambivalent relationship with SIL International and its members due to their underlying Protestant Christian goals, but a great deal of the basic infrastructure for linguistics (software, fonts, the *Ethnologue*, the **ISO 639-3** list of languages of the world and a very large number of orthographies, dictionaries, grammars and so on) was developed and is maintained by SIL International. Some Catholic missionaries also have good training and a very strong focus on linguistic work. Less academically oriented missionaries usually have excellent local knowledge and good language skills and can also give logistical and other assistance. However, a fieldworker should avoid becoming part of an expatriate missionary network; the goal is to spend time in the language community.

There are also indigenous Christian converts, sometimes missionaries in their own right, who can make excellent initial co-workers as they often have literacy skills in their own language, knowledge of languages of wider communication and are comfortable working with outsiders. Many of them are highly impressive individuals and leaders among their group; but note that they are likely to lead you into a social network with their fellow Christians, who normally have less traditional lifestyles and cultures than followers of a traditional religion. The same applies with any other proselytizing religion; for example, Islam is spreading in Africa and parts of Asia. Working closely with representatives of any one religious group puts a fieldworker in their camp.

Your main co-workers within the community may change through time; Chapter 11 discusses the kinds of skills needed in co-workers at various stages in field research. Initially, ability to speak a language which you know well in addition to the target language will be essential; but if you learn the language, this will gradually become less important. On the other hand, there will be people with whom you can only start to communicate effectively after you have some language knowledge.

If you are an insider to the group you are working with, you have a ready-made social network and introduction to the part of the group that you come from; it means that you have ongoing responsibilities to your community, and that your choice of co-workers and field sites may be partly predetermined. It also places you in an awkward position with parts of the group where your family or subgroup has disagreements or conflicts; and it means that you must not fail in giving back to the community. For a fascinating example of an insider researcher and his negotiation of these issues, see Perley (2011). There is also a substantial literature on the insider as anthropologist, for example, Reed-Danahy (1997), and on viewing fieldwork and contact with outsiders from an insider perspective, see Sahlins (1995) and Dentan et al. (1997).

Naturally one needs to develop personal empathy with one's direct co-workers and the community in general, but this should not be too close. It is best not to do something which you would be ashamed for everyone to know; a possible test might be whether your own grandmother would approve of your behaviour, or whether you would be happy for it to be discussed openly on the Internet.

Sometimes, an initial research plan may prove to be unfeasible or not as interesting as expected, in which case one may wish to change to a new and more promising topic. If this involves substantial changes to a project with funding, university approval, ethics approval, government approval, and in which others have helped you substantially, you should make your new plans known to those involved. If your initial research proposal is open to this kind of flexibility, such a change will be much easier.

3.2 COLLABORATION AND CONTROL

Principle 3, that the researcher should do some good, can include doing things which are academically important and contribute to provide data and advance linguistic and anthropological theories and models. More relevantly for the community, it should also include giving something back to the community in return for sharing their language and culture. Action anthropology, as developed by Sol Tax (1907–1995), making anthropology useful to the community, has a very long history (Daubenmier, 2008; Stapp, 2012). Collaboration and giving back are also a recurring theme in the recent literature on work in endangered languages, see, for example, Dwyer (2006), Rice (2009, 2011) and Gerdts (2010), and the need is not restricted to language work. However, with such communities, it is particularly relevant and urgent, as the object of the research is threatened with disappearance.

Rice (2009) in particular emphasizes the need for co-operation between outside researchers and in-group activists, and suggests some ways in which this can be effective. Hinton and Hale (2001), as well as other work by Hinton (1994, 2002; Hinton et al., 2002; Hinton, Huss & Roche, 2018), provide many concrete examples of this kind of work and how to implement it, as do many of the other works cited in Chapter 10 on field methodology. Most of them advocate a team approach, with each participant contributing different kinds of skills and work. Ideally, such projects should be driven by community wants and needs as expressed by the in-group participants, not just by the research goals of the fieldworkers.

Some team projects involving minority groups are top-down policy initiatives initiated from outside, but nevertheless provide some benefits for the groups investigated, such as the international UNESCO drive for mother tongue education (UNESCO, 2003b) and the classification of ethnic groups in countries such as the former USSR. These usually involve both outside experts and minority insiders, and can be valuable if national governments support and implement them effectively. Other team projects are more bottom-up, initiated and driven by the wishes of indigenous minority groups.

One example of a top-down initiative was the Tribal Research Institute in Chiang Mai, Thailand, which was established in 1965 as the Tribal Research Center (TRC), upgraded to an institute in 1984 and dissolved in 2002 when some of its staff and most of its materials were moved to a new Tribal Museum oriented towards tourists. It started as a joint initiative with paired teams of foreign anthropologists funded by various governments (Australia, New Zealand, the United States, the UK, France) and Thai anthropologist counterparts funded by the Thai government, each team doing in-depth ethnographic research with one hill tribe of Thailand. The TRC also provided a base for a number of other foreign anthropologists and linguists who did field research with the same groups, as well as other foreign social scientists and development workers. It was part of the Thai Department of Public Welfare and its Thai employees were Thai civil servants, mostly ethnic Thai and thus not members of hill tribe groups, but they each achieved close rapport with and deep understanding of the group they worked with. There was a controversy in the early 1970s in which the TRC was accused, quite unjustly, of being a US front for spying on hill tribes during the Vietnam War; but, although the funding for its foreign researchers came from members of the Southeast Asia Treaty Organization military alliance, its work was initially entirely ethnographic, with a strong agricultural focus, as well as linguistic and development-oriented. As its foreign support gradually disappeared, it became a normal Thai government organization, albeit an unusual one whose main function was research on minorities; most of the cadre of Thai anthropologists remained, and continued to do ethnographic and development work with the hill tribes. They provided a bridge between the hill tribes and the Thai government at a time when Thailand felt itself under threat from its eastern neighbours, and produced a great deal of valuable research – see, for example, Bhruksasri and McKinnon (1983).

A bottom-up team project which works from within the minority groups of Thailand is Inter Mountain Peoples Education and Culture in Thailand (IMPECT; www.forestpeople.org) which grew from a foundation set-up some years earlier by a Dutch anthropologist and became a separate organization in 1991. It does public relations and outreach work with and on behalf of ten hill tribes of Thailand, and runs a range of small-scale locally initiated projects, including cultural revival and alternative education (with subprojects on mother tongue education, cultural revitalization and curriculum development) and natural resources and the environment (including water and land management, environment protection, mapping). All of its funding comes from a range of foreign governments, including the Netherlands and Norway, and it is staffed and run entirely by members of the ten groups which it serves.

A team project can also involve scholars and local experts from a range of disciplines working in a single community on a joint topic, both outsiders and insiders; a botanist can collect, identify and prepare specimens of plants for archival collections, a linguist can collect accurate information about the words for the plants and narrative about how they are used, an anthropologist can investigate their meaning and importance in the society, a traditional herbalist can show all the scholars how to find, prepare and use them for medicinal and other purposes, and a pharmacologist can analyze their chemical properties. Some of the scholars may be local, others may be foreign. Such team projects can also focus on a wider range of subtopics, with scholars and community members working together to find ways in which they can benefit the society where they are doing the research.

In addition to the minority in-group members as individuals, families, groups and a community, the views of community leaders about what is an appropriate form of giving back should be taken into account. Many outsiders may also need to be consulted and convinced about these needs: local workers such as teachers and health workers, other government workers at all relevant levels in a range of functions (administration, education, health, development, welfare, forestry, police, military etc.), local outsider leaders, local, regional and national politicians and nearby local majority group members. Ideally, the goals of the fieldworker and the other stakeholders can mesh in synergistic ways to benefit everyone involved. The many stakeholders may not always be able to agree on everything, but the basic principle of doing good where possible should hold.

3.2.1 What Do Communities *Need*?

When indigenous group leaders meet at international conferences and discuss what their communities need, or when you ask individuals what their priorities are, there are usually two main types of answer. One concerns material life: desire for good healthcare, good education and a better life for the children and economic advancement. The other concerns social recognition: full and equal citizenship in a nation, rights to traditional land, self-determination and autonomy in that land. These are reasonable human aspirations, which normally come before concerns about language, culture and traditional identity. In a World Bank survey of 60,000 people from sixty countries living in poverty, Narayan et al. (2000), and summarized in Wolfensohn with Margo (2010: 345), found that some main concerns are well-being, having a voice in their own future and economic opportunity; but, the deepest concern is for their children's future.

Often, once material and social needs are met or on the way to being met, concerns about language, culture and identity start to become more prominent in a community. Unfortunately, this often means that language and culture are neglected while material and social progress are being pursued, and that the in-group language is not transmitted to children, in the name of economic advancement and their future. It also means that some of the most strident advocates for language, culture and other minority rights come from groups in developed countries, notably North America, Europe and Australia. Sadly, sometimes such leaders themselves have limited skills in the group's language, no matter how positive their attitudes may be; such leaders may be particularly sensitive about language as a key component of in-group identity.

In such developed countries, government policies about minorities and their languages are often quite supportive, official resources available for minorities are very substantial, and, in many cases, the majority groups are well aware of and sympathetic to the desires of their local minorities.

3.2.2 What Do Communities *Want* from a Researcher?

There is normally no specific organization or individual who can tell you what the community as a whole wants you to do for them; this becomes clear gradually as you interact with a range of people. If there is a recognised leadership, their wishes may reflect general views, or can sometimes be tendentious and controversial. It is crucial not to become involved in existing internal disagreements, and even more so not to create new divisions.

Sometimes these desires will be clearly expressed and widely held, in which case, a sense of expectation will develop, and the fieldworker will become enmeshed in obligations which can be difficult to fulfil. This can include a range of things which fieldworkers are unqualified to do and some which they should not or do not want to do; see further discussion in Section 3.4.

Given the widespread desire for education, many requests will revolve around preparing educational materials: creating or revising writing systems; preparing primers and other materials to teach the traditional language in school or to teach literacy to adults; collecting and disseminating traditional oral or written literature and so on. Most fieldworkers have other primary goals, and have no training in education or in publishing and would need help from experts in these areas to ensure that what they do is appropriate (Hornberger, 2008).

It may even be that people want materials to learn a world language such as English, or to learn the national language more effectively. Such materials are very much outside the expertise of a foreign field-worker, whose control of the national language may be less than perfect. As we saw in Chapter 1, it can be very hard to persuade a community that bilingualism gives a cognitive advantage and is actu-ally beneficial for learning the national language and English or other languages of wider communication, even though this is the general finding in fully bilingual communities around the world. Unfortu-nately, this seems counterintuitive to most minority groups who have suffered from educational disadvantage; hence, the ongoing loss of world linguistic diversity. On the other hand, it is highly desirable that good materials for learning these outside languages are in use. National and international experts in preparing such materials may wish to have some information about the first languages of the learners and about their cultural practices and how these differ from those of the majority; here is where the fieldworker may eventually provide some useful input to the educational system.

Some fieldworkers, such as members of SIL International, whose ultimate goal is Bible translation, may be very comfortable working with communities who want Christian religious materials in their language. Many others are decidedly not; and it is inappropriate to do things which are against your own beliefs. All fieldworkers have an obligation to document the range of activities within a community, even when this includes newer as well as more traditional religious activities; but many prefer to leave studies of the religion of converted groups to missiology. Some anthropologists do both; see, for example, Walker (2003) who devotes nearly a quarter of his anthropological monograph on Lahu religion to Christianity among the Lahu.

If you choose to do language planning work (Chapter 8), such as devising a writing system, choice of a dialect for writing, choice of vocabulary and structure for the standard and choices about new vocabulary, be sure that you are doing so with local agreement and participation, and that you know how to do these things. If this is unnecessary because these choices have already been made, you should conform to in-group practices and expectations about this; so, if there is an existing standard dialect with an orthography, it is best to use this if possible, to make your work accessible to literate community members, unless the orthography or other aspects of the standard have serious problems. Again, you should stay out of internal disagreements about such matters.

The most substantial thing that the outsider fieldworker can leave behind in a community is a cohort of trained and enthusiastic insider colleagues. Your co-workers must be paid for their work, but while they work with you as a team, they are also learning how to become independent researchers and may later choose to continue and to pursue other interests and topics. It is extremely valuable to have such experienced in-group colleagues, and fascinating to watch what they do on their own. They may be the most important people to listen to, as they understand your work, share many of your interests and are very likely to have important insights. If you are an outsider, you will eventually leave; even if you come back regularly, you are not there all the time, so your long-term impact is less than theirs. In the long run, even after you are no longer present, you should continue to encourage, guide and support them in their efforts.

Another valuable function of a researcher can be to create new wider networks, as we saw in the Bisu case study in Chapter 2: relinking members of the same group where contact has been broken, and thus strengthening self-esteem and increasing the possibilities for in-group marriage and language maintenance in the home. Networking similar groups, whether at a local level or more widely, is also valuable; for example, we have run a series of three increasingly broadly based workshops for language maintenance at a teachers' college in southwestern China which trains teachers for various minority areas; the first, mostly internal with a few foreign experts to energize and train the staff of that college and their students, the second, bringing in researchers and minority group members from around that province in China, and, the third, also bringing in people from the same minority groups in Burma and Thailand as well as from other provinces in China; the materials from all three workshops have been published in English and Chinese (Bradley, 2005; Xu, 2007; Bai & Bradley, 2011) for distribution to participants and for wider use.

Communities often have unrealistic expectations of 'their' fieldworker. They expect rapid results, and are often disappointed if language fluency comes slowly or not at all, or, when the fieldworker goes away, they may feel that the fieldworker is not committed or is not trying hard enough. If a language already has an orthography, as discussed further in Chapter 8, the community may be strongly committed to it and reluctant to change; if there is none, one can be devised in an appropriate and consultative way with stakeholders including local teachers and others, as discussed in Chapter 8. There are a few communities who do not want an orthography, sometimes for privacy reasons or because they believe literacy in some other language is what they need; such wishes should be respected unless their views change. Scholars know that a good dictionary takes many years of work and a deep knowledge of the group, its language, culture and environment; but a dictionary is often the first thing that a community wants once it has an orthography.

In many parts of the developing world, minority groups have most often encountered foreigners who are missionaries. If they have been converted, they may welcome the fieldworker as another missionary, leading to potential misunderstanding; if they have not, they may be suspicious that the research work is just a pretext for future conversion. Guérin and Lacrampe (2010) report on a situation in Vanuatu where the fieldworker was asked to produce a Christian hymnal; you may be expected to attend church services and even invited to give a sermon in church. Where different parts of a single community follow different religions, the situation can be delicate; associating with people of one religious persuasion can sometimes preclude work with others.

Other familiar outsiders are medical and development workers. Linguistic and anthropological fieldworkers must not pretend to have medical, agricultural or other knowledge which they do not have. On the contrary, they should be interested in traditional medical, agricultural and other knowledge, which is often even more endangered than the language and other areas of culture due to high regard for outside medicine and other modern technology.

3.3 RECIPROCITY

As we saw in Section 3.2.2, traditional language and culture are not the top concern in most places where an endangered language is spoken. Not everyone shares your enthusiasm about this, although, if you find some who do, that is a bonus. If they were not working with you, people would be doing some other work, so the first component of reciprocity is paying them for the work they do with you. The amount of such payments should be discussed and negotiated in advance, and should always be met or exceeded; increases are appropriate when a co-worker's skills have improved or local costs have risen. In some communities, the leaders may tell the researcher how much to pay people; in some, there may be a standard minimum hourly or daily wage which must be met or exceeded; and, in some, people may be reluctant to accept cash payments, so they will need to be reimbursed in some other way, such as by substantial regular gifts in kind: sacks of rice, chickens or whatever they need. In addition to cash payments or alternative gifts in kind, you should give additional culturally appropriate gifts at normal gift-giving times, such as at weddings and festivals; and you may also wish to contribute in cash, in kind or through your own work to any village or nearby projects to build or repair infrastructure.

In some places, the appropriate gifts may include alcohol and tobacco; this may be problematic if you need to account for your expenditure to a university or funding body, may cause problems if the speakers get drunk, may be a moral issue for you, and has well-known long-term health consequences. You need to be consistent and firm about this; if you don't smoke and feel that tobacco is too detrimental to health, don't buy it and give it out, and don't pretend to accept it when offered. You may also find groups or subgroups where tobacco and alcohol are banned for religious or other reasons; so don't assume that, just because some people like such gifts, everyone will welcome them. For example, it is illegal for anyone to take alcohol into much of the Aboriginal land in Australia.

If you live in the community, you may wish to live in someone's house. Initial hospitality is sometimes difficult to pay for, but, as soon as possible, you should discuss and agree on a cash or other payment for accommodation and meals. Again, the local headman may wish to be involved in this negotiation, or to determine an appropriate price. Having a house built in the village is a good idea; it will allow you to observe and participate in housebuilding, meet experts in various skills and record narratives about this. You can also pay and feed the people who do the work and listen to their conversation. A house is a private space to retreat to, and it is something for you to leave behind, for example, as a village cultural centre. Even if you have a house, it may still be a good idea to take meals with a family, both for the everyday conversation that you can participate in and to save you the time required for buying and preparing food; find someone who is a good cook and try to arrange this, with explicit payment arrangements from the outset. Where there are hotels or guesthouses and restaurants or food shops, those are another alternative; but you will spend less time with people in home settings. If you are travelling between villages, your network of local people will probably take you to a host in each place; again, try to sort out a rate of payment as soon as politely possible if you are staying any length of time, and give appropriate gifts to hosts who will not accept payment.

At some times of year, such as during harvest, it may be necessary to pay more; and at some times of year, such as during festivals and holidays, people may be unwilling to work, so the work schedule will need to be flexible. You also need to be careful not to overpay, which may make other people who do not work with you jealous, and create high expectations which you may not always be able to maintain.

Other forms of reciprocity include training community members in language and culture documentation skills, providing them with equipment to collect the kinds of things they find important (see Becquelin et al. (2008) for an example) and helping them to disseminate their own materials as well as what you collect. It may also be desirable to set up a local cultural centre, where material culture objects can be stored and information made available in hard copy and other forms.

As a high-prestige expert, you may be called upon to act as an advocate for the community. This can be a formal process, as when anthropologists and linguists are employed to prepare expert reports and participate in court cases on land rights, as has been happening in Australia over the last forty years; reports on the environmental and social impact of development projects such as dams, mines, roads, forestry, resettlement; educational and social policies and outcomes; and other kinds of studies. Governments and companies who wish to oppose the granting of land rights and/or proceed with development projects also employ experts including anthropologists and linguists; being on the other side of such a process is a quick way to ruin your relationship with the community where you work. Conversely, strident advocacy against government or company plans will place you in a difficult position when you want your visa or your research permit renewed, and can be dangerous in some parts of the world.

At a less formal level, researchers may be able to help communities to liaise with local, regional or even national authorities to achieve better education, health and economic outcomes. At the local level, this includes working with village teachers so that they understand the needs of their students better, taking people to appropriate health services, providing contacts for the sale of their crops or other products such as handicrafts and talking with government officials about needs, problems and conflicts – provided this is done in constructive ways. This can also be at a higher level; years of advocacy by linguistic researchers working in Thailand, including powerful Thai insiders as well as outsiders, has now led to a new national policy which recognises the need for mother tongue transitional education for minorities, well-regulated translation and interpreting services and various other important policy improvements affecting minority language rights.

Participation in local activities, in a nonintrusive way which meets community needs, can help to build rapport with the community. You may be able to teach in a school, help teachers to make the school experience more relevant for minority children, or prepare materials for the minority language to be used in school, even if only in a symbolic way – provided you have the knowledge and skills to do so. You can help individual children and groups of children with their studies. Some communities may want language lessons in English or another language of wider communication. This can even include physical work; for example, one of the authors spent time working together with a group of people from a Gong village in Thailand when the local government told the village to send a certain number of men to repair a road washed out during the rainy season; he has also helped to clear fields and build houses in Lahu villages in Thailand. You should not participate in activities which are private or sensitive unless invited, and should only help in ways which are possible for you and in accord with ethical behaviour.

Chapter 10 also discusses field methods from a methodological perspective, and the case studies in most chapters provide various examples of how to give back to the community where you work.

3.4 CONCLUSION

Some of the major issues concerning language policy impacting on a community, such as official decisions about the status and use of languages, the development of orthographies, dictionaries and other language planning work, are outlined in Chapter 8. Chapter 9 follows up on types of language reclamation possibilities in communities and how to design, plan and implement them successfully; case studies at the end of most chapters also give specific examples. Practical methodology for field research and types of research to consider doing are discussed in Chapter 10.

There has been a recent reaction among some scholars about the growing expectation that all research should involve collaboration with the community being investigated. For one thing, the group may not be organized in a way that allows collaboration – either because leadership and authority are absent or fragmented or because there is no in-group desire for any specific input from outside researchers. Second, an individual researcher often lacks the skills to make the kinds of input that a community does want. Third, as effective collaboration requires a major commitment of time and work from the researcher, it inevitably reduces the time available for primary research. Fourth, the developing expectation that data should be documented using specific and time-consuming methods, made accessible and placed in archives requires extensive additional work to prepare the data and thus may greatly reduce the amount of data that can be fully analysed.

Thus, the denigration of **lone ranger** or lone wolf research (Dwyer, 2006: 54; work done by a sole fieldworker who does not work in a team and who does not pursue collaboration with the community) as found in some of the literature (Dwyer, 2006; Gerdts, 2010; Rice, 2009, 2011), mainly concerning work in North America or by researchers from there, may be exaggerated. As Crippen and Robinson (2013) show with several examples, collaboration is often problematic, even for an insider, let alone an outsider. Having started from a position of reflecting on unanticipated local expectations of a fieldworker (Dobrin, 2008),

Dobrin (2014) comes to the conclusion that collaboration is not always appropriate or even possible.

It is normal in linguistics and in anthropology that research by masters and doctoral students is done individually and over a relatively limited time, and the thesis is supposed to be entirely based on the student's own work. This enforces a lone ranger approach, at least initially. Team research may be very productive where possible, but much of the best work starts in lone ranger mode and some of it continues in this way. However, the lone ranger's data should not just be filtered through a Tonto, a single insider co-worker; nor should the lone ranger remain aloof from the community where collaboration is possible and realistic.

CASE STUDY: NǀUU/NǁNG BY MATTHIAS BRENZINGER, WORLD CONGRESS OF AFRICAN LINGUISTICS, AND SHEENA SHAH, SCHOOL OF ORIENTAL AND AFRICAN STUDIES, UNIVERSITY OF LONDON

As of January 2018, the western Nǁng variety, Nǀuu, is spoken by four elderly speakers: Hanna Koper, Griet Seekoei, Katrina Esau and Simon Sauls. This is one of the indigenous click languages of Southern Africa, which include **click** sounds like the English expression of disapproval sound 'tsk'. A few years ago, ǁ'Au, an eastern variety of this language, became extinct when Hannie Koerant and Fytjie Sanna Rooi passed away. The four remaining Nǀuu speakers are siblings and live in the outskirts of Upington, in the Northern Cape province of South Africa, but they are not in daily contact with each other, mainly because of restrictions in mobility due to old age and infrastructure. Thus, Nǀuu is no longer used on a regular basis. Afrikaans is the dominant language in this part of the country, and it is also the mother tongue of all members of the ǂKhomani community. Even though ǂKhomani is an exonym, the Nǁng speakers and their relatives have accepted this name as their autonym. The last speakers of Nǁng are exceptional resources in at least two respects: they still speak a language of outstanding importance and they are also witnesses of a widely neglected past, the genocide of hunter-gatherers in Southern Africa.

It is generally assumed that humans originate from Southern and East Africa. While more than 100 indigenous click languages might still have been spoken by hunter-gatherer communities in this part of the world a century ago, only about a dozen of them are still used as community languages today (Brenzinger, 2013, 2014). Together with click languages spoken by pastoralists who arrived in Southern Africa a few thousand years ago, N‖ng was classified as a member of the 'Khoisan' language family. However, as more language data from these languages became accessible and with the progress made in improving the methods in historical linguistics, this language family proved not to exist (Güldemann & Vossen, 2000). Nevertheless, these genetically unrelated languages continue to be referred to as 'Khoisan', simply out of 'convenience'. We use the term 'indigenous click languages' as these languages belong to different language families.

Linguists considered N‖ng to be extinct for several decades (Traill, 1999: 27). However, in the late 1990s, Nigel Crawhall met Elsie Vaalbooi, who turned out to be a fluent speaker of N‖ng. Via radio, Elsie asked other N‖ng speakers to make themselves known and some twenty elderly people from various parts of the Northern Cape province of South Africa revealed their competence in different varieties of this language (Chamberlin & Namaseb, 2001).

Ouma ǀUna was among these last speakers and was fluent in the Nǀuu variety. She vigorously stressed the importance of maintaining the N‖ng language and culture. Twee Rivieren was her birthplace, which became a game reserve in the 1930s; all indigenous people, including ǀUna and her family, were subsequently forced out of their homes. Ouma ǀUna was instrumental in the ǂKhomani land claims, and, after a long struggle, the South African government compensated the members of the ǂKhomani community for the loss of their lands by granting them six farms in the heart of the Kalahari in 1999.

Their language, Nǀuu, with 114 phonemes, has one of the largest speech sound inventories in the world; forty-five **click** phonemes, thirty non-click consonants and thirty-nine vowels are represented in the Nǀuu orthography. The most striking phonetic feature of the language is the sets of bilabial clicks, also called 'kiss clicks', which only occur in two other languages.

By ignoring fundamental differences between hunter-gatherer communities in Southern Africa, all are commonly lumped together and referred to as 'Bushmen' or 'San'. Even though they do not share racial, linguistic or cultural features, hunter-gatherers in Southern Africa seem to have one aspect in common, a past that led to their economic and cultural marginalization and the extermination of entire communities in genocides. Traill (1996) insists that assimilation of the hunter-gatherers into so-called coloured communities and not genocide was the major factor for the disappearance of these people and for the loss of their languages. At the same time, he states: 'Wherever they found themselves in their homeland, intruders either killed them or treated them with utter contempt and, through a process of "taming", extinguished their ... identity' (Traill, 1996: 183). Speakers of some languages shifted to south-eastern Bantu languages; in the Northern Cape, many of the former hunter-gatherers abandoned their languages in favour of Afrikaans. Traces of these languages can be found in Afrikaans varieties, such as the one spoken by the Karretjie Mense ('donkey-cart people') of the Upper Karoo who 'perceive their spoken version of Afrikaans to be a Bushman language' (Prins, 1999: 48). More recent studies reveal that genocide of hunter-gatherer communities wiped out entire communities in the second half of the nineteenth century. The extermination of hunter-gatherers was not only by Dutch-speaking pastoralists; there was heavy involvement of Baster, Griqua and Khoi groups in the destruction of hunter-gatherer bands.

The digital Bleek and Lloyd archive (http://lloydbleekcollection.cs.uct .ac.za) constitutes a huge database for the ǀXam language, consisting mainly of texts recorded by Wilhelm Bleek and Lucy Lloyd with ǀXam prisoners in the 1870s. Few documents exist for most other related languages. Since the late 1990s, however, various linguists have recorded the Nǁng language as remembered and spoken by the remaining speakers. Various language documentation projects have focused on specific aspects of Nǁng, such as its sound system, selected morpho-syntactic structures and the lexicon, but also on discourse-based descriptions and analyses. There is a recent grammar of the Nǀuu language (Collins & Namaseb, 2011). Another important source with audio, video and text files is the Hugh Brody archive at the University of Cape Town.

Katrina Esau, also known as 'Ouma Geelmeid' and more recently as Queen Katrina, is the most active among the remaining Nǀuu speakers. For more than a decade, she and her granddaughter, Claudia du Plessis, taught Nǀuu as a team. In 2016, David van Wyk became involved in the teaching and, through his initiative, a Nǀuu language committee was established in December 2017. Katrina is non-literate and Claudia, David and another young woman, Mary-Ann Prins, are the only non-linguists who can actually read and write Nǀuu texts. Between thirty and forty children from the ǂKhomani community and the neighbourhood acquire Nǀuu phrases and songs in Nǀuu language classes, which take place three times a week for roughly two hours per day.

Since the beginning of 2012, we have supported community teaching efforts, working closely with community members in the establishment of a community orthography and the production of language teaching materials. In a community workshop in Upington on 24 March 2014, illustrated alphabet charts and other Nǀuu language posters with translations in English, Afrikaans and ǂKhomani Nama were launched and are being used in the community teaching efforts (Shah & Brenzinger, 2017). In 2016, an illustrated trilingual (Nǀuu, Afrikaans, English) reader in the Nǀuu community orthography was handed over to the community. The contents and format of the reader are tailored towards Nǀuu teaching conducted by the community. The reader is based on words, phrases and sentences recorded in interviews, but also on natural conversations. The twelve sections of the book feature different semantic fields and include games, prayers and songs. Nǀuu–Afrikaans–English and Afrikaans–Nǀuu–English glossaries include the Nǀuu terms used by Katrina in her language classes (Shah & Brenzinger, 2016).

Not Nǀuu, but ǀXam, which became extinct about 100 years ago, is the most visible related language in the country. On Freedom Day, 27 April 2000, the new coat of arms of post-apartheid South Africa was introduced with a written motto in this extinct language: *ǃke e: ǀxarra ǁke*, with an official English translation 'diverse people unite'. Very few people are able to read, let alone understand, this ǀXam phrase, which features prominently on all South African currency.

On Freedom Day 2014, Katrina Esau received the Order of the Baobab in silver: 'For her excellent contribution in the preservation of a language that is facing a threat of extinction. Her determination to make the project successful has inspired young generations to learn' (www.thepresidency.gov.za). While this award is an important recognition of the Nǀuu language revitalization efforts of Katrina and the community, much more governmental support would be required in order to prevent Nǀuu from following the path of ǀXam towards extinction.

DISCUSSION QUESTIONS

Your university ethics approval requires you to maintain the anonymity of your sources, but your consultants want to be identified as the experts who gave you their knowledge. What should you do?

Your initial topic does not work out; the field site is inaccessible or too dangerous, the community refuses to allow you to work there, the language turns out not to be spoken anymore or some other problem prevents you from continuing. What should you do, and whom should you tell before you do this?

SUGGESTIONS FOR FURTHER READING

The American Anthropological Association (2012) and the Linguistic Society of America (2009) provide two standard statements about ethical field research. These can be compared with the guidelines of your own institution.

Dorian (2018) is a recent overview by the doyenne of research on endangered languages and working with their communities, which provides a valuable reflection on how to do research in an appropriate way.

4   Identity and Attitudes

Some have carried, it, held it close, protected.
Others have pulled it along like a reluctant child.
Still others have waved it like a flag, a signal to others.
And some have filled it with rage
and dare others to come close.
And there are those who find their language
a burdensome shackle.
They continually pick at the lock.

Zepeda (2008: 64)

Identity is complex, multifarious and fluid. Groups define themselves and others with names, by group and other categories and their composition and with their attitudes (Llamas & Watt, 2010), and in many other ways (Fishman, 1977, 1989). These combine to form individuals' identities – overt and covert, often multiple and shifting. Where enough of this is negative, the result may be language endangerment. Thus, changing negative attitudes is one of the most important precursors for language reclamation (Chapter 9).

4.1 NAMES

One of the key elements in a group's identity is its name. Often there are several names: the **autonym** (the group's name for itself), one or more **exonyms** (names for a group in other languages, such as the majority language) and possibly some other former autonyms. Exonyms and even autonyms may become pejorative due to negative attitudes to minorities, and so there may be **neonyms** (new names), mainly, but not exclusively, autonyms, newly created to replace them.

Names come from a variety of sources; some are just names with no specific meaning (although people often invent plausible meanings and etymologies for these). Some autonyms are meaningful in the language, and exonyms can be meaningful in the language that they come from. There are also **toponyms** based on geographical names (Chapter 6), and names from other sources, not infrequently just the word for 'people' or 'human beings' or some salient word in the language. There is often major confusion in the literature about names and groups, usually due to alternative names for the same group. There may also be separate names for a group, its language and its territory, or all can be the same; or there may be no general name at all, just names for subgroups. A further level of confusion is that there are always superordinate names which subsume many distinct groups, and these are often popularly used among the majority as if they were the name of a group of people with one language: Aboriginal in Australia, *orang asli* ('original people') in Malaysia and Indian in the United States. Less comprehensive exonyms which still lump many groups together are widespread all over the world; sometimes these are embedded in official classifications of minority groups. There are also often distinct names for several subgroups within a group, which are sometimes said to be distinct groups; and, indeed with sufficient time and social pressure, they may become distinct.

In some cases, new exonyms are coined from minority language elements, as in the case of Zomia (Scott, 2009), intended as a toponym for the minority-inhabited highlands of mainland South East Asia and adjacent highland areas of South Asia and China, which is derived from Central Chin language terms *zo* 'middle' and *mi* 'people', found in the opposite order in the autonym of the largest Central Chin group, the Mizo of Mizoram in north-eastern India; the term *zo* 'middle' and **cognate** forms are present in the autonyms of many Chin groups in western Burma, eastern Bangladesh and north-eastern India. Chin is a collective Burmese exonym referring to a cluster of scores of Tibeto-Burman languages, spoken mainly in the Chin State and in Arakan. The related term Khyang (reflecting older Burmese pronunciation) is used for these groups in Bangladesh. In India, the exonym Kuki is still sometimes used to refer to Chin groups, although this has become somewhat pejorative, as has the Indian exonym Naga which subsumes some of the northernmost languages closely related to the Chin languages, as well as a large number of other Tibeto-Burman languages of Manipur, Nagaland, south-eastern Arunachal Pradesh and some areas of eastern Assam. The Indian exonym Naga has also spread into Burma, to refer collectively to the groups speaking similar or related languages in north-western Burma, although this is about to change in new official usage. There are also exonyms for many groups, some still in use; the Indian term Lushai for the Mizo (as in the Lushai Hills, the British administrative name for what is now Mizoram State in India) is still used to refer to the Mizo in Burma. There was a former Indian exonym Mikir for the group which is now officially referred to as Karbi (in the Karbi Hills of Assam) but also has the autonym Arleng, although Mikir still appears in the official list of tribes in India from 1950.

A similarly complex example is Mishmi, an Indian exonym for four distinct languages of north-eastern Arunachal Pradesh in India, also spoken by smaller populations in eastern Tibet and one also extending into northernmost Burma (Bradley, 2007a: 357). These are four languages in two distinct subgroups of Tibeto-Burman. One subgroup is Digarish, which includes Taruang (also known by the former Indian exonym Digaru Mishmi, as Taraung in Burmese, as Darang Deng in Chinese and under various other distortions of the autonym including Taraon, Tayin, Tawra or Tain). The other Digarish language is Idu, also known as Idu Mishmi or in Chinese Yidu, and sometimes by the exonym Chulikata ('cropped hair') which is seen in its ISO 639-3 code (clk). The other subgroup is Mijuish, which includes Kaman (an autonym; the Indian exonym is Miju; also known as Geman Deng in China) and the recently located Zaiwa language (also known in India from two clan names as Zakhring, seen in its ISO 639-3 code (zkr) and Mayol, Meyol or Meyor, and in Tibetan and Chinese as Zha). As we can see, the names for genetic subgroups also often come from old exonyms.

Ethnic groups are often categorized at different levels of diversity in different exonym systems. The degree of internal diversity within a nationality in China is much greater than in adjacent countries, so often several ethnic groups of Vietnam, Laos or Burma are subsumed into one national minority in China. Or the boundaries may differ in other ways; for example, the endangered Kucong language of far south-western China and nearby in north-western Vietnam (with the autonym Lahlu) is very closely related to, but not mutually intelligible with, Lahu of China, Laos, Burma and Thailand; Kucong is a local Chinese exonym. The Kucong of China were added to the Lahu nationality in 1989, while the Kucong of Vietnam were initially classified as the Cosung ethnic group, the Vietnamese pronunciation of the Chinese exonym, in the 1950s, but later renamed Lahu in Vietnamese official sources according to the Vietnamese pronunciation of their autonym; there are no non-Kucong Lahu in Vietnam (Bradley, 2007a: 397–8). The Laomian (Chinese exonym) of China and Burma call themselves Guba 'our people' and speak a language very closely related to Bisu further south in China and Burma and in Thailand, but were classified as Lahu in China in 1990 because they live among the Lahu and many can also speak Lahu (Bradley, 2007a: 400–1). Because Laomian and Bisu are very similar, Chinese linguists now regard it as one *yuyan* (the Chinese term usually inaccurately translated as 'language'; it actually refers to a cluster of related languages with a historical and cultural connection, like Chinese; for discussion see Bradley, 1992a).

Sometimes there are dialect differences without distinct names, and sometimes culturally distinct groups speaking the same dialect may have different autonyms in different places, such as the Laho Shi Banlan in Burma and Thailand, Laho Shi Nakeo in China and Laho Ahpubele in Laos and California, all speaking the same subvariety of Lahu Si 'yellow Lahu' (Bradley, 1979b); since moving to California and converting to Christianity, the Laho Ahpubele have started to call themselves Lahu Si or just Lahu, since they are the main Lahu community in the United States.

Dialect and subgroup names usually contain the name of the overall group and some additional element: geographical location, compass direction or some salient characteristic such as colour (usually of women's clothing). Where the subgroup name does not contain the overall group name, there is sometimes confusion about its inclusion in that group; for example, the Lao exonym for Lahu Ahpubele is Kwi, and this is officially a distinct ethnic group from Lahu in that country and in Burma; there is also another dialect of Lahu spoken in Laos and Thailand, Lahu Kulao also known as Lahu Hpu ('white Lahu'), which is referred to as Lahu in the ethnic classification of Laos.

Personal names are also a component of individual identity and often serve to identify someone as a member of a particular group. This is particularly true for surnames, transmitted across generations within a family, mainly patrilineally, but sometimes also or instead matrilineally. In some societies, personal names are also reused within the family. In many parts of the world, genealogies are essential and carefully transmitted cultural knowledge; they also provide insights into family and local history.

In Chinese, there is a limited set of almost exclusively one-syllable patrilineal family names which occur first in the name of every person in the Han Chinese majority group, normally followed by a two-syllable meaningful personal name; one-syllable personal names also occur but are now less frequent. Chinese people also have a baby nickname, often two identical syllables, and some take an additional Western given name. Members of most ethnic minority groups in China have adopted the basic Chinese pattern, and been categorized into one of the existing Chinese family names – sometimes on the basis of real or imagined descent from a Han Chinese male ancestor. Minority children whose parents do not give them a meaningful Chinese personal name get one when starting school. However, in many groups there is also an indigenous name. For example, most Nosu Yi, Nasu Yi and Nisu Yi have a two-syllable patrilineal clan family name followed by a two-syllable personal name; the Hani have two-syllable names which normally have the second syllable of the father's name as the first syllable of the child's name, plus another personal name syllable which will later become the first syllable in the names of a man's children; the Lahu have names based on which day in the twelve-day animal cycle or time of day one is born. Sometimes the choice of an official surname will reflect the semantic value of a person's minority-language name; so, a Lisu person with the clan surname /ŋwɑ^{55}/ 'fish' may have a Chinese surname similar to Chinese yú 'fish'; or, if living in Burma or Thailand, 'fish' in those languages; or, if Christian and English-speaking, Fish; or the choice may resemble the Lisu name phonetically; or the choice can be arbitrary. In China, once the surname choice is made, the patrilineal descendants keep the same Chinese surname, thus permanently disrupting other traditional practices such as those of the Hani and Yi; another form of cultural endangerment. As with language endangerment, the traditional naming pattern may survive for a few generations alongside the new one; just as immigrant groups often keep two forms of their name, one for group-internal use and one for use with outsiders.

Other kinds of names including place names, terms for cultural artefacts such as clothing, tools or musical instruments can also contain identificational elements which form an important component of local identity. Naming practices, how they reflect identity, culture and ethnicity, and how they change all need to be documented.

4.2 ETHNICITY AND GROUP MEMBERSHIP

Ethnicity is a sociocultural construct, is multifarious and its characteristics and components may shift through time due to social changes or in other ways. It can be deliberately or unconsciously deployed by a group to redefine itself, as Fisher (2011) discusses for the Thakali of Nepal. As he says, ethnicity is 'not a simple cultural given defined by primordial evidence such as language, dress, social organization, religion and the like. Individuals have access to numerous dimensions of identity – for example, those based on class, kinship, locality or religion – some of which become more important at certain times' (Fisher,

2001: 14–15). For the Thakali, major economic change (the loss of their traditional role as middlemen in trade between Tibet and India), greater integration into life in Hindu-majority Nepal and a diaspora of four-fifths of the Thakali population across Nepal and the world has led to competing traditional Thakali, Tibetan Buddhist, Nepali Hindu and modern identities affecting their self-definition of ethnicity and greatly reducing the need to speak the Thakali language, even within the in-group.

It is not always easy to define the membership of a group; the main popular criterion is family relationship. There is on the one hand the ethnic group, and on the other the speakers of the language, who are typically fewer, and often far fewer, than the number of people in the ethnic group, and often far fewer in the case of an endangered language. Then there are the people who marry into or out of the group; the latter may move away and cease to participate in group activities completely, the former provide a focus for a shift in group language use if they move in but do not learn the group language. When people move away, do they ever return? Do they use the language while away? Do their children learn and use it in the diaspora? The descendants of mixed marriages may have two identities, or more after several generations, if they choose to keep them. Many will privilege one of their possible identities over the others, or even hide some of their identities and 'pass' as a member of a larger or more prestigious group.

In some communities, there are legal definitions of group membership. In the Australian Aboriginal context, there are three criteria for Aboriginal status: personal identity, genetic descent and acceptance by a local tribal group. The second criterion is not restricted: the descent can be only a small part of one's genetic heritage; but the third criterion means that people can be excluded from the group by local leadership, whatever the individuals feel. In North America, each tribe or nation and its bands have a corporate existence, often with a defined territory (the reservation) and a tribal leadership which maintains a list of tribe members; the proportion of genetic descent required is sometimes fairly stringent, and there is more tendency to exclude people – for example because they come from a different area, such as the Tohono O'odham who come from Mexico, who are excluded from membership in the Tohono O'odham tribe in the United States, or even for misbehaviour. But no one is excluded for not speaking a group's language! On the other hand, the government of Taiwan recently proposed that social benefits and other positive discrimination for aboriginal people should be restricted to those who speak their traditional languages, but it is extremely difficult to institute testing for this.

Ethnic group membership is often a matter of national-level policy; most countries influenced by the USSR nationality model recognise a specific closed inventory of nationalities or ethnic groups: initially 176, later reduced to 69 in the former USSR, 56 in China, 54 in Vietnam, 59 in Laos and 135 in Burma (Bradley, 2007b). Typically, one nationality is the majority group, there is a small set of large minority nationalities with a recognised territory and then a larger number of smaller groups; in Russia and China, most of these smaller nationalities have a recognised territory at some lower administrative level. In Burma, the Bamar are the majority, there are seven large mostly collective ethnic groups with ethnic states (Arakanese or Rakhine, Chin, Kachin, Karen, Kayah, Mon and Shan) and 127 others. Each citizen of these countries is categorized as a member of one of these groups; this status is indicated in official documents such as identity cards, and membership of a minority group may confer some rights to special economic, educational and social advantages. Recognition as a nationality in the former USSR and China also conferred the right to use and develop the language, although general social attitudes and top-down national policies supporting the national language very often override this right, with the support of in-group leaders who themselves have had the maximum exposure to the majority language of anyone in their group.

In India, constitutional recognition of the special rights of tribal people is granted to tribes on a schedule (list) which has now reached 645, and is regularly revised upwards; within this list there are many additional subgroups within certain tribes, such as Kuki, Bhil and Gond, giving a substantially higher total of named groups. Elsewhere in the world, similar processes of recognising and involving minorities in national life have progressed greatly in recent years.

One of the major causes of language endangerment is passing into the majority, whether after mixed marriages or moving out of the traditional area. This can sometimes be reversed, but usually without the traditional language, as in the case of the Stolen Generation: large numbers of Australian Aboriginal children who were removed from their families and adopted into mainstream families, mainly between 1909 and 1969. Some are now returning to their roots, but completely without traditional language knowledge. Similarly, almost none of the members of China's minority nationalities who have reclaimed this status in the last thirty years can speak their traditional languages. Thus, demographic, political and social advances have not always served to advance traditional language maintenance and impede language endangerment; in reality, it is very often the most advanced and assimilated members of minority groups who have leadership positions.

4.3 ATTITUDES

A usual definition of attitude is the predilection to react positively or negatively to certain phenomena. In social psychology, 'Attitude is the predisposition of some individual to evaluate some symbol or object or aspect of his [sic] world in a favorable or unfavorable manner' (Katz, 1960: 168), divided into affect (what one feels), cognition (what one thinks) and behaviour (what one does) (Triandis, 1971: 2–4; Dawes, 1972: 15–16).

Linguistic and other social attitudes strongly affect the actual transmission and use of languages and the resulting range of fluency within groups (Chapter 5), the stability and cohesiveness of a language (Chapter 7), the formulation and implementation of language policy and the likelihood of its success (Chapter 8), and the likely outcomes of language reclamation efforts (Chapter 9). The various non-linguistic external factors discussed in Chapter 6 contribute to and shape language attitudes. For a more detailed discussion on this, see Garrett (2010).

As Gudkynst and Schmidt (1988: 1) point out, 'Language use also plays a major role in the development of social identity in general.' The social identity theory developed by Tajfel (1978, 1981) has been widely applied in linguistics and in work on the social psychology of language to identify and tease out the factors involved.

There are five key interrelated factors in attitudes about language identity: (1) ethnolinguistic vitality; (2) language as a core cultural value; (3) attitudes to bilingualism; (4) attitudes about the languages in the community and (5) views about the status and functions of languages. All of these vary along continua and include a range of different internal subfactors.

The first relates to the degree to which positive attitudes lead to the ongoing transmission of the language and culture to children: how solidly established and secure the community is in its values, activities and family structure. This also relates to the degree of strength of family, kinship and in-group ties, geographical and social mobility.

Language is not necessarily a core cultural value (Smolicz, 1981) in all communities; there are places where many components of culture, identity and values persist with the traditional language being lost, as happened over many centuries in Ireland until independence in 1921.

If functioning members of a group do not need traditional language skills to remain and feel part of the group, such communities are more at risk of losing their languages, even with strong ethnic vitality, positive policies and strong institutional support.

Bilingualism is sometimes viewed as difficult for children and detrimental to their progress in education and in later life. From bitter personal experience as late second-language learners, not all parents are convinced that bilingualism is desirable, and many choose to transmit only a majority language to their children. Although it is well-known in academic circles that bilingualism is closely related to greater cognitive flexibility as well as obvious communicative advantages, this is not the usual popular belief. However, in some communities, bilingualism is normal and expected; then, the prospects for language maintenance are much more positive. In others, it is strongly discouraged, or monolingualism in a national language may even be enforced, alongside negative attitudes to other languages, especially those of indigenous minorities.

Factors 4 and 5 are intertwined, with deeply embedded attitudes often reflected in language policy choices. Attitudes include both aesthetic and practical judgements: is a language beautiful, able to express intimate thoughts; is it useful in one's daily life; is it appropriate for use in education, does it give access to individual socioeconomic progress; is it OK to speak a language in the presence of outsiders who do not understand it? Many of the non-linguistic situational factors discussed in Chapter 6 are often relevant; does a language have long historical continuity, an established written standard and great written or oral literature? Such things provide prestige and improve the prognosis for language survival. There are both minority in-group attitudes about their own language and about other minority, majority and global languages, and also majority attitudes about minority languages in general and about specific languages; for example, although knowledge of foreign national languages is widely valued for instrumental purposes, some minorities and their languages may be particularly stigmatized, like Rom across Europe; the pejorative meanings associated with exonyms for this group, such as gypsy, often reveal such attitudes. There is often a clear social hierarchy of languages, with endangered languages at the bottom. Around the world, recent moves in the direction of more enlightened policies aiming for language rights, political correctness, social inclusion and equality mask underlying negative attitudes to minorities; but such covert attitudes nevertheless remain important factors in language maintenance. Another subtype of attitudes is about the structure and content of languages: is a language hard or easy to learn and use, complex or simple, impure or incomplete because it contains many loanwords, are complex social choices embedded in a language making it difficult to avoid culturally inappropriate behaviour?

Attitudes are directly reflected in choices made by parents and families to transmit languages to their children, in the choice of languages used in various domains, and cross-generational proficiency differences, as discussed in Chapter 5. They are also affected by factors from the non-linguistic situation and language policies discussed in Chapters 6 and 8. Fortunately, most policy change is now in the direction of greater recognition of minority linguistic and other rights; but, due to prior negative policies and existing covert attitudes, in many cases it is already very difficult to preserve endangered languages without major effort.

Changes in policy can allow groups to access resources for language maintenance, if other positive attitudes and motivation are strong enough; apparently near-terminal endangerment situations such as Irish and Welsh can be reversed with enough effort, if positive attitudes are still present and policy is supportive.

4.4 WELL-BEING AND HAPPINESS

Well-being is a complex composite of positive moods and emotions, satisfaction with lifestyles, individual and group fulfilment and positive functioning, combined with the absence of negative moods and emotions such as anxiety. As this is a relatively recent construct, there is not much relevant literature on this area of attitudes and their effect.

Marmion et al. (2014: 29–30) suggest three main components of well-being nominated by members of a range of Australian Aboriginal communities when asked how traditional language use improves their well-being and thus promotes language maintenance. The first is Belonging: strengthening the sense of identity and sense of belonging to tradition, culture, ancestors, spirits, family, community and land (cited by 57 per cent of respondents). Second is Empowerment: strengthening self-esteem, pride and positive feelings in general (cited by 38 per cent of respondents); and third is Communication: allowing people to communicate with each other (cited by 5 per cent of respondents). Walsh (2018) follows up and discusses how health, both physical and mental, is improved by efforts to reclaim traditional languages.

Bhutan is a nation which has chosen to strive for national happiness, rather than solely for economic development; this is a form of well-being under another name. This aim is reflected not only in the economy, but also tourism, foreign relations, education and other areas of national life. This includes a focus on continuing traditional cultural activities such as archery, clothing or architecture. National identity and unity are promoted through spread of the national language, Dzongkha, which is greatly expanding its use in eastern areas of the country. This has the effect of endangering some of the smaller languages in the nation; thus, pursuit of happiness at the national level may not necessarily lead to positive outcomes for language maintenance of all individual languages.

4.5 MEASURING IDENTITY AND ATTITUDES

Direct measurement of attitudes and other components of identity is extremely problematic; often unrealistically positive self-report reflected in surveys or public comment differs from actual behaviour, greatly exaggerating claims about identity, language knowledge and language use. This goes with a tendency for awareness about language endangerment to be delayed: adults do not worry about the vitality of their language because they still speak it, even if their children cannot, and so transmission may be broken and the language is already severely endangered before the community feels the need to react (Schmidt, 1990). Methodologies for investigating language attitudes, names and group membership are discussed in Chapter 10, and ways of viewing language transmission, language abilities and language use are found in Chapter 5. Any study of language attitudes should be based on direct observation, not just on questionnaires, interviews and existing government statistics.

There are various questionnaires used in work on the social psychology of language which have been widely used to investigate minority attitudes and identity. For a very early survey, see Agheyisi and Fishman (1970). One widely used questionnaire is the Subjective Vitality Questionnaire derived from the work of Giles et al. (1977), as discussed in Johnson et al. (1983) and Ryan et al. (1984), with a recent overview by Noels et al. (2014). Another is the Multigroup Ethnic Identity Measure (Phinney, 1992; revised in Phinney & Ong, 2007), with a recent overview by Brown et al. (2014). Marmion et al. (2014) include the questionnaires used to collect information about current Australian Aboriginal language attitudes. Most work within these models has been based on questionnaires, mainly administered in first-world urban settings, especially to investigate the identity, attitudes and language and culture vitality of immigrant minority groups; although the last is different. Some revisions are required to apply such methods in rural third-world settings where most language endangerment is now occurring. Another fundamental issue is that self-report of attitudes using such methods may not reflect actual beliefs and behaviours.

As suggested by the poem at the beginning of this chapter, by a leading in-group Tohono O'odham linguist who has spent her career working towards language maintenance, language attitudes and identity come in many guises: nurturing, compelling, symbolic, confrontational and constraining, among others. By use of focus group discussion, surveys and observation of language use choices (Chapter 5) and surveys, better understanding of attitudes may develop – although self-report in face-to-face discussion with outsiders and in questionnaire-based surveys may not reflect real attitudes.

4.6 ECOLOGICAL RESILIENCE AND RESILIENCE LINGUISTICS

Resilience is a much-used term for successful adaptation to a new situation which initially has adverse consequences, something which is required more and more in the modern world. In ecology and bioscience, Resilience Thinking (Walker & Salt, 2006, 2012; Gunderson et al., 2010) is a way of viewing ecological change: the observation that ecosystems move through stages in reaction to environmental change, that a range of external factors contribute to such changes and that their input to change can be measured. Furthermore, and crucially, an ecosystem may re-establish itself in a new state which shows resilience, typically a new equilibrium which differs from the original state. The same model has also been used to understand change in human social systems and ecosystems: the anthropology of resilience (Berkes, 2008), which so far is not very widely applied.

Resilience Thinking observes that ecosystems move through four phases: (1) growth, (2) conservation, (3) release and (4) reorganization. Crossing the threshold between phases can result in very rapid and drastic changes, particularly when entering a release phase – which in linguistic terms corresponds to language endangerment. Systems may adapt to the release by reorganization, which in linguistic terms corresponds either to complete language shift and monolingualism in a new, dominant language, or some form of multilingualism, with or without overt language maintenance or reclamation efforts for the former language (Chapter 9). The long-term outcome of a reorganization is a new stable phase which may lead to growth; so this is a cyclical process, as has been seen repeatedly over long timescales in our planet's ecosystems. However, the timescales of human linguistic resilience are much shorter; one, two or a few generations, or less in a particularly catastrophic release phase brought on by natural or human-induced disasters. Furthermore, from the perspective of a language which is lost to its community, the new stable state without the language is an ecolinguistic disaster parallel to the extinction of any plant or animal species due to environmental change. However, it has more wide-reaching consequences for our human ecosystem, as discussed in Chapter 1, and the identity and attitudes of group members; groups may simply cease to exist, even though their genetic descendants persist as speakers of other languages with other identities.

The transition between the conservation phase, when things appear to be stable and safe, and the release phase is unpredictable and based on multiple input factors. Just as in ecosystems, signs of stress may be apparent even early in a linguistic conservation phase, and accumulate until release begins; the transition is subtle and hard to detect, and, as we saw in Chapter 2, attempts to impose a universal sequence and discrete categories on language endangerment in the release phase are problematic.

Various types of major external and internal factors which may move languages towards release are outlined in Chapter 6. These include many large-scale sociopolitical and historical factors: colonialism and the dissemination of colonial languages over the last five centuries, the more recent development and centralization of nation-states with a national language, and most recently globalization and the spread of world languages. The seven main clusters of non-linguistic factors are (1) demography, (2) geography, (3) politics, (4) economy, (5) history, (6) education and (7) culture. In different settings these factors may have differing degrees of impact. Resilience Thinking attempts to assign values to factors conducive to ecological change and calculate their combined impact, but in a human ecosystem this may be more difficult. In resilience linguistics we are not just looking at sea or air temperatures, precipitation, forest cover, vegetation type and other externally measurable facts in a time sequence. Some factors, such as population, geography and history are directly observable, with some caveats, but, like endangerment itself, may be difficult to scale appropriately. Economic factors might be thought to be objective facts, but many societies speaking endangered languages may be partly self-sufficient and some may be producing cash crops not measured in official statistics; conversely, economic factors promoting release and reorganization, such as increasing integration into a cash economy and dependency on outside goods, are more easily quantifiable. More subtle internal social factors such as culture, identity and attitudes are also crucial; these can be observed and sometimes measured. Each individual language is spoken in a situation which combines all of these factors, leading individuals to have the kinds of attitudes discussed in this chapter and to make language choices which we will discuss in Chapter 5.

This is not to suggest that we should strive to resist all forms of linguistic change; see Schumpeter (1976: 84), whose creative destruction, 'competition from the new', leads to social renewal. A language permanently in conservation phase will eventually become archaic, leading initially to reduction in its use and its restriction to use in limited domains and eventually either to release and language shift or some other form of renewal – for example, the use of a more modern variety of the language for some purposes in **diglossia** (Chapter 8) or changes induced by policy and planning to modernize the language and thus return it to a growth phase.

In all languages, there are cyclical processes of linguistic change, greatly accelerated during the process of language loss in a language endangerment situation, as shown in Chapter 7. Resilience linguistics is the application of the Resilience Thinking model to linguistics, helping us to understand the processes of language endangerment and the factors which contribute to it more clearly and to assist communities in responding to ecolinguistic change and threats to the persistence of their languages, and, where appropriate, to reverse the shift through reclamation activities as outlined in Chapter 9.

The case studies in this volume suggest different possible approaches in resilience linguistics; other case studies are in Hinton and Hale (2001), Bradley and Bradley (2002), Bradley (2005, 2010, 2011a, 2011b), Grenoble and Whaley (1998, 2006), Jones and Ogilvie (2013), Hinton, Huss and Roche (2018) and elsewhere. The generalization is that linguistically resilient communities become or remain multilingual. They do not cling solely to the past, but they respect themselves and their traditional identity and are willing to make some efforts to retain the parts of their heritage which they have positive attitudes about, including, in most cases, all or part of their language, which they continue to use in some domains (Chapter 5) and which may require some renewal for use in modern domains, preferably based on solid language policy and effective planning and implementation (Chapters 8 and 9).

Clearly, the application of resilience linguistics is not intended to resist or reverse the spread of knowledge and use of regional, national and world languages, as these are part of the path to economic opportunity. Rather, the intention is to aim for a new stable multilingual situation, where each language is used in appropriate situations, and minority groups have multiple identities and positive attitudes about all of them: as members of an ethnic group with a language and culture; as residents of a region with local characteristics including perhaps a regional language; as citizens of a nation-state with a national language; as adherents of other types of groups, such as an organized religion (sometimes requiring the use of a particular liturgical language) or other nonlocal group using an additional language; or as users of a language of wider communication such as English. With contact and intermarriage, individuals can also have multiple overlapping minority, regional, national and other affiliations. The challenge is to make these all positive, additive resources, and not to allow the more widespread languages to displace the smaller ones. Ideally, all individuals will develop multilingual and multicultural skills without weakening their connection to their roots and the language and culture associated with it, and younger individuals will return to or expand use of their background language.

4.7 CHANGING ATTITUDES

Languages become endangered because of negative attitudes; if a language is to persist, these negative attitudes must be overcome. Attitude change can only come from within the community; it cannot be imposed from outside. An outsider researcher can help insiders to develop skills, resources and self-esteem and help in advocacy. Supportive educational and other official policies and good language planning and development work can be very helpful, but it is the insiders who will ultimately decide. An outsider should not become too involved in and committed to the process of attitude change, as pointed out by Matras (2005). The key to the future of every language is positive in-group attitudes leading to language transmission to and the development of language skills in the children of the community; this is further discussed in Chapter 5, and various strategies for language reclamation are outlined in Chapter 9.

One component of language policy formulation which is aimed at promoting positive attitudes about endangered languages, both inside a community and among national leaders, educators and other outsiders, is prestige planning (Sallabank, 2011: 283–8), as discussed further in Chapter 8. This usually starts as an in-group movement, often spreading from one minority group to others, and is rarely imposed by a top-down policy from the national level. However, the general policy of international bodies such as UNESCO and UNICEF in favour of mother tongue education as a human right for all, including minorities, is a rare exception. Where such policies gain traction, their implementation also requires support from positive attitudes; if parents reject mother tongue education as another manifestation of marginalization, it can fail and thus further reinforce negative linguistic attitudes.

CASE STUDY: MINANGKABAU

Minangkabau is an Austronesian language of West Sumatra province in Indonesia. It is the north-westernmost in a chain of Malayic languages including Riau Malay to the east and Jambi and Musi (Palembang) to the south, all very closely related to Malay in and across the Straits of Malacca which forms the basis of standard Indonesian and standard Malaysian, Singapore and Brunei Malay. The name is said to be a **compound** of *minang* 'victorious' and *kabau* 'water buffalo'.

There are nearly 8 million ethnic Minangkabau; nearly 4 million live outside West Sumatra. This includes about half of the population of Negeri Sembilan state in West Malaysia, just south of Kuala Lumpur (who are now officially classified as *bumiputra* (indigenous) Malay), as well as large numbers in many cities in Sumatra, elsewhere in Indonesia. For example, Jakarta has over 300,000, and there are substantial numbers in every city in Sumatra as well as Bandung in Java. Outside West Sumatra, the highest proportion is in Pekanbaru, the capital of Riau province to the east of West Sumatra, where they are 38 per cent of the city population, or nearly 350,000.

One reason for the Minangkabau diaspora is a long tradition of *merantau*, migration for work by men. Traditionally, women owned the land and stayed at home in this matrilineal society, but women are increasingly also migrating. They had a long tradition of trade from their gold and other mines, were converted to Sunni Islam in the sixteenth century and came under direct Dutch rule after 1838; they played a leading role in the Indonesian independence movement, and many are among the leading figures in modern Indonesian life.

While they are recognised as the fourth largest ethnic group in Indonesia, the language is under threat. It has almost disappeared into

Malay in Malaysia, and is not fully maintained among many migrants outside West Sumatra. Even in West Sumatra where the vast majority is Minangkabau, the language is being replaced by Indonesian in many domains, and transmission to children is decreasing, especially in cities and towns.

Minangkabau is written in a Romanization, but this is not taught in schools, which only have limited teaching about culture. To prepare children for school in Indonesian, many parents, especially in cities, now speak Indonesian to children in the home. The language has a number of dialects; the dialect of the capital, Padang, is the standard. It is also used to a limited extent as a lingua franca by speakers of some surrounding languages such as Mandailing Batak to the north and Jambi to the south as well as by local Chinese and others in cities and towns in West Sumatra.

Apart from many lexical items which are unrelated to the corresponding Indonesian and Malay forms, a large part of the lexicon shows regular sound changes, such as 'a' > 'o' in word-final position, as in *limo* (Indonesian *lima* 'five') and *mato* (Indonesian *mata* 'eye'), as well as changes between 'e' and 'a' other than word-finally, as in *ampek* (Indonesian *empat*) 'four' and *bali* (Indonesian *beli*) 'buy'. There are also consonant changes, such as the loss of 'h', as in *ari* (Indonesian *hari* 'day') and *tau* (Indonesian *tahu*) 'know' and 's' > 'h' in word-final position, as in *abih* (Indonesian *habis*) 'finish'; also various shortenings of multisyllable words such as *baso* (Indonesian *bahasa* 'language', originally an Indic loanword). These changes are often eliminated as the language converges towards Indonesian/Malay; for example, the Malaysian place name Negeri Sembilan comes from Minangkabau *nagari sambilan* ('village nine', nine villages), with three 'e' changed to 'a' reflecting the Malay form. There is an extremely comprehensive Minangkabau–Indonesian–French dictionary (Moussay, 1995) based on an extensive newspaper corpus, including a full list of **toponyms** from West Sumatra (Moussay, 1995: 1247–328).

Like many major languages of Indonesia, Minangkabau has a complex system of speech levels. The four speech levels are known as *kato nan ampek* (Indonesian *kata yang empat*) 'word – relative marker – four'. These include *kato mandaki* 'word upward' used to elders for respect, *kato mandata* 'word level' used to people of the same age for empathy, *kato manurun* 'word downward', the simplest speech level used to younger people and *kato malereang* 'word slanted', avoidance language used to in-laws. While their knowledge is highly valued, and nearly all adults claim to use them, this knowledge is declining and many younger people who can speak Minangkabau do not control the system.

Thamrin (2015) did a large-scale survey of language attitudes, learning and use in six locations in West Sumatra: two cities in the central area with high levels of Indonesian language contact and use: the capital Padang (PD) and Bukittinggi (BT); one city with medium contact: Payahkumbu (PK); and three towns in more traditional areas with less intensive contact, Lubuk Sikaping (LS), Pulau Punjung (PP) and Muaro Sijunjung (MS).

A total of 200 ethnic Minangkabau children aged eleven to eighteen from these six locations reported whether they regarded Indonesian or Minangkabau as their first language. Table 4.1 shows the results. L1 indicates first language.

The same children reported where they learned to speak Minangkabau (Table 4.2).

A total of 200 parents of these children reported on their own use of Minangkabau and Indonesian in a large number of domains, on a **Likert scale**: all Indonesian, 1; mainly Indonesian, 2; both equally, 3; mainly Minangkabau, 4, and only Minangkabau, 5 (Table 4.3).

Most children are addressed by their parents using Indonesian or mainly Indonesian in the three locations where the most children report Indonesian as their first language. Even where parents do sometimes speak to their children in Minangkabau, many children still feel themselves dominant in Indonesian. However, many parents still speak to each other mainly in Minangkabau at home – hence the possibility for children to learn it there. It is only in the two large towns that school is said to play any role in children's learning of Minangkabau,

Table 4.1 *Children's first language (%)*

Location	PD	BT	PK	LS	PP	MS
Indonesian L1	68.4	75	55.9	62.5	50	37.5
Minangkabau L1	31.6	25	44.1	37.5	50	62.5

Table 4.2 *Children's learning of Minangkabau (%)*

Location	PD	BT	PK	LS	PP	MS
Family	26.3	50	47	50	53.1	56.3
Friends/society	57.8	37.5	50	46.9	43.8	40.6
School	15.8	12.5	2.9	3.1	3.1	3.1

Table 4.3 *Adults' domains of use of Minangkabau*

Domain	PD	BT	PK	LS	PP	MS
To spouse at home	3.55	3.38	4.23	3.91	4.66	4.38
To children at home	1.95	2.25	3.06	1.72	4.25	3.34
Post office	1.71	1.78	1.94	2.56	1.84	2.56
Doctor	1.84	1.91	1.91	2.31	2.41	2.44
Bank	1.50	1.91	1.59	2.22	2.25	1.84
Write to friends	1.74	2.03	2.94	2.47	2.56	3.09

Table 4.4 *Adults' attitudes about Minangkabau, six locations*

Location	PD	BT	PK	LS	PP	MS
L1 to children	0.29	0.39	0.42	0.25	0.50	0.28
Should speak	0.49	0.94	0.70	0.83	0.88	0.94
Proud	0.81	0.94	1.00	1.00	1.00	1.00

but school has not succeeded in making people comfortable about writing in it, except where the language remains strongest. Formal spoken domains are mainly Indonesian domains in all locations, even for adults with full knowledge of Minangkabau, and especially in the highest-contact areas.

The survey also asked a number of questions about language attitudes, which reveal interesting patterns; the data is reported for the 200 adults surveyed in Thamrin (2015). Table 4.4 is based on rating No as 0 and Yes as 1; so 1.00 means all responses were Yes, 0.50 means that half were Yes and half were No. The first question is whether adults should speak Minangkabau as their first language to children, the second is whether an ethnic Minangkabau person should speak Minangkabau and the third is whether the person is proud of speaking Minangkabau.

A very positive language attitude is reported except in the two high-contact cities, but somewhat less positive views are reported about whether speaking Minangkabau is essential to identity and much more negative views concerning whether it should be spoken to children, sometimes even in locations where the language is currently well-maintained. The judgements about what should be spoken to children may suggest a negative future trend for transmission of Minangkabau.

˙ In summary, Minangkabau is still spoken by nearly 5 million people, but in restricted and gradually reducing domains, with partial loss even of the family domain, incomplete transmission to children and greatly reduced knowledge of the range of traditional speech levels. Its future is likely to be a continuing convergence towards Indonesian, which is easy as the two languages are very closely related.

DISCUSSION QUESTIONS

Briefly define your own identity. What are its key components and what is their relative importance to you? Are you a member of multiple groups, and do you assume different identities in different settings?

In a particular setting very familiar to you, what kinds of issues would arise in measuring community attitudes about languages? Would you expect people's answers to be accurate, and, if not, in what ways would they be likely to be inaccurate?

Pick a language listed in the *Ethnologue* with multiple names, and try to find out from other sources what types of names these are: autonyms or exonyms, names for all or part of the group, names with specific meanings in the language or in nearby languages, obsolete or pejorative names; discuss.

SUGGESTIONS FOR FURTHER READING

Bradley (2002) is a more detailed outline of some of the attitude factors in language maintenance, as discussed in Section 4.5.

  (2010) contains two case studies applying the resilience linguistics model to two languages, one critically endangered, the other currently safe but becoming vulnerable.

Fishman (1977) is the classic overview of the components of ethnic identity and how they relate to language and language shift.

5   Language Knowledge and Use

For community members, language loss is not an abstraction ...
Perley (2012a: 137)

You feed the child with the language as soon as it is born.
Burke Museum of Natural History and Culture (2016)

5.1 KNOWLEDGE

From the perspective of an individual, personal life history, capacities and choices determine their abilities in whatever languages they speak. The outcome for the languages in their repertoire is often that an individual's knowledge of the dominant language in the larger society will increase, while their knowledge of their in-group endangered language may cease to develop after a certain age, and may even contract. The process of language endangerment is an overall collective outcome of the choices made by individuals, families and communities to acquire and use another language rather than a traditional in-group language, more of the time in progressively more situations.

The ability of any normal mature individual in a community whose language is endangered falls along a long range from fully fluent with the ability to use a language in every relevant domain discussed in Section 5.3, to no ability to speak or understand a language at all. At one end of the continuum are the fully fluent speakers with maximal traditional cultural knowledge; in the modern world, most of these tend to be mature adults, often older ones. Within cultural knowledge, there is individual specialization. Some people know more about some things; some women may know about growing plants for use as thread, making thread, dyeing, weaving and sewing traditional clothing, and many will know about plants which can be gathered from the environment for food, medicinal or other uses. Some men may know more about hunting, animals, making and using tools and weapons. Some will be experts in a traditional craft: making baskets, being a blacksmith, building houses and so on. Ritual specialists have specific religious and other cultural knowledge which may be essential for everyday life within a fully traditional setting, but which may be vulnerable to abandonment in the face of new lifestyles and outside influences. There are also mature speakers who are fluent but have less cultural knowledge, and thus may have gaps in their lexicon and less ability to be an active participant in traditional settings.

In an endangered language setting, the semispeaker has less than fluent control of the conservative form of the language, although he or she may be able to function fully in everyday life using the language. There is often a long continuum of ability within the semispeaker group, with structural consequences explored further in Chapter 7. Furthermore, as discussed in Chapter 2, the attitude about the language ability of semispeakers whose speech differs more from that of the fully fluent speakers may differ greatly between communities. In some, semispeakers with relatively innovative speech patterns are accepted and recognised as full speakers and members of the community, and a new stable semispeaker variety of the language may even develop, as in the case of Baby Gumatj, also known as Dhuwaya (dwy), among the Yolngu community at Yirrkala in East Arnhem Land, northern Australia. Other societies may have less positive attitudes about semispeaker speech, preferring a 'pure' conservative variety.

The least fluent semispeakers may have very limited productive knowledge, although they may actively use a range of phrases and words without much ability to produce new phrases; perhaps they should not be classified as semispeakers, even if they are able to function to a very limited extent, as they have no capacity to produce new utterances and the innovative content of what they say can only be produced in the replacing language.

It is not so unusual for there to be members of the community who can understand a great deal of the language, but do not currently speak it themselves; these are often termed **passive understanders**; while they may choose not to produce speech, they may nevertheless have some insights about the language and their knowledge should not be disregarded. If circumstances change, a passive understander may choose to start to produce speech; for example, in some Ainu (ain) communities in northern Japan, after the oldest and most fluent local speakers have died, less old and formerly silent passive understanders have taken over the role of language expert – which means that they were keeping their knowledge unexpressed in deference to more knowledgeable elders, presumably because they respect their elders and regard their own abilities as less authoritative.

Different communities differ greatly in their attitudes about speech and understanding abilities representing different parts of this continuum, as we have seen in the previous chapter; even within a community there are often various attitudes to less fluent and less traditional speech forms. Obviously, the more critical and negative the overall community attitudes are about semispeaker speech, the more likely semispeakers are to fall silent in this language, and thus become apparent passive understanders; and the less likely a semispeaker speech style is to be accepted as worthy of ongoing community efforts for maintenance. Negative attitudes to semispeaker speech may restrain the otherwise rapid progress of structural change, but at the risk of speeding the disappearance of the language as children are discouraged from speaking in an innovative way, but have not been exposed to enough input of the conservative variety and may feel that they do not have the ability to speak in a more conservative way. This is particularly true if their own parents are semispeakers.

5.2 ACQUISITION

This is not the place for an extended discussion of the processes of first-language acquisition, nor for a discussion of second-language learning of an endangered language, as is taking place for all speakers in some types of endangered language reclamation such as renativization and revival, and for some individual speakers in other types (Chapter 9); the general literature on these topics is very large. Some of the structural consequences of the acquisition and learning processes will be outlined in Chapter 7. What is most relevant here, and also considered further in Chapter 8 from the perspective of language policies and their implementation, is how and where the endangered language is being acquired.

All endangered languages, and most other languages of the world, are spoken by people who speak more than one language, and are thus bilingual to a greater or lesser degree – bilingualism is normal. Bilingualism is also one of the major topics of research in linguistics; for a recent overview, see Ng and Wigglesworth (2007).

It is now believed that first-language acquisition is most efficient, and perhaps can only take place, up to puberty, so this is why it is particularly disastrous for the survival of languages that many families are making a choice not to transmit the family background language to their children in the home during childhood. Often this is due to a mistaken belief that using a dominant language in the home will confer an educational and social advantage on their children. Unfortunately, this belief is sometimes reinforced by observing **developmental** issues arising in bilingual language acquisition, which is often slower and may initially appear 'confused'; and by parents' own recall of traumatic experiences which they encountered due to lack of ability in the dominant language. For example, because they were effectively monolingual and had no knowledge of the dominant language when they started school, and may even have been punished for speaking their own language there.

The reality is exactly the opposite: a great deal of the recent research in bilingualism shows that this is a grave mistake, as bilingualism acquired in childhood is not only fully fluent in both languages, but also confers a variety of cognitive and other advantages on the bilinguals. Ng and Wigglesworth (2007: 61–7) summarize these as cognitive flexibility and metalinguistic awareness; metalinguistic awareness includes awareness of the arbitrariness of language as well as structural awareness of differences between languages in sounds, words, sentences and meaning. Another advantage of bilingualism is that learning of additional languages is greatly facilitated, both in speed and in the level of fluency achieved. Language workers and educators need to make parents and the society as a whole aware of these advantages, and urge parents to transmit their in-group language to their children. One way to promote this is to highlight the cognitive advantages for learning additional languages: a powerful motivator in a globalizing world. For example, Yuan (2005) clearly demonstrates that ethnic minority students in China who speak their own group's language in addition to Chinese do significantly better in study of English as a foreign language than monolingual Han Chinese students and also do better than ethnic minority students who do not speak their traditional languages and are monolingual in Chinese.

Not just the age of acquisition is important; it is also desirable to have this take place in as many of the domains discussed in Section 5.3 as possible, including the family domain. Reinforcement through early school-based learning can be important, and Language Nest programmes, such as those discussed in Section 9.1.1 can be extremely useful, but this kind of domain alone is not enough; and the materials and teaching must be supportive of the speech variety also used in the home, which is a problem where there is denativization (Section 9.1.6). In-family language use between grandparents or parents in the presence of children can be useful for transmission, but children need to be addressed directly in the group's language and expected and encouraged to respond in this language when addressed.

Less relevant in early stages of endangerment, but more relevant where younger members of a community who do not speak their community's endangered language are trying to revitalize and improve their knowledge of it, is the very substantial literature on second-language pedagogy and techniques for success in developing and retaining second-language skills.

While there is considerable individual variation in second-language learning ability, if the learning starts after puberty, this learning will normally never reach the stage of full native-like fluency in all areas of structure. Some of the literature suggests the strong plasticity version of this: that the critical period prior to puberty is the only time when a language can be acquired fluently. Other studies suggest that age of acquisition is not an absolute constraint on achieving substantial fluency: that the period prior to puberty is a sensitive period, but that successful learning to a relatively fluent level after then is possible; see, for example, Birdsong (2005). However, even if post-puberty late learning achieves apparent fluency, there are usually residual second-language learning effects in the sound system and gaps in vocabulary and cultural knowledge.

As we have seen in Section 2.1, in many communities whose languages are more endangered, childhood first-language acquisition of those languages has already broken down; only adults of the parents' generation or older can speak the language at all. In others, language is only transmitted to some children during childhood: in locations where the language is better maintained, in families who value and use their traditional language more, and often most effectively to first-born children who initially have no siblings to talk to, and to only children, especially in societies with grandparents present in the household or where the **nuclear family** is the basic unit. Where female social networks are strong, language transmission may be stronger among females; males, usually with less dense networks often including more outsiders, may have a lower propensity to in-group language transmission and maintenance. One positive outcome of urbanization is that many children around the world are now left behind in the care of grandparents in rural settings while their parents work elsewhere; so these children are extensively exposed to their language, endangered though it may be. Multigenerational family structures also support language transmission.

In Chapter 9, there is a brief discussion of the nativization process whereby a contact language develops. Some scholars view this as a linear process starting with a **pidgin** and developing into a **creole**, but this is not universally so. The processes of pidginization and creolization is again the subject of a very substantial literature; for one approach to the stages in this process and the consequences of how children acquire a creole, see Thomason and Kaufman (1988); for another view, see Ansaldo (2017). As we have seen in preceding chapters, creoles are very often regarded by their speakers as substandard varieties of the dominant language which is the main source of their lexicon; for example, Torres Strait Creole in north-eastern Australia is called Broken (English) by its own speakers. For this reason, creoles may be relatively unstable and undergo rapid change, like endangered languages, and may also be particularly susceptible to becoming endangered, unless they achieve institutional support, such as for Tok Pisin in Papua New Guinea where this creole is the official language of the nation and is even replacing many indigenous languages, such as Taiap or Gapun (Kulick, 1997).

There is also a great deal of research on the effects of attitude and reasons for learning on the effectiveness of language learning. Gardner and Lambert (1992) divide this into integrative and instrumental motivation; integrative motivation is basically the desire to use a language within a society and to be a member of that society, and instrumental motivation is the desire to use a language for communication purposes as an outsider. Another approach is Valdes and Figueroa (1994) whose circumstantial and elective categories formulate this differently. Elective bilinguals are individuals who choose to learn another language, often in an artificial setting such as a classroom, but who usually remain dominant in their first language; circumstantial bilinguals are groups who learn a second language for survival or success in new circumstances. In nearly all endangered language settings other than revival (see Section 9.1.2), use of the in-group language is integrative and circumstantial, and use of the dominant language is instrumental and circumstantial, and potentially later integrative. Thus, the process of endangerment from this perspective is an outcome of the dominant language becoming progressively more and eventually absolutely essential for survival and success, being used in more and eventually all domains, and the resulting loss of the competing circumstantial and integrative basis for the endangered language.

5.3 USE: DOMAINS

Domain is the technical term used here to refer to specific situations in which a language is used. Another early term for domains was settings, from Hymes (1964). Apart from the terms setting and domain, the term situation has also been used. More broadly, a complete description of a speech domain includes all the components of the acronym SPEAKING from Hymes (1974), in which S stands for Setting and Scene, P stands for Participants, E is Ends, A is Act Sequence, K is Key, I is Instrumentalities (also known in more recent literature as style or also as register), N is Norms and finally G stands for Genre. Setting is the physical time and location of a speech event; Scene is the sociocultural context. The meaning of Participants is clear enough; however, the exact background, status and relationships of the participants is crucial and needs extensive investigation, as has been recognised within work in Labovian variationist sociolinguistics when using their equivalent alternative term Speaker Characteristics, for example, Labov (1966, 1972, 2001). Ends are the purposes and outcomes of speaking; Act Sequence is the discourse structure and cultural expectations for the components and order of these components of the speech event. Key is the tone – degree of seriousness, playfulness. Instrumentalities are the types of linguistic forms used: formal or casual, slow or rapid, conservative or advanced and standard or nonstandard. Norms are the social rules for the type of speech event and how participants should interact during it. Genre is the type of speech event: conversation, narrative and so on, with a vast range of subgenres. All of these together form part of the social knowledge for which Hymes coined the term communicative competence: knowing what it is socially appropriate to say and how to say it in a stylistically suitable way according to the expectations within a particular society, in each domain that speech events normally take place.

The term Style is a major topic of research within Labovian variationist sociolinguistics; this includes components of Hymes' Setting, Scene, Norms and Genre in the usage of many scholars, as well as other things such as social networks and relationships among Participants; for an overview, see Rickford and Eckert (2001). Some early work within variationism also extended the term Style to refer to the overall category of domain or setting. A considerable amount of recent work within this paradigm focuses on the relationships of Participants in a Setting, the community of practice: a network of people who share Norms and interact often within a particular Setting and Scene, with speakers constructing and performing their social affiliations and identities through speech and in other ways such as dress.

The key concept of variationist sociolinguistics and its subfield sociophonetics is the Linguistic Variable; variables are the Instrumentalities of the earlier Hymes model: the linguistic forms which have more than one possible alternative, used in ways that reflect Speaker Characteristics and Style in a systematically patterned way. For example, the (h) variable of English in most words is written as 'h' and pronounced as /h/ in most non-British varieties of English, as in words like 'hear', but is variably not pronounced in most British varieties of English, making this word sound the same as 'ear'. This so-called h-dropping happens less frequently in more formal styles and the speech of higher-status speakers, more frequently in more casual styles and the speech of lower-status speakers. Like most Linguistic Variables, the situation is rather complex, with some frequent words such as 'he' showing a different pattern (with frequent omission of the /h/ even in many non-British varieties). Conversely, the name of the letter 'h' itself and other similar words which do not have a pro-nounced /h/ sound in standard English also have the possibility of a form with a hypercorrect pronunciation containing the /h/ sound in the speech of those who do variably 'drop their h', reflecting social aware-ness of the prestige and formality associated with the presence of /h/ and going beyond the standard by using it inappropriately, so 'ear' is sometimes pronounced with the /h/, like 'hear'. This process has been ongoing for many centuries; the pronoun 'it' used to be 'hit' but has now lost its /h/ even in written standard English. In general, during the process of language endangerment, there are many variables and a very large range of individual differences in the range and pattern of variation, as discussed further in Chapter 7. Unfortunately, not much systematic work has yet been carried out on variation within endangered languages; but for a masterful exception, see Dorian (2010b) concerning East Sutherland Gaelic, a very distinctive variety of Scots Gaelic, and see also Stanford and Preston (2009) and Hildeb-randt et al. (2017).

When younger people lack full control of the required range of styles, as is very often the case for many more and less endangered languages, their speech may be culturally inappropriate, even if they do control the everyday informal style, if they use a culturally 'wrong' form of speech to someone of different status. For example, there are elaborate vocabulary and structure differences, sometimes known as registers, within many languages. The norm used to be that they were used to elders and to members of traditional high-status groups, as in Balinese (Suastra, 1995) or Javanese. But many younger speakers do not know these registers sufficiently well to use them, and thus may either shift to the national language, Indonesian, so as not to speak to elders or high-status individuals in a socially inappropriate form of their in-group language, or not speak to them at all, rather than violate social norms which they are aware of but cannot follow. Others who do not control the appropriate register may choose to use what are inappropriate speech forms in such cases, which is regarded by many speakers who do control the formal registers as rudeness and lack of complete knowledge of the language. In this sense, even a language with over 100 million speakers like Javanese can be partly endangered, due to the reduction in use and loss of formerly widespread components of the language like formal registers and the loss of some domains of language use in such areas.

Domains are often categorized into a hierarchy from maximum intimacy and informality to maximum social distance and formality; the exact degree of informality or formality for a particular domain may differ between societies. For example, in many societies around the world, a formal and respectful style is required in the presence of and especially when speaking to certain categories of relatives; and, conversely, with other categories of relatives, one may be expected to interact in a much more informal, intimate and joking style. For that matter, silence may be the most appropriate action for some younger or lower-status speakers in some domains.

Another important way to characterize domains is in terms of the social relationships of the Participants: within the family, among friends, among neighbours, with strangers, with high-prestige and powerful people and so on. Another is in terms of the Setting: in-group Settings in the home and the local community, as well as out-group Settings such as education, outside work and various types of transactional situations. A third cross-cutting parameter is Genre: traditional Genres which are appropriate for activities such as births, weddings, funerals and festivals and modern Genres for non-traditional activities. The Setting and Genre of religion can fall along a continuum between traditional and modern: some religions may have a fixed liturgical language and set of SPEAKING conventions which comes as a package with the religion, which may be adapted in different ways in different communities, as Ostler (2016) has discussed in his usual insightful and entertaining manner; local in-group religions may be based entirely in local tradition; and a range of intermediate possibilities is also found. A fourth parameter is whether and how the domain uses written material as opposed to entirely oral expression, some written and some oral content, or is entirely written. This includes various types of media, with oral (and sometimes visual) media for listening, such as radio, TV and webcasts; and written media for reading such as newspapers and other text-based media, textbooks and literature.

Another Genre issue is the form of expression; for example, there may be distinct patterns for Genres which include music as well as lyrics; also, there are different kinds of music with more or less language content for different Settings: religion, entertainment or introduced outside subgenres such as rap music. The specific and often important role of music in maintaining and reclaiming endangered languages is exemplified in a number of studies in Ostler and Lintinger (2015).

One universally salient Participant characteristic is gender. In principle, females are usually more directly involved in early nurture of children and so may have a greater input to mother tongue acquisition; and female social networks tend to be closer, so females may also maintain an endangered language better than males of a similar background. As the normal way to learn a mother tongue is in the birth family, these female speech models are essential for language transmission.

Of the domains characterized mainly in terms of the relationships between Participants, those which are the most intimate and long-lasting, although, as we have seen not always the most informal for all types of interlocutors, are within the family – especially the birth family of blood relatives and in some societies also relatives by marriage. Within this, generation (+2 generation: grandparents and their siblings; +1 generation: parents and their siblings; 0 generation: oneself and one's siblings and cousins; −1 generation: children, nieces and nephews; −2 generation: grandchildren, great-nieces and great-nephews) is one important factor; how widely within this range the family network actually interacts differs across societies. Another factor is age, both absolute (as an uncle can be the same age as a brother) and by order of birth. Within each nuclear family of more than one child, there can be elder and younger brothers and sisters, and sometimes for language transmission birth order is relevant: the first brother, second brother, third brother, first sister, second sister and so on; also first child, second child and so on. Once there is more than one sibling, children interact with each other extensively, which may be detrimental to the preservation of a language if the parents and society have not established a solid basis for language use. From a kinship point of view, in addition to many other individual and external factors, the ideal language expert in many societies is the eldest or only daughter whose mother is the eldest or only daughter in her family, as long as the family has an ongoing positive attitude to the language and transmits it during childhood. Interaction with relatives by marriage may be close or distant, frequent or infrequent, and like or unlike interactions with the corresponding birth family relative who is the connecting spouse. Family connections can be institutionalized through genealogy, which forms a link with the past and the endangered language associated with it. Some domains across generations may have nonreciprocal language use: parents or grandparents speak the in-group language to their children or grandchildren, who answer in the out-group language; and some intimate domains may favour **code-switching** between languages; this is especially frequent within the same generation. In both cases, all participants need to know both languages for such interactions to work.

The friendship domains are also intimate, and may be more informal than some intra-family domains involving interaction across generations or between people related by marriage. In some societies, the neighbourhood domain is relatively close and informal; this is often particularly so in rural and traditional societies. A similar pattern can be maintained even in an urban setting when a group migrates but chooses to live in residential concentrations and maintain social networks linking its members; and often these networks are regularly linked back with the original source location of the group. Paradoxically, displaced groups may sometimes be more conservative and successful in maintaining an endangered language than in the 'homeland', see, for example, van Engelenhoven (2002, 2003) concerning some languages which are now more vital in the Netherlands than in their original areas of Indonesia, and Stary (2003) for the survival of Manchu from the north-east of China in far western China, under the separate name Xibo but speaking essentially the same language. The basis of the Endangered Language Alliance in New York City (www.elalliance.org) is that such displaced groups often provide a valuable and easily accessible resource for documentation of endangered languages.

A more distant kind of domain is interaction with strangers; but not all strangers are the same. Some are in-group members who may be recognisable from their traditional dress; some are strangers who are dressed in lower or higher status non-traditional ways, regional, national or foreign. In many societies, females are more likely to maintain many aspects of traditional clothing; so they can thus immediately be identified as in-group even though they are strangers, while the males are more likely to wear non-group-specific out-group clothing; females may also be more likely to have skills in the endangered language. When interlocutors are strangers who are not identifiable as in-group, the initial tendency is to assume that they are outsiders and to choose an out-group language to interact with them. In many societies, the initial part of the Act Sequence of meeting a stranger precisely includes establishing the identity and background of everyone involved; in others, this is less formalized and structured. The final Participant characteristic is status. There are traditional in-group high-status roles such as village headman or traditional religious leader, and somewhat lower-status roles such as traditional healer, shaman, craftsmen and experts such as blacksmiths, fishermen or weavers and other types of social roles. Some societies have traditional hierarchical hereditary caste, clan or other subgroups: from a two-way distinction of aristocrats and commoners to hundreds of originally occupation-specific castes in South Asia. In the case of the Nosu in China, there were formerly five stratified clan clusters: a very small number of *nzymop* 'big ruler' former royal clans, more *nuohop* 'black bone' former aristocrat clans, and many *quhop* 'white bone' commoner clans, *mgapjie* 'outside slave' former farming serf clans and *gaxy* 'fire-foot' or *gaxygalot* 'fire-foot fire-hand' former domestic slave clans (Harrell, 2001: 93). Traditional hierarchies may be made irrelevant by social or political change, as in the case of the Nosu since 1958 (Winnington, 1959).

Another high-status role sometimes fulfilled by an insider is religious leadership; for example, Christian pastor or priest, Islamic imam or Buddhist monk. Some religions promote dominant languages, others choose certain local languages, including some which are endangered, and use them. Sometimes religion can become a strong domain for use of an endangered language. Alternatively, sometimes one local language is chosen by outsider missionaries and imposed more widely; such mission languages can then become a new local **lingua franca** used in church and later more widely, and threaten or replace other languages in the area, as has happened with Lisu now used by Christian Nusu and Anong in north-western Yunnan in China. Another widespread phenomenon is the development of new composite religions combining indigenous and outside influences; these may be highly supportive of an endangered language if the new religion uses and supports the language and is seen as an upholder of traditional community values; one good example is the long series of Lahu indigenous messianic religions (Walker, 2003: 505–47) incorporating a substantial Buddhist component (Walker, 2003: 310–61).

Out-group high-status roles in frequent contact with groups speaking endangered languages mainly relate to education, health and other government services, including teachers, nurses, doctors and other types of government officials. In some cases, in-group and out-group roles may overlap: the traditional headman may also serve as the government's political village leader, some teachers, health and other government workers may be local or from the in-group. If so, high occupational status may override in-group language knowledge: the local in-group teacher or doctor may choose not to speak the endangered language in the school or the health clinic. The endangered language also usually lacks much of the vocabulary needed for such domains.

In mixed interactions where some Participants do not speak the in-group language, there are substantial differences between societies about how willing people are to continue to speak in the in-group language, whether the non-speakers are local or outsiders. Some groups who are already bilingual may immediately switch to the out-group dominant language, even if all but one of the Participants speaks the in-group language; others may be more willing to continue in the in-group language. For an endangered language, once transmission has broken down and some in-group family, friends and other local in-group people do not speak it or have only limited ability, the choice not to speak the endangered language in their presence will rapidly eliminate most possible domains for that language, other than interaction between older speakers where the younger non-speakers are not present.

The earlier discussion of Settings as a parameter in the use of languages in a domain has been partly integrated into the discussion of Participants. One type of setting not yet discussed, which is gaining more and more prominence as societies become less self-contained and self-sufficient, is the transactional domain: buying and selling things. Another is the work domain; paid work and work for outsiders is now usual. Education and health services are other large and growing domains. In all of these types of domain, language shift is likely when outsiders are involved. Modern transactional domains, supermarkets, shopping malls, public transport as well as paid work outside the community, education and health services or military service do not favour use of an endangered language.

On the other hand, there can be official formal education in minority languages, including some which are endangered. This may take the form of transitional bilingual education, using the mother tongue as a bridge to the dominant language in preschool or early primary school, or ongoing education in the minority language through school. In some cases, it is not just the language, but other subjects, which are taught using the minority language as medium of education. In the maximal case, the entire curriculum is delivered in the minority language; for example, there are minority-language medium streams up to university level in a number of larger minority languages in

China. After this training, graduates are well-prepared to be teachers or government workers in their own areas. Another example is the widespread tribal college system in the United States, where language reclamation and documenting and preserving cultural activities are among the main goals. Where the government is not involved, some groups choose to have private education for their children in the endangered language; such classes are usually run in a local institution such as a church or meeting house, with a local teacher. Thus, education need not always be a negative for an endangered language.

Traditional hunter-gatherer and agricultural work and artisanal production can be strong domains for the continued use of an endangered language. So also can local traditional markets, small local shops and other places where outsiders are few or non-existent. Many societies around the world have indigenous health and medical practices known to local experts and transmitted through the local language which often have valuable knowledge of the medicinal effects of parts of plants, animals and other local substances. This kind of medical and other cultural knowledge is often more endangered than local languages.

Settings which can be supportive of endangered languages include traditional activities of all kinds. This includes celebration of the stages of life (e.g., birth, reaching adult status, marriage and funerals) and also seasonal festivals, religious holidays and celebrations of historical events. In many cases, these become an opportunity not just to use the language and carry out traditional activities, but also for public display and even for attracting tourists and gaining outside income. However, when outsiders are present, there is pressure not to use the endangered language in their presence.

Religion, as we have seen, can be a local, an outsider or a blended domain. It may be more or less prominent within a society, and more or less important to individual members of the society. In many societies, religious activities play a key role in seasonal festivals and life transition events; in others, these are community events without religious content, or family events only. Some societies have members who adhere to different religions, dividing and weakening a community.

Finally, there are some Settings of internal dialogue: the language of dreams, the language in which one counts and does arithmetic or the language of daydreaming. Another Setting is speaking to animals including pets and domestic animals, who do not normally reply with speech except in traditional stories. The main example of Key which affects language use is the expression of emotion: happiness, sadness, anger or love. Whether these are internal or externalized and spoken, most are informal and relatively likely to be done using the endangered language; although counting and arithmetic may be done in the language in which they were learned.

One systematic study of domains of language use is Moser (1992) on the Central African Republic, where the main languages in use are the ex-colonial prestige language, French, the national vehicular language, Sango, and a variety of ethnic languages from several distinct language families, some of them endangered. After collecting data on speaker background and language knowledge, she asked about the use of French, Sango and ethnic languages in thirty spoken domains on a four-point scale from 3 (always) to 0 (never). The domains considered included five within the family, five within the local network, five in the domain of religion, life cycle activities and local traditional activities, five formal domains of interaction with medical and government outsiders, five in transactional domains, and five intimate domains including dreams, quarrels, to animals, with a traditional healer and local meeting places.

Music is a universal Genre; the instruments, scales, musical practices and subgenres differ widely but are also subject to wide diffusion. Some music is without words; although sometimes the music can stand for words, as in the case of Lahu gourd flute courtship music (Bradley, 1979c) and Lisu four-string plucked 'banjo' dance music where there are words associated with the music which are never sung but whose **tones** are represented by the music.

Where music has lyrics, these may be in an archaic or stylized song style of the language, which may be affected by the need to fit in with the music; or music can be written to fit the lyrics. The form and content of the music and lyrics will be affected by the subgenre: religious music may follow the pattern required by the particular religion, such as four-part harmony and translated lyrics for Christian choral music. Songs or religious chants which are entirely oral may be strikingly similar in structure and content to songs and chants which are written in a nearby community speaking a related language which has a writing system; Lisu oral songs, some now written down and published, have the same seven-syllable line structure with two parallel lines and overlapping links between adjacent lines as some Nisu songs which are written down, but were probably originally performed and remembered orally.

Modern innovations have spread around the world; many societies now have rap music, with casual rapid speech and staccato rhythm, similar to the original African American subgenre. Amplified guitar, bass, drums and sometimes organ playing eight-tone scale music is also widespread. In Lisu, there is a lot of soft rock, mainly modern love songs and Christian religious songs. This includes audio as well as video and even some karaoke, with subtitles in Lisu to sing along. These are completely unlike the original five-tone scale indigenous songs with their stylized lyrics in seven-syllable lines.

Recording and dissemination of recorded music has advantages and disadvantages. It can be good for preserving traditional best practice, although there is more of a tendency to record in innovative outside subgenres. However, once excellent recordings of traditional musical performances are available, this reduces demand for live performance by traditional musicians, thus reducing their income and their incentive to continue playing and to keep the skills for making and maintaining their instruments. One innovation which makes music more accessible, but eliminates its value as a symbol of a group's language, is 'tourist music': replacing the lyrics with dominant language lyrics; ironically, this is often what is performed for outsiders when they want to experience something exotic and local. There has also been a lot of instability over the last twenty years in the ways of disseminating music and video; the latest method of using the Internet to download it can be problematic for traditional indigenous groups, whether their language is endangered or not. Technology is an issue; some societies still use audio cassettes as a medium for music.

Some Genres are based on writing, and thus producing and using them requires literacy. One measure of the health of a language is its use in print media such as textbooks, religious books and other media disseminating information such as public signage, posters, newsletters, newspapers, magazines, websites and other forms of literature. Advertising of commercial products in any such media is extremely rare in endangered languages; using major global, national and regional languages emphasizes the modernity and high status of their products and services. Conversely, use of print media makes it possible to write down, preserve and disseminate traditional oral literature: songs, poetry, proverbs, riddles and stories.

There are media which use the spoken mode, such as radio and recorded media (audio cassettes, various formats of disks or on the Internet), or both spoken and visual modes like television, movies and discs, computer games and the Internet. Some of these are used by communities speaking endangered languages, mainly in developed countries.

The Internet has made it possible for those with computer and Internet access to communicate using whatever language they choose.

This includes reading such as web browsing and downloads, and writing including social media. Many people create written, oral, picture, video and other kinds of outputs which are disseminated, again through social media or websites. Increasingly, this is moving to the much more democratic and widely available medium of the mobile phone, with SMS text, Twitter and so on. Internet use via computer requires electricity and Internet access as well as a computer, but a mobile phone can be recharged and can generate and receive text, and smartphones and tablets also have even more Internet capacity. These new domains have created a new genre of written language which is much more informal, full of acronyms and other abbreviations, and uses a large array of emojis like ☺ to express feelings and attitudes. For some endangered languages, this has created new networks of users. For others without access to this technology, this is another example of the disempowerment of small marginal groups around the world: most of the Internet content is in dominant languages.

Other new domains also do not support language diversity. For example, global positioning system navigation devices speak only a small subset of the world's languages, and so must be listened to in those languages. Games like Pokémon Go typically use a very restricted range of languages. Speech recognition software to produce written text or for telephone access management can only deal with a few spoken language inputs. New devices have manuals and controls only in a relatively small range of languages. Thus, endangered languages will continue to be marginalized as such new domains become more widespread.

5.4 DEACQUISITION

A less well-documented linguistic process, but one highly relevant for the understanding of the processes involved in language endangerment, is language attrition – decrease in language ability in a formerly spoken language due to long-term non-use. Like language endangerment itself, this has gone through a number of terminological changes, including Lambert and Freed (1982) who called it loss of language skills. Later, Seliger and Vago (1991) used the term first language attrition, Hyltenstam and Viberg (1993) regression, and Schmid (2001) attrition. No positive or neutral term has yet been proposed to refer to this process; the antonymous positive terms refer to improvement or at least non-decrease in language ability: retention as opposed to loss, progression as opposed to regression and development or retention as opposed to attrition.

Because many endangered languages have ceased to be used in a range of domains, or even all domains, some languages are best known to older speakers who have not used the language for many years; thus, their usage may reflect attrition effects, and communities wishing to pursue some form of reclamation as well as scholars wishing to document such a language need to be aware of this possibility, consider what the likely areas of structural attrition may be, given the likely original pattern and the corresponding pattern in the replacing language, and seek out the speakers with the minimum of attrition effects in their speech. Ideally, this requires as much information as possible about the replacing language, the endangered language and their structural differences. In some cases, information from closely related languages may be used with care for hypotheses about the likely former structural properties of an endangered language.

Most of the study of language attrition has taken place in developed-country settings among speakers of two major non-endangered world languages, usually involving two European languages and especially some other European language and English; see, for example, all of the previously mentioned studies.

Attrition studies show that decrease in ability can be related to some of the factors which tend to increase language endangerment. Children who cease to have contact with their original first language prior to adolescence and have thus not acquired it completely may lose it completely. This means that well-intentioned programmes to give children preschool or school exposure, like Language Nests, may be ineffective unless there is ongoing supportive use of the endangered language in and especially outside school settings. Pre-puberty adoption of children to a foreign country at an early age prior to complete acquisition, with no further contact with the original first language, appears to lead to complete loss; this is analogous to moving out of the traditional community to live in a town or city with no further contact with the endangered-language community, which does occur for some individuals but is not as widespread as the situation where some contact is maintained, even if the medium of communication must be the dominant language. In some of the case studies in Schmid (2011), negative experiences associated with the original society are recalled, which are likely to have led to negative attitudes about the language as well, and thus favour attrition. She also notes that adolescence is a time when youth seek to integrate themselves into peer groups and may wish to adopt the norms, including the language, of their peers, rather than that of their parents and background, so language shift may result. Finally, there is a cluster of attrition-related factors related to age, such as age of onset of attrition (when a language ceased to be used regularly), time since this onset that the individual has been in the second-language environment and current age. It is often suggested in the literature that there is a reversion to the first language in old age; some scholars reject this, despite widespread impressionistic and self-report data to the contrary. If older speakers who acquired an endangered language up to puberty and were originally fluent but ceased to use the language long ago have undergone attrition due to non-use, can they revert to their fluent speech as they age? Or is attrition irreversible? And how do the negative effects of age on cognition, memory, speech production and perception affect the speech of an older endangered language speaker? These are all interesting and important questions which we need to consider when making our choices about sources of data on endangered languages, where we normally seek out the oldest speakers for our research; we also need to consider their life histories, which may make them more or less able to provide data which is less affected by language attrition.

Another issue here is whether the language has been fully acquired by an individual; or, if not, what developmental characteristics of incomplete acquisition can be identified in their speech. When a language ceases to be regularly spoken, or undergoes loss of many of its domains of use, speakers who were not fully exposed to sufficient fluent input for long enough may have acquired only a non-adult developmental stage of the language, which, as we have just seen, is also more likely to be lost completely. This is quite apart from the issue of ability to interact in the language; a speaker may have substantial **communicative competence** but speak in a developmentally non-adult way.

The most obvious attrition effects are in vocabulary. Some of the attrition effects distinguishing fully fluent speech by speakers who have continuously used a language and those who have not may include problems in active or even passive recall of vocabulary, use of large numbers of **integrated** or unintegrated words and phrases from the replacing language and other structural effects discussed in Chapter 7. Communities differ in how they regard loanwords; some are more open to them, others reject them and regard them as interlopers; endangered language communities are no different.

5.5 FLUENCY

Measuring fluency and proficiency can be problematic. When asked directly about subjective self-reported language ability, many people will exaggerate how well they speak, some will belittle or deny any knowledge of something they do speak more or less well, and most people lack the metalanguage and self-awareness to discuss this in an explicit, detailed and scalar way. If we instead rely on judgements by others, this has the same problems, and the additional problem about who is doing the judging and their own abilities and attitudes about the endangered language. In some communities, elders may expect very high levels of conformity to their own speech in order to rate someone as fluent; in others, semispeaker speech of greater or lesser similarity to the traditional conservative speech variety and with greater or lesser ability to express the full range of what people want or need to say may be fully accepted by all. If we use questionnaires with **Likert scale** ratings for fluency, like Kayambazinthu (1995) or Thamrin (2015), this still has the same problem: all of these are subjective judgements which may be strongly affected by individual and community attitudes.

The same issues arise in rating and comparing ability in the dominant language in which speakers of the endangered language are bilingual. If school, government and other settings have convinced people that their abilities in the dominant language are less than fully fluent, there may be considerable under-reporting of these abilities; conversely, if skills in the dominant language are required for some desirable purpose, there may be an over-reporting. We also need to be clear about what kind of knowledge we are asking about, as often people regard the written language as primary, and report mainly about relatively lower skills in that, when their speaking and listening ability may be much stronger.

Naturally, skills in each language will be much better for domains or situations where people normally use that language, so it is necessary to determine fluency in conjunction with investigation of domains of language use; for example, how well do people feel that they can function in a government office in the dominant language, in a traditional ceremony in the endangered language? And how is their individual and collective fluency in such domains judged by others – for example, by the government officials who regularly interact with them or the local leaders who run traditional ceremonies?

There are also developmental issues involved for young children who have not yet achieved full control of the sound system and grammar; naturally, they cannot be judged to be fully fluent and their speech should not be expected to show mature adult-like patterns, but they may have a greater or lesser degree of age-appropriate fluency. Where children are not exposed to enough of the endangered language in the home and community, naturally, the full development of the language will suffer, and then adults may make negative subjective judgements about children's levels of fluency. Alternatively, adults may be willing to accept a greater range of developmental ability, just as they may be more or less willing to approve of adult semispeaker speech.

5.5.1 Testing Language Skills

For objective assessment and measurement of language fluency and proficiency, we must first explicitly distinguish the four skills involved: speaking, listening (comprehension), reading and writing. Speaking and writing are active skills, listening and reading are passive skills, and all four can be and often are tested separately. This is the fundamental basis of most modern language testing.

There are objective testing procedures which measure ability in specific areas of language structure, provided they are well designed. Monolingual testing of vocabulary can use pictures: naming pictures or matching a set of words to a set of pictures. Nouns are easier to test in this way, verbs can be more problematic: a picture of a person standing, reaching up and picking fruit from a tree while holding a basket containing already picked fruit can have multiple 'correct' verbal answers: standing, reaching up, picking, harvesting, gathering or collecting. Bilingual testing of vocabulary can ask for translation equivalents (although this has major methodological problems as the range of word meaning in one language differs from that of the 'translation equivalent' word in another) or monolingual testing can ask for synonyms, antonyms, hyponyms, and so on to investigate depth of lexical knowledge.

Testing ability in the sound system of a language can obviously only be done in listening mode, to determine whether all the sounds of a language can be accurately perceived and distinguished; and in speaking mode, to determine whether the sounds are produced in a manner able to be understood, and preferably an accurate native speaker-like manner. In most languages, there is variation in the ways that particular sounds are pronounced; for example, the 't' between vowels in English which in words like 'letter' can be changed to a short sound similar to 'd', or the 't' at the end of the word which can be omitted if there is another consonant pronounced before it as in 'mint', or changed to a **glottal stop** at the end of a syllable after a vowel in many local varieties of English in England as in 'hot'. Another example is the English 'h' sound, which is often omitted in words such as 'he', 'him' or 'his' in all varieties, and sometimes in all words in many local varieties in England: 'appy' for 'happy', as discussed earlier. So test designers need to be aware not just of the standard slow and careful pronunciation of sounds in words, but of rapid speech casual forms as well as some regional alternatives. Decisions about which pronunciations to recognise and accept in testing may be particularly problematic in language endangerment situations where the sound system is in the process of changing and variation both between speakers and in the speech of each individual may be particularly great.

The counterpart of pronunciation for reading and writing is spelling; if a language has an established written standard, testing this is not problematic. Spelling tends to change slowly if at all, and may thus represent a more conservative form of the sound system of the language. For more on writing systems and how to devise and if necessary reform them for endangered languages, see Chapter 8.

Words and the formation of words, also known as morphology, refers to those units of speech which have a meaning when said alone; in writing systems which use spaces, there are often spaces between words, while each word is written together, without spaces. Some languages have relatively simple word structure, other have more complex patterns and structures with several component parts (also known as **morphemes**) within the word; for example, the English plural **suffix** '-s' as in 'cats'. Sentences and the formation of sentences, also known as syntax, refers to the way words are put together into longer strings to express a complete meaning; again, this may be more or less complex. The ways in which sequences of sentences are linked together to form a cohesive whole is referred to as discourse. Morphology and syntax are popularly referred to together as grammar; these areas of structure are explored further in Chapter 7. Much of the testing of language ability in all four skills investigates different aspects of grammar. There is a very large number of widely used grammatical terms, some of which are derived from terms originally used in Latin grammar; but we must be extremely careful not to impose the grammatical structure of one language (such as Latin) mindlessly on the structure of other languages. Testing grammar is near universal, although requiring knowledge of the appropriate terminology is less so. Grammar tends to be tested mainly in reading and writing mode, although speaking and listening tests also exist. Many of the standard tests used to assess foreigners' ability in national languages test mainly grammatical and vocabulary knowledge in reading and writing. Obviously a language whose writing system does not indicate word spaces and/or whose word structure is particularly simple, like Chinese, may not lend itself to testing morphology in depth; likewise, for a language whose syntax is relatively straightforward, testing may need to focus on other areas. Tests tend to contain relatively short passages, and thus may not lend themselves to investigating discourse structures at all.

The final area of structure normally tested is the area of meaning: both the meaning of words and parts of words (also known as semantics), the social rules for the appropriate use of language (communicative competence, what to say in a particular situation) and the way language relates to events in the world and logic (pragmatics). This can be tested in all four skills.

Translation used to be a prominent component of language testing, and teaching using the so-called grammar-translation method was widely applied; this is still found in some educational systems around the world, for example, what is known as 'intensive reading' in English classes in China. This is basically teaching students to parse sentences in the source language – that is, break them down into grammatical components – and know the technical terms for those components, and then translate them into another language following the grammar of the target language. Like testing grammar, the testing of translation, especially in reading and writing skills, is relatively simple to implement and thus still quite widespread; although it can be difficult to assess adequately, as there may be various more or less accurate alternatives for the target language translation.

The form of the test can be an issue. A written test relies on literacy; this will be a barrier for many potential testees. Many people may have limitations in educational background in the dominant language of the test and/or be unfamiliar with the written version of an endangered language, or their writing skills may be at a lower level than their reading skills. So-called objective written testing based on the dominant language and the cultural assumptions of the dominant group is just another type of problematic and confronting written materials frequently encountered by speakers of all minority languages, such as government forms, written health and other important information, public information signage. If the test is entirely oral, again the issue is whether testees have adequate knowledge and listening comprehension of the language variety or varieties used in the test, as well as the relevant speaking ability to give answers. In both cases, there may also be issues related to familiarity with the appropriate vocabulary and style expected in testing.

The formulation of questions and the types of required answers may also cause different kinds of problems. Multiple-choice tests, often where more than one answer is plausible, are easy to assess, but may be completely unfamiliar and confusing. **Cloze** tests filling gaps in sentences may be equally unfamiliar, and can be of greatly differing degrees of difficulty; for example, in some languages the relevant missing words must contain extensive **inflectional** material, in others (or where the relevant missing words do not include inflectional material), the task is much simpler, and, again, there may be multiple possible appropriate answers, although the assessment may favour just one. Testing based on translation from one language to another requires both receptive and active skills in both languages: listening and speaking for an oral test, and reading and writing for a written test. Possible 'correct' translations may be quite diverse and not so simple to assess objectively. Testing which requires open-ended answers may be difficult for those who lack the appropriate metalanguage and stylistic range, even if their skills in the language tested are solid; these can also be extremely difficult to assess. For monolingual tests of skills in an endangered language, the metalanguage required for testing may not exist at all, and the process of testing may be completely unfamiliar for people with limited exposure to education, or even traumatic for those who have 'failed' in testing situations in the past.

The widespread old-fashioned translation method of assessment is still most appropriate when testing for one specific purpose: verifying and accrediting the ability of individuals to work as translators or interpreters. These are very different skills; a translator of written material can work slowly or quickly, with access to more or less additional outside resources, while an interpreter must convert spoken material from one language to another immediately, whether consecutive (where the speaker pauses while the interpreter interprets) or simultaneous (interpreting while the speaker continues without stopping). Best practice is exemplified by Australia's National Accreditation Authority for Translators and Interpreters (**NAATI**; www.naati.com.au), which has four types of constantly revised tests at three levels for a large number of languages: translation from X to English and English to X, also interpreting both ways.

Another important procedure valuable in making language policy decisions in language endangerment situations as well as elsewhere is objective and carefully designed and controlled testing of intelligibility between related speech varieties when listening to short narratives, as discussed further in Section 10.2.4. Some sources describing one valuable standard method, the Recorded Text Test or RTT, are Casad (1974, 1991), Blair (1990) and O'Leary (1994).

Since speakers of an endangered language are almost always bilingual, it might seem that interpreting and translation services are not necessary for them; however, many speakers of an endangered language would have difficulty understanding and being understood in crucial medical and legal settings such as a hospital or a law court, and older speakers with lower levels of bilingual skills may even need assistance in other domains. This need is not often adequately dealt with by governments, although the Australian government telephone interpreter service provides on-demand interpreters for nearly 150 languages by telephone nationwide, see www.tisnational.gov.au.

Testing fluency in a national dominant language mother tongue situation is normally carried out with children as they progress through school, and often relies primarily on assessment of reading and writing skills, although listening skills are absolutely essential for school learning as well, and nearly all school systems have some form of continuous assessment of speaking ability. Even for mother tongue speakers of non-prestige regional or social varieties of the dominant language, school normally also requires learning of the sounds and grammar of the 'standard' high-status sociolect. In **diglossia** (Chapter 8) the literary variety of the language is different from all modern spoken varieties, including the prestige spoken variety of the dominant language, which raises particular problems for endangered-language speakers learning a diglossic national language whose control of the spoken variety of the national language may be at a lower level. For all early education up to the end of primary school, there is also an emphasis on facilitating the developmental aspects of first-language acquisition. Another of the main aims of all levels of education is to develop and enrich various fields of knowledge ('subjects' such as mathematics, science or history) and the vocabulary and concepts associated with them.

One of the main educational issues in many countries is that speech varieties in many regions of a nation may be regarded officially as 'dialects' of the standard, even though they are actually distinct languages. This leads to young students whose mother tongue is a regional 'dialect' which is actually a distinct (although often related) language having the 'standard' language imposed on them from the start of education; as education starts well within the age period for fluent first-language acquisition, most children cope with this and eventually become fluent in both speech varieties. However, the 'dialect' then has less prestige and may be associated with old-fashioned activities and attitudes, so such regional 'dialects' may lose domains of use and become endangered. For example, in Italy, this hollowing-out of regional languages such as Friulian, Venetian, Sicilian or Sardinian and their subvarieties has led to massive expansion in the use of standard Italian and greatly reduced knowledge and use of regional languages, so most are gradually becoming endangered.

There is no testing of fluency in endangered languages carried out in schools which do not teach them. Even where a local endangered language is taught, the assessment may not carry the same weight in educational progress as knowledge of the main school language. Primary schools are ill-equipped to assess speaking and listening skills in languages which are unknown to most school leaders and teachers. Teaching materials may also be inadequate or non-existent. While there is always a tradition of testing skills in the dominant school language, this almost never exists for an endangered language. Since existing tests in the dominant language emphasize reading and writing skills as developed in school, this is often what newly developed tests for ability in an endangered language tend to focus on, neglecting incipient speaking and listening skills which parents and grandparents can use and reinforce with the students.

Methods of teaching second languages, most typically a foreign language of wider communication such as English or French or a major regional language, vary greatly. Unlike mother tongue teaching where basic speaking and listening skills are assumed and developed but not explicitly tested, these place a great deal of emphasis on developing and assessing these speaking and listening skills, although they also develop and assess reading and writing. There is usually a covert assumption that second-language learning and second-language teaching methods are not necessary where there is a dominant national language, but this is often not true.

There are very widely used tests for proficiency in English as a second language: the US Test of English as a Foreign Language (TOEFL) and the UK International English Language Testing System (IELTS), which test all four skills, including a brief interaction with a trained tester to assess speaking and listening skills. However, most similar tests are like first-language mother tongue tests which assume that literacy as achieved through formal education is primary and do not test speaking or listening ability or test it only to a limited extent.

Where the second language in school or religious institutions is a language of prior history, such as Latin or Ancient Greek, or a historical language of religion such as Classical Arabic, Biblical Hebrew, Sanskrit, Pali or Ge'ez, teaching may focus almost exclusively on reading. Such learning is more effective where the local language is a lineal descendant of the historical language, like Italian from Latin, modern Greek from ancient Greek, modern spoken Arabic varieties from Arabic and modern northern Indic languages like Hindi from Sanskrit. It can also reinforce and enrich vocabulary development; conversely, lack of familiarity with vocabulary from the relevant classical languages, even where these are not closely related to the mother tongue, can create educational barriers (e.g., the lexical bar of Corson, 1985). For those whose mother tongue is not the national language, this sets up another layer of difficulty: Pali loanwords in Thai or Burmese for non-Buddhist mother tongue speakers of endangered minority languages in those countries, or Arabic loanwords in Swahili for non-Moslem speakers of endangered languages of Tanzania.

Where transmission has ceased in the home and endangered-language teaching in schools is developed, its aims are often like those of teaching a second language from scratch. Sometimes, there is no written form of the language and the goal of the teaching is mainly for children to learn speaking and listening skills; even where a written form exists, care must be taken not to make this the primary target of education. Where mother tongue models are available in the home, even if only from grandparents or old people generally, this can greatly facilitate and support school learning, but schools cannot adequately substitute for active spoken use of the language by children in the home, family and community from an early age. Where the endangered language is still being acquired by some children in their homes, these children can be a resource and model for others. This will also help these children to feel proud of their language and feel more positive about their identity. It is particularly important to reinforce and reward achievement in the endangered language in a meaningful way. This is the idealistic goal of testing for ability in endangered indigenous Austronesian languages of Taiwan.

There have been some attempts to measure ability in two languages using well-designed and carefully administered testing. For example, Ding (2016) investigated listening and speaking ability in Nosu and standard Mandarin Chinese among eleven adults aged fifty-six to eighty-four representing the grandparent generation, eleven adults aged thirty-six to forty-six representing the parent generation, and twelve youths aged seventeen to twenty-three; a further group of ten monolingual Mandarin Chinese speakers aged eighteen to twenty-five was also tested using the Chinese version of the test as a control. The sad finding is that the Nosu language, with nearly 3 million speakers, fully established orthography based on a modified traditional indigenous system (Bradley, 2001, 2009, 2011c), extensive educational support and widespread public use both written and spoken, is nevertheless in decline. Despite widely implemented education in the new Nosu orthography since the late 1970s, neither older nor younger speakers could be tested using the Nosu script as their knowledge of it was not sufficient.

Ding (2016: 194–204) showed that the oldest group had very high levels of Nosu ability. Middle-aged speakers had similar high levels of Nosu, while youth had a great deal more internal diversity in their Nosu ability. In the Chinese test, Chinese and Nosu youth had similar high scores, while Nosu middle-aged adults showed a wide range of levels. All but one of the oldest Nosu group and three of the middle-aged group had limited ability in Chinese and could not be tested in Chinese. Among Nosu youth who grew up in a traditional area, measured ability in Chinese was higher, sometimes by a wide margin. If these results represent language abilities in the general Nosu population, the prognosis for the Nosu language is eventual endangerment, despite its large speaker population and extensive policy and other public support, as the current youth with their strong Chinese and more limited Nosu abilities move into the parent generation. Ding also found substantially lower levels of Nosu ability for three additional Nosu youths tested who had spent much of their childhood in the provincial capital, with limited exposure to Nosu outside the home, and for a small group of speakers of Suondi, a distinct variety classified as part of Nosu but who speak a quite distinct language. Being tested in Chinese is a familiar task for all the youth and the middle-aged who have had substantial education, so these scores may therefore be higher than the Nosu scores due to practice – but this is no reason for complacency.

5.6 CONCLUSION

This chapter has considered how speakers know an endangered language: how they learn it, when and where they use it, how they may lose what they have already learned and how their level of proficiency in their two or more languages can be measured. We have also seen that such measurement of relative ability in the bilingual's languages can reveal trends in language vitality in a directly quantified way, sounding the alarm while remedial action is still relatively easy. The learning and unlearning processes are similar to the parallel processes for non-endangered languages, and much of the information about domains of use and differences in degree of fluency show that endangered languages represent an extreme case of widespread linguistic phenomena, with interesting consequences for linguistic structure which are explored in Chapter 7, and important implications for how to implement language policy concerning endangered languages discussed in Chapter 8.

CASE STUDY: DOMAINS OF LANGUAGE USE IN MALAWI

One detailed case study investigating language use in a range of domains is briefly summarized here. The information is from Kayambazinthu (1995, personal communication).

In Malawi, the prestige ex-colonial language is English, the de facto (and de jure from 1968 to 1994) national language is Chichewa as spoken by the Chewa group, and there are twelve other indigenous languages, some of them moving towards endangerment. One of these, Tumbuka, was used as the Christian mission language in the Northern Region, and has become a lingua franca there. All these languages are closely related Bantu languages; eight of them are also spoken by substantial groups in neighbouring countries. Kayambazinthu (1995) conducted a survey of 450 households from four groups, including the national majority Chewa, northern Tumbuka as well as Yao and Lomwe groups. This survey included questions on language acquisition, knowledge and use in a large number of domains in three comparable neighbourhoods of three urban centres in different regions of Malawi. Her questionnaire had fourteen questions on the Participants and their Speaker Characteristics, five on self-judged best language and language use, eleven questions on knowledge and use of the national language, Chichewa, the same eleven on knowledge and use of English and again the same eleven on knowledge and use of the indigenous language of their own group. All of the scalar questions were on a five-point **Likert scale** from 1 (not at all) to 5 (like a native speaker). This was followed up by forty-five questions on languages spoken and listened to in various domains, one question on languages listened to on the radio, four questions on reading domains and eight questions on writing domains. Since this survey was conducted, the language policy of Malawi has fortunately become more supportive of indigenous languages other than Chichewa, although Chichewa continues to dominate national life, alongside the ex-colonial language, English. The domains investigated in Malawi include six family domains, eight friend/neighbour domains and four domains with strangers, as well as four traditional domains, four work domains, five religious domains, eight transactional domains and six domains interacting with high-prestige insiders or outsiders such as a traditional chief, a doctor or a government official.

Nearly all the non-Chewa adults surveyed claim their ethnic language as their mother tongue (Kayambazinthu, 1995: 127), but domain data reflects a major generational shift: for the Lomwe, the second largest group, it is reported that nearly four times as many of the parents of the people surveyed had fluent Lomwe, while only one-fifth of their children are reported to have fluent Lomwe; for Yao, the third largest group, the parent generation has more than double the proportion, and the children's generation has less than one-fifth; and, for Tumbuka, the fourth largest group, the parents had about 1.4 times the number of fluent speakers, and the children had a bit over half. This outcome may be partly due to the survey having been done in three urban centres, where people have extensive exposure to other indigenous languages, especially Chichewa, as well as to education, which also disseminates English, and government policy, which at the time favoured Chichewa. On the other hand, there is also extensive report of knowledge of indigenous languages other than Chichewa and one's own ethnic language; most Chewa, presumably especially those living in the Northern Region where Tumbuka is the local lingua franca, report knowledge of that, mainly as a second, third or fourth language; and substantial numbers of each of the other three main groups report knowledge of the other two languages as well; this is particularly the case for Lomwe and Yao claiming to know each other's languages. Monolingualism is obviously rare in Malawi; but it appears that there is a substantial shift away from non-local indigenous languages underway in urban populations. Table 5.1 shows reported ability and use of one's own group's ethnic language.

Note that there are some contradictory self-reporting issues here: a substantial number of people report that they cannot speak their ethnic language at all, but report in answering other questions that they do use it and that it is their mother tongue. Evidence of shift is seen in the greater report of understanding than of speaking knowledge. There is clearly exaggeration of having no speaking knowledge at all, as well as modesty or uncertainty about having full speaking and understanding fluency, even among the few people who report exclusive use.

Table 5.1 *Knowledge and use of ethnic language in Malawi (%)*

Reported ability	Speaking		Understanding		Use	
	Male	Female	Male	Female	Male	Female
Never/not at all	24.1	17.5	–	–	14.4	8.7
Sometimes/a little	–	–	14.4	8.7	21.3	29.7
Often/fairly well	3.7	3.5	2.3	4.4	13.6	12.2
Usually/very well	72.2	79	83.3	86.9	40.9	45.4
Always/native	–	–	–	–	9.8	3.9

Of the forty-six oral domains investigated, six are within the family, six are with friends and acquaintances, two are with neighbours, four are with strangers, six are with high-status insiders or outsiders, four are traditional activities, four are work domains, five concern religion, eight are transactional and the final one is listening to radio; at the time of the survey, radio was only in English and Chichewa, although now the other three languages discussed here are also used.

There are clear generational differences of language use in family and friendship domains (Kayambazinthu, 1995: 349). This includes adults from all groups surveyed. This also reflects the national policy at the time of the survey. We can see that, for the adults surveyed, code-switching is increasing dramatically, Tumbuka and particularly Yao use is decreasing, Lomwe and other indigenous languages are hardly used even within the nuclear family in towns, and Chichewa use is increasing. Use of Chichewa by females is slightly less than by males, and use of English is still a small proportion but is on the increase, as shown in Table 5.2.

Comparing the Tumbuka and the Yao groups, shift away from the ethnic language outside as opposed to inside the home is shown in Table 5.3 (Kayambazinthu, 1995: 360). Tumbuka appears to be used substantially less outside the home to one's spouse and slightly less outside the home by younger parents to their children; to friends, there is an unexpected age difference, with older people using less Tumbuka with Tumbuka friends outside the home than younger people; perhaps it is becoming less unusual for Tumbuka to be spoken publicly in Mzuzu, the Northern Region city surveyed. Yao is used equally as much inside and outside the home to family members, but there is a substantial decrease in its use to Yao friends outside the home.

The use of ethnic languages by members of that ethnic group in a variety of non-family domains including the religious domain (Kayambazinthu, 1995: 73), the friendship domain (Kayambazinthu, 1995: 183), domains with strangers (Kayambazinthu, 1995: 200), the transactional domain (Kayambazinthu, 1995: 212), the work domain (Kayambazinthu, 1995: 374) and the government domain (Kayambazinthu, 1995: 371) are also interesting. Recalling that one quarter of the sample is from each group, results reflect the proportion of members of that group who use that language, virtually all of whom claim to be mother tongue speakers of their ethnic language. Tumbuka is used to some extent outside the family domain, but Yao and especially Lomwe are used much less, unless one is aware that one's interlocutor is of the same group. In Tables 5.4–5.7, the percentages given are the proportion

Table 5.2 *Use of ethnic language: generational differences (%)*

Language	To elders		To siblings		To spouse		To children	
	Female	Male	Female	Male	Female	Male	Female	Male
Chichewa	46.7	38.7	51.6	40.2	52.0	48.6	59.4	59.1
Tumbuka	26.6	22.7	19.1	19.7	14.6	14.8	10.7	12.6
Yao	15.9	21.3	11.2	16.2	6.6	7.6	4.6	5.1
English	–	–	0.9	3.9	4.0	2.9	5.1	4.5
Code-switch	5.1	8.9	12.6	13.1	22.7	26.2	20.3	18.7
Lomwe	5.6	8.4	3.3	5.7	–	–	–	–
Other	–	–	1.4	1.3	–	–	–	–

Table 5.3 *Age and use of ethnic language: home and outside (%)*

Age	Group	To spouse	To children	To friends
16–26	Tumbuka	−16.8	−1.9	0
	Yao	0	0	−5.3
27–37	Tumbuka	−25.7	−1.9	0
	Yao	0	0	−18.6
38–48	Tumbuka	−10.3	0	−7.8
	Yao	0	0	−8.9
>48	Tumbuka	−33.3	0	−2.5
	Yao	0	0	−21.8

Table 5.4 *Use of ethnic language in friendship domains (%)*

Domain	Tumbuka	Yao	Lomwe
Close friend/same group	74.0	66.8	25.2
Close friend/different group	5.4	2.7	0
Acquaintance/same group	74.1	67.3	0
Acquaintance/different group	3.6	0	0
Neighbour/same group	93.7	69.4	20.8
Neighbour/different group	23.4	8.1	0

Table 5.5 *Use of ethnic language in outsider domains (%)*

Domain	Tumbuka	Yao	Lomwe
To a White	2.7	0	0
To a well-dressed African	18.8	0	0
To a non-well-dressed African	29.7	0	0
At the post office	27.0	0	0
To a nurse	28.8	0	0
To a doctor	21.6	0	0
To a government official	4.5	0	0

of members within a group who use their ethnic language in that domain.

Note that, despite many people claiming to speak the languages of other groups apart from Chichewa, it seems that they rarely do so. Even within the Lomwe group, ethnic language use is quite low; Yao is

Table 5.6 *Use of ethnic language in transactional domains (%)*

Domain	Tumbuka	Yao	Lomwe
Shop	33.9	0	0
Market	29.7	0	0
Bus	25.5	0	0
Bank	15.5	0	0
Supermarket	28.8	0	0
Indian store	11.0	0.9	0
Kantini (local store)	33.9	0	0

Table 5.7 *Use of ethnic language in work domain (%)*

Domain	Tumbuka	Yao	Lomwe
Colleagues/personal	19.3	0	0
Colleagues/general	13.1	0	0
Colleagues/work	4.8	0	0
Boss	0.0	0	0
Meetings	0.0	0	0

used about two-thirds of the time between Yao, and Tumbuka somewhat more but not all the time.

The reported usage of Tumbuka in these domains, low as it is, is presumably mainly confined to Mzuzu City in the Northern Region where Tumbuka is widely spoken. Yao and Lomwe are obviously not considered appropriate in such domains.

It can be seen that Tumbuka is used to some extent in the transactional domain, again mainly within the Northern Region. Lomwe and Yao are hardly used at all.

In these work domains, Tumbuka is used even less of the time, and Yao and Lomwe not at all.

Concerning level of education, those with more education use their ethnic languages less, even in the family (Kayambazinthu, 1995: 375); Chichewa, English or code-switching are used instead. In four reading and six formal writing domains, there was no use of anything other than Chichewa, English and code-switching, while two of the eight writing domains show substantial use of Tumbuka and some use of Yao when writing to relatives and friends; for example, 89 per cent of ethnic Tumbuka say they write to uneducated relatives in Tumbuka, and to uneducated friends 58.9 per cent (Kayambazinthu, 1995: 369–72); Yao is lower, with 12.5 per cent writing to uneducated relatives in Yao, but very rarely (0.9 per cent) to friends.

This study was carried out under the government led by Dr Hastings Banda from 1964 to 1994, which very strongly favoured the use of Chichewa as the sole national language alongside English, the ex-colonial language, and banned other indigenous languages in 1968 while promoting Chichewa nationwide and using it as the medium of education in schools in the first four years. The policy has changed twice since. The Yao president elected in 1994 rapidly introduced the use of other indigenous languages of Malawi (Kayambazinthu, 1995: 119–22), in some cases too rapidly for effective use. This included Tumbuka as a medium of education up to Standard 4 in the Northern Region and Yao and Lomwe as semi-official languages in education, government and radio. The effect was to strengthen the position of Tumbuka in the Northern Region, but Yao and especially Lomwe continue to decline in Malawi, although a closely related variety of Lomwe is spoken in Mozambique, and another different variety in Tanzania; Yao is also spoken in Mozambique and Tanzania (Kayambazinthu, 1995: 126–34; Simons & Fennig, 2018). From 2014, the focus returned to English. The education law of 2012 as implemented in 2014 made English the medium of all government education from the beginning; private education is also English-only. This change led to extensive protests in favour of mother tongue education by university education students and others. The reality is that teachers still use local languages, especially Chichewa and Tumbuka, in the early years of school. Grass-roots activism for Tumbuka continues, but Chichewa and especially English continue to dominate national life.

DISCUSSION QUESTIONS

What are some of the issues involved in working with older speakers, both practical and linguistic?

As language acquisition in childhood is most effective, what are some steps which local authority figures (teachers, health workers, other government workers, local businesses) could take to improve the status and transmission of an endangered language?

What are some additional domains not already discussed which would be relevant for a community that you are familiar with?

SUGGESTIONS FOR FURTHER READING

Kayambazinthu (1995) is a wide-ranging study of language policy and language use in Malawi.

Thamrin (2015) is a large-scale study of attitudes to and domains of use of Minangkabau in West Sumatra, Indonesia.

6 The Sociolinguistic Setting

Though I cannot tell you in my mother tongue
Please accept my sorrow and joy
I am also a child of the high grassland
I have a song in my heart
In the song are my father's grassland
And my mother's river

Buren Buya'er (Xi Murong) (2013),
translated by David Bradley

Apart from the various nonlinguistic factors included in the indices of language endangerment discussed in Chapter 2, there have been many previous studies listing, classifying and discussing sociolinguistic setting factors, such as Ferguson (1962), Fishman (1962, 1985), Kloss (1968), Haugen (1972), Kibrik (1991), Edwards (1992), Krauss (1992), de Vries (1992) and many more.

The major nonlinguistic factors which relate to language endangerment are demography, geography, politics, economy, history, education, culture and other external human and environmental factors, also individual speaker background characteristics. Also highly relevant are acquisition of the language and domains of language use, as discussed in Chapter 5, and crucially attitudes and identity, as discussed in Chapter 4. Linguistic factors discussed in Chapter 7 are also relevant. Often 'facts' about minority groups and their endangered languages are contested, as will be discussed in the conclusion of this chapter.

6.1 DEMOGRAPHY

Demography includes both absolute group and speaker populations, percentage and age distribution of language knowledge within the population, trends in population increase or decrease, concentration of the population in the traditional area who are members of the group and what other groups are represented in this area in what proportions.

In many groups whose language is endangered, people who identify as group members do not all speak the language. Some others may not identify as group members. Census statistics on ethnic background are often based on self-report of ethnic identity; those who do report a particular ethnic identity may also claim to speak the group's language, even if they do not.

When it is advantageous to have a particular ethnic identity, some people will reclaim it and some outsiders may also try to claim it. Such demographic expansion may even be negative for a language, diluting the proportion of the group who do speak the language.

Other demographic-linguistic characteristics are also relevant: the proportion of monolingual speakers and the proportion of children learning the language as a mother tongue in the home. The extent of knowledge of other languages, proportions of people who speak particular other languages as well as or instead of the group's language, proportions of people with formal education and to what level and in what language(s) and what types of language (local lingua franca, regional lingua franca, official/national language(s), languages of wider communication, languages of religion and so on) are also relevant. A similar factor is age, gender and geographical distribution of language knowledge, as discussed in Chapter 5.

The demographic aspects of migration also need to be understood. The migrant population may be a substantial proportion of the group, and may be a major resource for the group, remaining in regular contact and continuing to use and transmit the language. Migrants often tend to congregate in specific locations, or they may be more dispersed. If they congregate, they may be a high proportion in their neighbourhood, and be highly visible and active in these locations.

6.2 GEOGRAPHY

There are three main geographic factors: location, concentration and isolation. Some groups live entirely in one isolated location where they are the only local population; other groups live in many locations, mingled with other groups and in easy and regular contact, or anything in between. Groups who live in more than one location may be entirely within one nation-state and may have local minority status, or live across more than one nation-state, and possibly with difficulties in ongoing contact.

Some groups have lifestyles adapted to particular ecological zones – high mountains, river valleys or grasslands. Often geographical distribution reflects economic preferences – trade routes, where certain crops can be grown or fishing resources. It may also reflect the availability of land in an area, or land where they have been concentrated or relocated.

Land is often associated with the ancestors and history; the ancestors remain in the land, they watch over it, and traditional history tells about the links of the group to its land and the associations of various local geographical features. Geographical features with cultural significance may include large features like rivers and mountains, also smaller features such as rocks, trees, springs and so on. There may also be permanent human artistic efforts such as pictures on rocks or more portable artistic objects, as well as local features created by humans such as buildings, travel routes or irrigation systems.

One key social factor in geography is marriage patterns: do people normally marry within a village, or are there specific marriage links with specific other villages? There may be ongoing marriage network links between different locations.

Some factors link demography and geography. A group may be the entire population of its core area or a higher or lower proportion, whether traditionally or due to recent in-migration. The lower the proportion in the core area, the more likely there is to be language endangerment. The proportion of the group which has migrated away, and whether there is ongoing contact, are also relevant.

Other factors link geography and economy. An environment which can sustain the population is a positive. Communication networks such as roads, navigable water bodies and convenient transport and telecommunications are an economic positive, but also increase contact. With easy communications, outsiders can move in and contact increases.

The crucial geographic factor is recognition of rights to land. Providing land rights and reserved territories is widespread in many countries, based mainly on ethnicity and tradition but also sometimes explicitly on language. The exact location and characteristics of the traditional area, whether recognised or not, is relevant: is the language spoken in one remote village in the Himalayas where everyone speaks the language, like the Tibeto-Burman Kanashi language in Malana village in north-western India, or was it traditionally more widespread? Malana does not welcome outsiders, and remains isolated in an area otherwise speaking Hindi varieties. Is the group mainly sedentary, or does it move frequently into new territory, such as with swidden agriculture? How possible is it for outsiders to move into the area, and are they doing so? Is the area isolated by mountains, rivers or deserts, or are there fewer or no barriers between the group's area and those of other groups? How good are local communications, and how have they changed recently? For example, in China seventy years ago, there were many minority villages of distinctive non-Han Chinese groups in remote mountainous areas which had no roads and which were mainly self-sufficient, but now roads reach everywhere, and cash crops and wage labor have become widespread, reducing the local adult population, many of whom have moved to work in towns and cities elsewhere in China and come back to visit once a year, if that. Thus geographical change has also led to economic change.

Through history, there has also been forced movement of peoples based on their ethnicity. Some examples include many American Indian groups moving to what is now Oklahoma in the 1830s, the eastward removal of the Crimean Tatars and Volga Germans in the former USSR in the early 1940s, and very recently the Rohingya moving from Burma to Bangladesh. In some cases, 'ethnic cleansing' has reconcentrated a group and reduced contact with former dominant groups whose languages and cultures were endangering their own. However, the refugee experience is often overwhelmingly negative.

Such forced movements often led to language shift, although some groups have persisted with their languages through adversity and re-established links between those who were moved and those who managed to stay behind, such as the Cherokee in the United States. Some Cherokee of what is now called the United Keetoowah Band moved west into Arkansas and Oklahoma out of their traditional lands in what is now North Carolina, Tennessee and adjacent areas starting in the early 1800s; most were forcibly removed to north-eastern Oklahoma in the late 1830s where they now form the Cherokee Nation, and a few managed to remain behind in North Carolina where they are now the Eastern Band of Cherokee Indians. These three Cherokee groups are now in contact and attempting to reclaim and spread knowledge of their language and indigenous script. Demographically, there are nearly 300,000 recognised members of the Cherokee Nation descended from the 15,000 who were moved in the late 1830s and about 14,000 of the United Keetoowah Band, mostly in Oklahoma; also, about 15,000 descendants of the 800 who remained in North Carolina. Over 800,000 people claim Cherokee ancestry in census statistics, but most are not enrolled on one of the three tribal rolls.

6.3 POLITICS AND POLICY

The political status of minorities and the policy concerning their languages are separate but often related. Increasingly around the world, there is official recognition of minority groups and their status and rights. Specific territories are assigned to minority groups, as reserves, reservations, autonomous areas, with some local political control and representation at higher levels. This does not necessarily lead to positive moves for the languages of these groups; the leadership is often drawn from the assimilated elite, who are sometimes not concerned about language and may not speak it fluently or at all.

Fishman has suggested a number of political parameters which are relevant for the relative tolerance of a political system for multilingualism. These include ideology, type of government (constitutional, totalitarian or authoritarian), power distribution (articulation and aggregation), type of party system (one, two or many), political leadership (degree of importance of individual personalities), type of bureaucracy and degree of separation of powers (legislative, judicial, administrative); few subsequent studies have followed this up, but it is certainly worth further consideration.

Many nations have recently moved to recognise minority languages for official purposes, although in most cases not all indigenous languages. Language policy in some developed nations also supports the continued use of migrant languages. At the international level, UNESCO and UNICEF have been promoting a policy of early mother tongue education for all, including linguistic minorities, since 1952, but this is not widely implemented. For more discussion of language policy and its implementation and effects, see Chapter 8.

6.4 ECONOMICS

A traditional minority society may be economically self-sufficient. More usually, such societies are linked into the surrounding economy, selling their surplus products and buying things they cannot produce, things easier to buy than to produce locally such as cloth, or locally unavailable things like steel tools. Where a society does not produce enough food and needs other outside inputs, but has no cash income, wage labour for outsiders, often eventually leading to economic migration, may result.

Economic anthropology has long measured work inputs and production outputs in traditional societies. Marketable outputs include traditional gathered forest, river and sea products such as sea cucumber, traditional herbal medicines and other wild animal and plant products. There are also crops and domestic animals and their products which can produce a local surplus; some cash crops are entirely produced for sale. Often, transport and marketing consume a high proportion of the value of such products.

Mining is an economic activity which has grave consequences for minority groups in many parts of the world, leading to influx of outsiders, loss of land and environmental degradation. One example is the mining of jade, rubies and emeralds in northern Burma; this is largely done with fairly dangerous low-technology techniques by members of local minority groups, with frequent injury and death. Similarly, land clearance for plantation cash crops such as oil palm in Malaysia and Indonesia or sugar and pastoral land in Latin America has been disastrous in the traditional areas of minority groups. Many small indigenous groups with endangered languages are now protesting about these depredations, and, in January 2018, during a visit to Peru, the Pope added his voice to these protests, in particular concerning the destruction of the Amazon rainforest, but also more generally.

Various kinds of outside work are open to members of minority groups. This includes peak agricultural labour during harvest and other seasons, other unskilled labour, factory work, sex work, and, in some countries, compulsory or voluntary military service. Some parts of colonial armies were mainly recruited from minority groups. British, French and other colonial forces from minority and other backgrounds participated extensively in the First and Second World Wars. Sometimes these forces were stationed in remote locations; various Chinese dynasties sent minority group units to the areas of other minority groups as they were more trustworthy there. In some cases, this led to the long-term survival of a language in the remote garrison which disappeared in the original homeland, as in the case of Xibo, a Manchu garrison moved to north-western China in 1764, who still speak a modern variety of Manchu, although Manchu is now almost entirely gone from its traditional area in north-eastern China.

A less detrimental and expanding source of income is tourism, being the 'exotic other' for local majority and international visitors. This has developed very rapidly in the last thirty years, and is a major source of income and a driver of rapid cultural change. Some of this income goes direct to small-scale local enterprises: guest houses, restaurants, craft sales, guided tours, adventure activities such as rafting and climbing or cultural performances. Tourist enterprises run by outsiders also provide some cash and other income to local people.

Migrants are often a major source of financial support for their home communities; many remote villages in northern Nepal have for nearly two centuries relied on remittances from local men from a number of minorities serving as Gurkha soldiers, many of whom eventually return to become leading figures in their communities, and others of whom remain overseas and establish international networks for their minority and its economic and social advancement.

Most of these economic benefits require direct contact with outsiders, usually conducted through an outside language; it is most unusual for outsiders other than missionaries to show much interest in minority languages, although there is a small amount of literature which attempts to facilitate outsiders accessing these areas and communicating directly with larger minority groups in their languages. A lot of this was compiled by Christian missionaries in colonial times, and is sometimes surprisingly useful. Some recent efforts are of spectacularly poor quality; some are much better. There is also a large literature in the local majority language for government officials who may be expected to learn a local minority language; for China, see, for example, Luo (2013) for Sani, a component of the official Yi nationality who live mainly in Shilin county, eastern central Yunnan. Usually such materials are for larger minority languages which are not currently endangered, but Bradley et al. (1991, 1997, 2008) does include very brief information on endangered Bisu, Gong and Mpi in Thailand.

6.5 HISTORY

Some groups take little interest in their history; others devote a great deal of attention to it. There may be experts who maintain aspects of group history and recite, perform and sometimes write it for the group; in other societies, historical knowledge is more widely distributed but there are still some recognised specialists. History can be traditional, revised, borrowed or even invented; some societies have an anti-history attitude and claim they have no history, as Scott (2009) has indicated. Where it exists, the preservation of historical knowledge should be a priority; this knowledge is fragile and often not valued highly during rapid social change.

One major component of the history of many groups is the literary riches which the written or oral tradition contains. For example, it may be embedded in a funeral song, life cycle songs and stories (relating to birth, maturity, marriage, household establishment or death), stories about ancient rulers, wars and cultural heroes, religious rituals, fortune telling or other traditional stories. Cultural history is also embedded in songs, proverbs, riddles, jokes and humorous stories such as the widespread Trickster genre. Sadly, much of this knowledge is not being passed on and may disappear if not documented soon. In some traditional societies, such oral material has been partly written down in an indigenous or outsider-developed script. It is highly instructive to compare oral versions preserved among groups speaking related languages and these written versions; for example, there are many parallel Nisu and Lisu texts such as the funeral song, with the former written and chanted by a shaman at the funeral and the latter oral. But even the written texts are vulnerable, as in many cases such as Nisu, the number of people who can read and understand them is now very small.

There is often a substantial amount of historical knowledge at the individual, family, clan and local level. Villages may have a traditional origin story, with geographical origin information. Families need information about relationships to know who cannot marry and sometimes who should marry. The degree of importance placed on this, and the amount of knowledge about it, differs from society to society. Many societies have family or clan surnames with documented descent relationships; sometimes there are genealogies which trace relationship back to real or fictive ancestors. For example, the Akha and Hani have patrilineal genealogies where the last syllable of the father's name is normally the first syllable of all his sons' names, as do some other groups in south-western China who speak related languages; the term for this in Akha and Hani is also the word for 'joint'. Traditional Akha and Hani people memorize their genealogy of up to sixty generations, and greatly enjoy comparing these with those of other Akha and Hani to see how many generations back they are related. Most of these genealogies converge after about eighteen to twenty generations or approximately 400 years since the Akha migrated south-westward away from the Hani area. The earliest ten or so names in these genealogies are gods; from about the tenth on they may have been real people, for Akha starting with the cultural hero Sm Mi O, then his son O Toe Loe. The Nosu of south-western China also keep similar very long individual genealogies, sometimes written but also always oral; many clans are now collecting and publishing these. Many Nisu manuscripts are also genealogical. Nisu, Nosu, Hani and Akha are all related Ngwi languages, see Bradley (1979a), and all show the same pattern with the last syllable of the father's name used as the first syllable of the son's; in the Nisu and Nosu cases, these are preceded by a clan surname which is the same through the entire genealogy. Genealogy may also be private and sensitive, as is the Māori *whakapapa*.

Marriage is both a builder and a destroyer of history. In some cases, descendants of a marriage with an outsider from the dominant group, especially a man, will not be part of a society. There may also be some ongoing contact, and in a few cases outsiders marry in, live in a community and become an integral part of it. In many cases, history is mobilized to assert and justify geographical claims. Continuity of specific aspects of culture is also a major component of the historicity of a group; culture creates history. The historicity of a group is often a strong component in and reinforcement of its positive attitudes and identity.

6.6 EDUCATION

Education is a crucial battleground for language transmission. Many education systems around the world attempt to eliminate the use of minority languages, with sanctions for using anything other than the school language, usually a national or other official language, in any school-related setting. A national education system prepares citizens to be productive members of society, with instruction aimed at literacy in the official language(s) of the nation. Education also transmits majority views about history and culture and disconnects children from their heritage.

There are often special residential schools for 'Indians' or other marginalized groups, with children removed from their families to distant places usually with children from many different groups, forbidden to speak their own languages and punished for doing so, given new majority-style names, dressed in majority-style clothing and sometimes later placed in low-level work (girls as house servants and boys as labourers) in majority areas after limited study. These have now disappeared from countries such as the United States (where Bureau of Indian Affairs schools were widespread from 1879 to the early 1960s), Canada (where similar schools operated from 1883 to the early 1970s) and Australia, but they persist in other places. A few of these have persisted as local schools, under the control of a local group, with completely changed policies concerning language and assimilation.

An unacceptable practice was the total removal of young children from their families on paternalistic grounds which assumed that traditional societies were less desirable for children and assimilation into the majority society would provide a better life, into residential homes or adoption into individual majority families. This practice was widespread in many countries, such as in Australia from 1905 to the early 1970s where the members of these Stolen Generations have no traditional language skills, even though they can now re-establish links with their birth families and are welcomed back into their original Aboriginal groups. As we have seen in Chapter 5 and will further discuss in Chapter 9, the school can also be a key adjunct in transmission of an endangered or other minority language, and many innovative types of preschool, in-school and supplementary language and culture education are in use around the world now.

6.7 CULTURE

This is the broadest and most diverse of the setting factors, and includes, among others, factors concerning human relations, human and other roles, material culture, activities, belief systems, taxonomies and other systems embedded in language. The degree of distinctness from surrounding cultures and similarities suggesting contact are also relevant; also the direction of diffusion of cultural influence and the approximate chronology of cultural change.

Human relations factors include the obvious areas of **consanguineal** and **affinal** relationships and family structure and behaviour; types and size of these and other relevant social networks; family, social, skill-related and other organizations; hierarchical structures within the society: social differentiation and stratification, contact and trade with outside groups and so on.

Roles include all kinds of leadership – political, religious, social, family, types of relevant work and artistic specializations and in-group expert roles and so on. Some roles are intermittent and more or less frequent, while some roles are supported by the society so they allow the individual not to do other kinds of work. Decisions about who should carry out such roles are made in various ways – self-selection, community consensus or inheritance. Some roles require training and are thus often preceded by apprenticeship and practice. Other kinds of roles are ascribed to ancestors, animals or deities in many societies.

Material culture includes both practical and artistic elements. This includes all the artefacts and utensils of every kind used in daily life and for special purposes. Activities include regular life sustenance activities, traditional or innovative; family or other in-group life cycle and other activities; leisure-time activities such as festivals and feasting, sport and play, music, dance and song and passive spectating of all kinds; language-related activities using oral and written genres; and specific cultural behaviours such as gestures. Many activities require the use of some material culture artefacts by individuals with special knowledge: music usually requires instruments and skilled players, dancers often wear special clothing and have special knowledge, and sport and play require balls, sticks and other utensils as well as practice.

Belief systems and taxonomies include religions; views concerning moral and other desirable or undesirable human characteristics; culturally defined taxonomies such as kinship, colour, taste and other categories expressed through language; socially determined cosmologies; beliefs and knowledge concerning illness, disease, medicine and curing, and any rituals and special experts associated with this; ecological knowledge about climate, soils, bodies of water, plants and animals; the appropriateness of talk or silence at certain times; frequent and appropriate topics for conversation and general or relationship-specific taboo topics; and so on. A full discussion of many of these topics is beyond the scope of this volume.

6.7.1 Human Relations

Small societies tend to have dense and multiplex networks (Milroy, 1980): most of the same people regularly interact with each other in a variety of different settings. Families may be nuclear, with only parents and their children, or extended, with three or even more generations living together; or other arrangements. New households may tend to be established with or near the husband's family, with or near the wife's family, or neither, and this will also affect the strength of different kinds of family networks. Other relevant network types are at the neighbourhood, village or higher level; also groups based on friendship, on shared age, school, work or other links, on social roles such as craft guilds. Some societies have an internal hierarchy, like South Asian caste systems.

Human societies reckon consanguineal relationships in different ways: **patrilineal** or descent through men; **matrilineal** or descent through women; or bilateral, descent through both males and females. These may divide society into larger or smaller subgroups; for example, the Māori in New Zealand have large *iwi* 'bone, tribe' groups which include various *hapu* 'subtribe' and *whanau* 'family' descent groups. Kinship factors and their importance in daily life are relevant for a group's identity and its language.

Higher-level organizations create wider networks: for a specific minority group and general minority organizations at a regional, national, transnational or international level. Networks involving outside contact for trade, government, school and so on are less favourable to language persistence.

6.7.2 Roles

Societies have a variety of types of leadership roles – political, religious, social and family – and functional skilled roles, such as in-group medical, artistic and craft experts, such as blacksmiths, potters and weavers. Many such traditional skills are being lost around the world as they become less relevant in modern life. New roles are also developing, but many of these involve connecting the community with the outside and are thus not inherently supportive of traditional language and culture.

6.7.3 Material Culture

Material culture includes a wide range of practical and artistic elements. As noted earlier, this includes food, clothing and other artefacts and utensils of every kind used in daily life and for special purposes: for hunting; fishing; gathering; cultivation; food preparation, cooking and eating; clothing of all types for all kinds of purposes and the things needed to make them; instruments for music; artefacts for sport and play; architecture and arrangement of houses, public buildings and villages and the tools and materials needed to build them; all other kinds of buildings and artefacts used in religion; healing; and art of all types,the equipment and materials used to produce it and the special symbols and motifs used in it.

Food is extremely diverse: what is eaten; preparation, cooking and eating implements; and food dishes, some every day and some for special occasions, such as the flat oval-shaped cooked and pounded glutinous rice cakes with sesame eaten only during traditional New Year celebrations by many related Ngwi groups such as the Lisu, Lahu and others in south-western China and nearby in South East Asia. Food and its associated artefacts may be more persistent than language in some societies, especially migrant communities; they may be also be a strong symbol of identity.

Clothing can also be remarkably distinctive, and is often a major symbol of group identity. In many societies, the clothing of women is more dramatic, but this is not universal. Children often have special types of clothing and are carried or cared for in specific types of artefacts, and appropriate clothing may change through the life cycle: married women often wear clothes which differ from those of unmarried women. Traditional artefacts and skills associated with producing clothing are at great risk, although they can be redeployed to meet outside demand, like Bai batik in western Yunnan, south-western China. Clothing may change, disappear and be revived; the Gong and

Bisu in Thailand have recently recreated their traditional clothing and wear it at public events.

Practical objects used in agriculture, animal husbandry, hunting, fishing and gathering are of great diversity and interest: tools, traps, nets, baskets and carrying bags; likewise, household items such as furniture, bedding, storage and cooking implements and pots, eating utensils, items for washing and grooming, and household and community religious artefacts. There are also musical instruments, equipment for sport and play, artefacts involved in traditional medicine and many other kinds of things.

Most societies have their own distinctive house and public building arrangement and architecture, with traditional building materials, methods and tools. Villages and houses may be arranged, oriented and decorated according to traditional patterns. The position, arrangement and artefacts at the village religious location may differ greatly, but are also usually a strong reflection of the culture: a building, a rock, a tree or grove of trees, a ritual dancing ground and so on.

Artistic expression creates a variety of objects, in various kinds of medium: painted, carved and so on. Some of these also have practical functions, others are for ritual purposes, and some are entirely for artistic expression. One such type of artefact is jewellery of all kinds, also pottery and others.

Museums collect cultural artefacts and display them, usually outside the community; often these were collected some time ago and are thus particularly valuable as traditional artefacts. In many cases, communities are now requesting and often receiving their return. Communities and families may also have collections, sometimes including family heirlooms; it is very interesting to see which artefacts are displayed by the members of the group, and to discuss the history and artistic merits of these objects.

The artefacts created during our research are also valuable: photographs, video and audio files, transcriptions of material accompanying cultural activities, personal, family and group history, and even ethnographic and linguistic notebooks. Providing these in a usable form to the community as well as archiving them in an appropriate way is important.

6.7.4 Activities

As noted earlier, activity is a very broad category which includes daily life and special events. Some kinds of activities, such as some life cycle events, religion, sport, music and dance, language-related activities such as singing, reciting traditional literature, storytelling and dramatic performances may be public events performed or led by experts. Others are private events where an individual, family or small group participate in small-scale daily and leisure-time activities. The traditional ways that children play and the artefacts for play are often distinctive. The same is true for sport and other ludic activities which continue beyond childhood. Specific sports are a focus in some societies: archery in Bhutan, wrestling in Mongolia, various individual, competitive and team games around the world played with a ball and other implements such as sticks, including Irish hurling, Iroquois lacrosse, Central Asian polo played on horseback and many others.

There are some language-related activities such as telling riddles, proverbs and stories, fortune telling and recounting traditional history, genealogy, singing and dramatizations. Songs range from simple lullabies to epic poetry about cultural heroes; songs and music may be a powerful symbol of identity, as in the case of the Saami *joik* genre.

Feasting is an important collective activity in some societies; for example, Russell (2001) shows that this is a major component of group identity among the Tagal Murut in Sabah. A more contemporary food-related activity is selling 'exotic' minority food to the majority in tourist settings. Similarly, music, dance and other kinds of dramatic performances may be both traditional activities as well as a possible source of status, work and profit.

A diverse range of special activities is usually carried out during human life cycle events such as birth, coming of age, courtship and marriage, and death, among others. Every society also has festival activities; some relate to the annual production cycle, others to the lunar or solar cycle of the year, including a new year festival, or to longer cycles. For example, in Shaochong village, Shiping county, southern Yunnan there is a local Nisu village festival celebrated every twelve years on the first Day of the Horse in the Year of the Horse (1992, 2014, 2026 and so on). The village has complex and consistent traditional activities with a village procession, twelve shamans reading simultaneously and various other activities.

Festivals are a place to display traditional skills in music, song, dance, sport, craft and language. Some ongoing Celtic examples based on traditional activities in north-western Europe are the Irish Feis at various times of year and the annual Welsh Eisteddfod in early August; revived examples are the Scots Mòd in October since 1891, the Bréton Fest, such as the one at Quimper in late July since 1923, and Cornish festivals in Cornwall and around the world such as the language-oriented Gosedd meetings since 1928 and the traditional Golowan (midsummer) festival in Penzance on 23 June up to the 1890s, revived in 1991, among other Cornish festivals. Another European example is the annual Saami Day on 6 February celebrating and commemorating the first Saami congress across national borders in 1917; the festival has been held annually on this date since 1993.

International events concerning language, such as UNESCO's International Mother Tongue Day, 21 February every year since 1999, celebrate the world's linguistic diversity; these promote and praise language reclamation and maintenance activities around the world, sometimes with local offshoots, and award prizes. The Comité International Permanent des Linguistes, a UNESCO-affiliated organization, has had a focus on language endangerment since 1991 and has held very frequent workshops, conferences and other events focusing on this topic since 1992, and also awards prizes to linguists who make an important contribution to language reclamation.

6.7.5 Systems

Belief systems and taxonomies include religion and other types of cosmological systems; views concerning moral and other desirable or undesirable human characteristics; culturally defined taxonomies such as kinship, colour, taste and other categories expressed through language; beliefs and knowledge concerning illness, disease, medicine and curing, and any rituals and special experts associated with this; ecological knowledge about climate, soils, bodies of water, plants and animals and how to deal with them appropriately; and other kinds of socially relevant category systems. For further discussion of these topics from a linguistic perspective, see Chapter 7, particularly Section 7.4.

Time taxonomy categorizes days, years and other culturally specific time units like weeks. The elaborateness of such systems differs widely; in some Tibeto-Burman languages, this extends up to eight days and years in the past and in the future, with distinct lexical forms not related to numbers (Bradley, 2007c).

Another universal system is kinship, which also regulates many aspects of human activity. Kinship terminology systems are also extended beyond the specific referents in all societies, but in different ways. These kinship systems may also reflect cultural preferences such as marriage patterns; for example, in Lisu, the preferred marriage partner is a mother's brother's daughter or father's sister's son, and much of the terminology such as for uncles and aunts, cousins, nephews and nieces reflect this. For example, the term for mother's brother's wife is the same as the term for father's sister; the term for a cross niece or nephew who can marry your child (and one of whom should) differs from the term for a parallel niece or nephew who cannot. Some kinship categories related to birth order are elaborate, such as the Northern Lisu system with nine specific given names for first-born to ninth-born males and nine different given names for first-born to ninth-born females; interestingly, the terms in this system appear to be borrowed from Anong, a language which Lisu is in the process of replacing (Bradley, 2007d).

Some other cultural taxonomic systems are also universal but diverse; examples include colour, taste, disease, dimensions and so on. Others are more restricted, such as taxonomies of smells which are found in a number of languages spoken by hunter-gatherers. Like kinship, some other such terminology systems are extended beyond their specific referents. Berlin and Kay (1969), in discussing and generalizing about the wide range of observed colour terminology systems, emphasize their universal and hierarchical nature, but do not venture into the fascinating area of cultural extensions; for example, in English, blue for sad, yellow for cowardly and green for inexperienced.

There are various physical manifestations which accompany speech; these are diverse, sometimes relatively culture-specific and often not documented by linguists, who usually describe only speech. These include gestures such as pointing, waving, saluting, nodding; facial expressions; body orientation; gaze and other eye movements; gait; standards for eye contact; and loudness. Some are very culture-specific and are therefore more readily noticed, such as the Tibetan preference for covering the mouth with one hand while speaking politely to someone of high status; others may be subtle.

Many societies have an established taxonomy about their language; there may also be a system of categories of literary genres and more or less specific structures for some of these genres. For example, Lisu has a very strong preference for a pattern of paired seven-syllable lines in its oral songs, proverbs, riddles and other genres, which is also carried across into modern Christian Lisu written literature. For an extended example, see Bradley et al. (2008). In Nisu, the four main genres are ritual texts, fortune-telling texts, genealogies and moral texts. Other genres such as popular stories were not traditionally written.

6.7.6 Combinations of Factors

There is a great deal of interplay and overlap between some of these areas. For most societies, food production is a sustenance activity using tools to carry out activities. Food preparation and consumption then uses artefacts to prepare culturally appropriate meals; food is eaten in social settings by members of a network according to cultural rules.

Special food is needed for life cycle celebrations, festivals and feasting, along with other activities.

Similarly, while producing or performing oral or written materials is an activity, this is carried out within a social setting within culturally determined systems. Writing also produces material artefacts. Furthermore, when we or any insiders or outsiders make recordings or videos of oral performance and then distribute these within a society, an artefact is created. The written materials and the oral performances may show virtuosity and have artistic elements; and the performers may wear special clothing and use various artefacts and gestures.

Cultural knowledge of many of these types is being lost around the world, but in many societies there are pleasant memories about former lifestyles which can motivate a community to document and maintain their language and many aspects of the culture embedded within it.

6.8 EXTERNAL FACTORS

Human societies are usually dynamic and constantly changing. Various external factors influence minority language persistence. These include effects from other human societies, environmental factors and combinations of the two.

The external human factors can sometimes be positive, but are more often negative. They include peaceful contact for trade, which increases contact and may also impel economic changes. Sometimes the effects are drastic, as where timber is removed from an area leading to land degradation and possibly flooding, or where new cash crops replace local subsistence crops. Trade may also lead to the decline of traditional crafts; it is much easier to buy cloth and pots than to make them.

At the time of the shift from hunter-gatherer lifestyles to mobile herding and sedentary agriculture starting about 12,000 years ago (12K YBP), there were major cultural changes which fundamentally increased productivity, allowed some societies to expand greatly and gradually decreased the number of distinct human societies and languages. Human genetic change may also have played a role in the success and expansion of some societies. For example, it has recently been suggested that a genetic modification among the Proto-Indo-European population circa 5K YBP eliminated adult lactose intolerance, so this society could rely on milk and cheese as well as herding and agriculture (Garnier et al., 2017) while spreading and dominating sedentary populations.

External human incursions have often been violent. One of the most disastrous incursions for the persistence of existing languages and cultures was European colonialism from about 1500 to the mid-twentieth century. Many colonialized peoples lost positive self-identity and gradually shifted to the colonial languages. There were many new contact languages which developed during such contacts as a result of Nativization (Chapter 9), but, as these have lower status, they also tend to disappear through decreolization, an often neglected area of language endangerment.

Throughout human history, small groups and their languages have even been subject to extermination; one recent example is Maku'a or Lovaia, the only language of its Papuan subgroup family, which was drastically affected during the war accompanying the Indonesian take-over of Timor Leste in 1975 and the subsequent resistance; speakers decreased from fifty to three elderly speakers by independence in 1999 (Hajek, 2002) and it is now no longer spoken.

Disease has often resulted from human contact through history. The Black Death, which devastated Europe in the mid-fourteenth century, probably came from an Asian source via the Silk Road. Many populations without resistance to measles and other European diseases were drastically reduced during colonial expansion. Colonialists moving to unfamiliar areas were also susceptible to local diseases, so this was not a one-way process.

Another very widespread external influence is religion; most major world religions proselytize. An external religion may also bring a liturgical language, such as Arabic for Islam, Sanskrit/Pali for Hinduism and Buddhism and, until fifty years ago, Latin for the Catholic Church. Some external religions support indigenous languages; the original motivation for SIL International was to produce Bibles in as many languages of the world as possible. Conversion to an external religion leads to increased outside contacts and influence, often favouring language shift. Conversely, there are existing, developing or new indigenous religions in many parts of the world, which may be a strong positive factor for a group, its identity and its language.

In many societies, outsiders marrying in have expanded the gene pool; this can be positive, where a group is so small that all available in-group spouses are too closely related to marry, as happened to the Gong in western Thailand, almost all of whom have had to marry outsiders for over fifty years; this has nearly eliminated the Gong language. Some societies assimilate outsiders who marry in, particularly females but also sometimes males, provided that they join the group, speak the language and practice the culture; this has happened with the Lisu in

China, Burma and Thailand over several hundred years, which has made Lisu much more vigorous, but has severely endangered some of the wives' languages, such as Anong in Fugong county, north-western Yunnan, and some of the husbands' languages, such as Laemae nearby in Lushui county. There was a large influx of Yunnanese Han Chinese ex-soldier husbands to the Southern Lisu population in Burma and Thailand from about 1920 to 1960. About half of the Southern Lisu have a Chinese surname inherited from their recent Han Chinese ancestor, rather than a Lisu patrilineal clan name, but few speak Chinese or identify as such.

Another anthropogenic change is technology. This has sped up and increased communication, eliminated some kinds of traditional work, created many new kinds of work requiring dominant-language skills and otherwise disrupted many aspects of life in most societies. Technology can be used in positive ways for many endangered languages, especially in the developed world, but this is not usually the intended or main outcome. Conversely, the German measles vaccine and the cochlear implant have greatly reduced the deaf population in many developed countries, thus reducing the user population of various deaf sign languages.

Environmental factors include short-term and long-term problems with negative effects on local populations, potentially endangering languages. Short-term disasters, one main component of anthropology of disaster, include tectonic effects such as volcanic eruptions and earthquakes with resulting tsunamis and landslides; also weather-related issues such as drought, excessive rain leading to floods and excessive heat or cold. In some cases, disasters combine: a landslide may block a river temporarily, but eventually the blockage collapses and there is a disastrous downstream flood, as happens fairly frequently in the Himalayas. Floods can also be anthropogenic, like frequent floods in central Thailand in part due to deforestation of upland watersheds.

Long-term environmental problems can lead to the collapse of ecosystems, affecting the languages spoken in an area. One example is the collapse of the Mayan Empire in the ninth century, resulting from long-term drought, over-reliance on a small number of crops, overpopulation and internal conflict, and its breakdown into a large number of distinct modern languages, many of them endangered. Non-anthropogenic long-term change such as ice ages and sea level changes also led to major population movements in prehistoric times; for example, the entry of humans to the Americas was facilitated during the period from 16.5K YBP to 11K YBP by a land bridge across the Bering Strait. We may be on the verge of a similar population movement, with disastrous effects for island and coastal peoples and their languages due to anthropogenic climate change and the resulting sea level changes.

6.9 SPEAKER BACKGROUND CHARACTERISTICS

Sociolinguistic surveys collect information about the background of the speakers and attempt to correlate speaker background with linguistic behaviour and attitudes. Surveys of language endangerment also need to do so, and ensure that their sample represents the community accurately. The survey should also investigate the non-linguistic factors already discussed as well as language attitudes (Chapter 3), language knowledge and language use (Chapter 5).

Speaker background tends to correlate with differences in speech and social behaviour. This includes the speaker's language knowledge, their household language repertoire and language repertoires among their ancestors, and where, when and how much their languages are used. Geographical, historical, educational and cultural factors are also relevant: where the speakers and their parents and ancestors lived; family and other kin group history, order of birth in the family and other kin-related factors; education of the speakers and their family members; social roles of the speakers and of their family members and ancestors; and so on.

Speaker background surveys used in postgraduate theses which we have supervised provide examples of how to investigate non-linguistic and linguistic factors. Moser (1992) is a survey of language use in the Central African Republic, where French is the ex-colonial language and the indigenous creole Sango is a widespread lingua franca. She asked nine background questions: name, age, birthplace, residence, schooling, occupation, ethnic group, church language and best language. Kayambazinthu (1995) is a survey of language use and attitudes in Malawi, where English is the ex-colonial language, Chichewa is the national language and various related Bantu languages are also spoken. This was discussed in detail in the case study in Chapter 5. Her eleven speaker background questions are gender, age, marital status, occupation, education, ethnic group, birthplace, residence (with a supplementary question, for how long), religion, mother tongue, and other languages (with a supplementary question about order of acquisition of these other languages). Thamrin (2015) investigated Minangkabau language attitudes and use in West Sumatra, Indonesia, as discussed in the case study in Chapter 4. She studied two groups, adolescent youths and their parents, and used slightly different speaker characteristics questions for each group. For both groups, she asked five questions: age, residence, how long in that location, how they learned Minangkabau and what other languages they use. For the youth group only, she asked eight additional questions: name of school, father's and mother's occupation and level of education, mother tongue and parents' mother tongue. For the adult group only, she asked two additional questions: occupation and spouse's occupation. In different locations, the major relevant factors may differ; so, every study must make a judgement about which to investigate. In-depth fieldwork will reveal a nuanced and extensive set of local setting factors, which should then be discussed with members of the community.

6.10 CONCLUSION

The large and varied inventory of non-linguistic factors discussed in this chapter include some which are relevant in most language endangerment situations, and others which are less widespread. The richest array of relevant factors, not surprisingly, relates to the culture of the group who speak the endangered language. The factor which shows the strongest effect on individual language behaviour and the greatest individual differences within a group is often speaker background.

Often the 'facts' about minorities are contested. Majority groups may have a range of ideas, some of them based on inaccurate stereotypes. Within the majority, there may be very different views; these may be linked with political views, personal interests and other characteristics of the particular majority group member. Often, inaccurate majority perceptions may lump a number of minority groups together, such as the popular view that there was one Australian Aboriginal language, not hundreds. Members of minority groups may also have different views.

Old and often inaccurate 'facts' often persist and are used long after they are no longer correct. As we will shortly see, the Ket speaker population was estimated at about 1,000 in 1991 (Kibrik, 1991), enumerated at nearly 600 in the 1990 census and nearly 200 in the 2010 census, but the actual figure is now under fifty. Part of this is based on inaccurate over-reporting in census surveys, part on over-optimistic estimates by scholars and part on a decrease over nearly thirty years. Minority activists may make exaggerated demographic claims about group numbers and speakers of a language. During successful efforts to achieve official status for their language in India, the Bodo group claimed up to 8 million ethnic Bodo in Assam in the 1980s. This was facilitated by incomplete census data mainly due to ethnic-based unrest among the Bodo which prevented the 1981 census from taking place in many parts of Assam. The exaggerated number included many ethnic Bodo who do not speak the language, members of several related groups, plus a few million more to strengthen the case.

Rights to traditional land are also very often contested. This is a key concern for many groups, often of greater immediate concern than preserving language and culture. The presence of a language which continues in use and historical and cultural links to land are major components in documenting and establishing these rights, as in all Australian land claims, where expert anthropologists and linguists with long-term connections to a community can assist.

The documentation of the sociolinguistic setting of the language community should be a core component of our work. This is a topic which is often of great interest to community members, who may have very important information and views. It is also essential to understand the setting of a language and work within it to help to strengthen and reclaim its use within the community.

CASE STUDY: KET

Ket is the sole remaining language of the Yeniseian family of languages, also sometimes called Yeniseic, formerly widely spoken by numerous small groups along the middle and upper Yenisei River in central Siberia. Apart from Ket, no other Yeniseian languages are still spoken. Ket is a recognised nationality of Russia, as it was a recognised nationality of the USSR. The autonym of this group is /ke'd/ [kɛt^{353}] which simply means 'human being'. It was formerly sometimes known to outsiders as Yenisei Ostyak; Ostyak is a former Russian exonym, possibly of Turkic origin, for various central Siberian groups, especially the Khanty who speak a Samoyedic Uralic language. The Ket nationality also includes descendants of speakers of Yugh, a closely related Yeniseian language whose last speaker died in the 1970s; the Yugh are also sometimes known as Sym Ket, the Ket of the Sym River and Sym village, and, in contrast, the Ket were formerly sometimes known as Imbat Ket. The name Yugh comes from the Ket name for the Yugh, /juk/.

The ethnic Ket population has been around a thousand since the 1836 Russian census. The 2010 census of Russia gives a population of

1,219 which includes the non-Yugh-speaking ethnic Yugh. Russian language statistics are based on a census question about mother tongue; the response is often by ethnic background, not what people actually speak. In the USSR census of 1990, nearly half of the Ket claimed to speak Ket, and Kibrik (1991: 272) suggested that 80–85 per cent could speak it but avoided doing so; this was not correct. The 2010 census suggests 199 speakers, which is also an exaggeration; scholars estimate about fifty fluent speakers. There are no monolingual speakers; all ethnic Ket speak Russian fluently, and most speak only Russian.

Ket has three dialects, Southern, Central and Northern. The Central dialect is critically endangered, partly due to the displacement of most speakers from the former village of Pakulikha in the 1960s (Georg, 2007: 26–7); this dialect was the basis for a short-lived Romanization developed by Nestor K. Karger used in education from 1934 but suppressed in the late 1930s like other Romanizations in the USSR. Northern Ket is also critically endangered, has almost no remaining speakers and is less well described. Southern Ket has more remaining speakers than Northern and Central Ket combined, but all fluent speakers are old. A Cyrillic script representing Southern Ket was developed by Heinrich Werner and has been in use since 1993. In 1991, the language was still being taught as a subject in five schools (Kibrik, 1991: 272), and until recently it was taught on demand to children in the school in Kellog, in the Southern Ket area; but the Ket language teacher in Kellog has now retired.

The Yeniseian languages were also formerly spoken further south. They have long been in contact with a wide range of languages: Turkic to their south and west, Samoyedic to their north and Tungusic Ewenki to their east. The Xiongnu Empire of what is now Mongolia circa 200 BC appears to have included some Yeniseian speakers among its population; see Vovin (2000) and Vovin et al. (2016); the latter suggest that the variety represented there was similar to Central Yeniseian Pumpokol. Turkic contact started over 2,000 years ago, see Timonima (2004). Turkic groups moved northwards into the southern part of the Yeniseian area from circa AD 552, the first identifiably Turkic Empire. There was also Mongol contact via Turkic groups since the period of the Genghis Khan Empire from the early thirteenth century. Substantial Turkic northward migrations since 1230 into the south and west of the Yeniseian area brought even closer contact. Since before 1600 there has been gradually increasing contact with Russian, especially since 1800, and Russian then became the lingua franca of the area. Russian has completely replaced all other Yeniseian languages.

The Ket and other groups in the area were settled in permanent villages in the 1930s, and their traditional lifestyle ended. During the Second World War, there was a major influx of outsiders into Ket villages, especially displaced Volga Germans and Balts. Many ethnic Ket born since 1930 have had limited exposure to the Ket language and have used mainly Russian as children, except with their parents; most of the fathers of this generation were away during the Second World War and many did not come back. All Ket children were sent to Russian-speaking boarding schools in the 1950s; this was perhaps the final trigger for the shift away from speaking Ket.

Vajda (2001: map 3) lists all ethnic Ket villages, from north to south: Northern Ket Kureika, Maduika, Svetlogorsk, Goroshikha and Sovrechka, with some in other northern mixed locations (Stari Turukhansk); Central Ket Turukhansk, Kostino, Farkovo, Baklanikha, Vereshchagino, Surgutikha and formerly Pakulikha and Baikha; and Southern Ket Verkhneimbatsk, Kellog, Bakhta, Sumarkovo, Sulomai, Baikit and Bor; also formerly in Lebed', Alinskoe and Yelogui. The Yugh used to live further south in Vorogovo, Zotino and Sym. A few are scattered elsewhere in Siberia and Russia. As of 2001, there was an ethnic Ket majority in only three villages: Northern Ket Maduika and Southern Ket Kellog and Sulomai. Villages with over a quarter ethnic Ket include Northern Ket Goroshikha, Central Ket Baklanikha and Surgutikha and Southern Ket Kangatovo. Villages with over a tenth ethnic Ket are Northern Ket Kostino, Central Ket Vereshchagino and Southern Ket Bakhta and Sumarkovo. Elsewhere, the proportion of ethnic Ket is even smaller. The former Yugh villages now have extremely low proportions of ethnic Ket and almost no Yugh.

According to reports from scholars, there are no fluent speakers under thirty-five and most are over sixty, with the main domain speaking to one's parents and a few people under seventy-five still using the language in daily life. Russian has almost completely replaced Ket, even among those who can speak it. This is despite the existence of Ket teaching materials since 1993 and their former use in some local schools. Some formerly fluent speakers who served as language consultants are now semispeakers who no longer use the language regularly. Georg (2007: 25) reports that spontaneous use of Ket by those under forty at the time of his fieldwork in 1999–2001 was rare; Krivogonov (2016) reports equally limited use by those under sixty in 2014. Passive understanding is now mainly restricted to those over thirty-five. All fluent speakers who assisted in the Ket dictionary (Kotorova & Nefedov, 2015) are now over seventy; this included sixteen Southern Ket speakers, seven Central Ket speakers and four Northern

Ket speakers, but at least six of these twenty-seven have already passed away. An overall current estimate is about forty speakers of Southern Ket, fewer than ten speakers of Central Ket and a couple of speakers of Northern Ket, including semispeakers.

Of the other Yeniseian languages, Yugh was last spoken by members of the Ket nationality living in Vorogovo and Yartsevo villages along the Sym River south of Ket, and formerly nearby in Sym, Bor and Zotino. The last of these speakers could not understand Ket. By 1995, there were forty-seven Southern Ket and one Yugh in these villages, but no Yugh speakers. Yugh was fairly well documented by Castrén (1858), supplemented by Werner (1997); the group's autonym was [djuk]. Ket and Yugh represent the Northern subgroup of Yeniseian.

Pumpokol was a village south of the Yugh-speaking area, just north-west of modern Yeniseisk. Their former speech appears to have been a distinct language; apparent lexical similarity to Yugh may be due to confusion in early data. Most scholars link it with Arin, a language formerly spoken south-west of modern Yeniseisk, also on the west side of the Yenisei River. Both of these Central Yeniseian languages have been extinct since the mid-1700s.

Southern Yeniseian languages were formerly spoken south-east of modern Yeniseisk on the east side of the river; they include Kott as described by Castrén (1858) who collected data on two dialects in the 1850s from the last five speakers in Agul'skoe village; there is also limited earlier data on the Kyshtym village variety and on Assan, extinct since the mid-1700s. Werner (1997) contains a summary of all available information on Kott. Anderson (2004: 9) suggests that Kott may be more conservative than Northern Yeniseian in retaining some two-syllable stems.

Other Yeniseian languages may formerly have been spoken further south, prior to Turkic conquest of that area circa AD 552. Some modern Samoyedic and Turkic language speakers along the Yenisei River may be partly descended from Yeniseian language speakers, and a tiny number of older speakers of other nearby languages also have limited knowledge of Ket.

The Southern Ket dialect is well documented by Vajda (2004) and Georg (2007) as well as the Kotorova and Nefedov (2015) dictionary; Georg and the dictionary also include Central and Northern dialect data. The verb morphology of Ket and other former Yeniseian languages is extremely complex. Southern Ket also has a **tone** system with four basic tones which is most unusual in Siberia. The Ket Cyrillic orthography indicates tones 2 and 3, but not tones 1 and 4 which are both unmarked; thus it is slightly underspecified.

Ket, as the last surviving Yeniseian language, is an example of the loss of genetic linguistic diversity that is resulting from language endangerment. It is also typologically unusual for its area, with a tonal system more similar to those of some Tibeto-Burman languages, and has an extremely interesting and complex grammatical system, particularly the verbs. Documentation is as advanced as it can be, but there is currently no effort to continue using the language and it will soon cease to be spoken.

DISCUSSION QUESTIONS

How important is it to document endangered languages which are the sole or one of the few members of a language family, or which have typologically unusual structures? Discuss.

What are some additional non-linguistic factors not mentioned earlier which may also affect the vitality of a language? Do these fit into one of the categories proposed here, or do they suggest additional categories?

Is it possible to assign a consistent weight to the various non-linguistic factors in language endangerment discussed in this chapter, and create a standard index like some of those outlined in Chapter 2? Discuss.

SUGGESTIONS FOR FURTHER READING

Georg (2007) is a thorough study of Ket, including detailed bibliography and sociolinguistic background as well as a structural outline of this dizzyingly complex language.

Lewis (2011) outlines the FAMED (functions, acquisition, motivation, environment, distinct niches) framework which attempts to create an index combining attitude, domain, acquisition and other issues.

7 Linguistic Processes

> Our languages, our stories:
> They express and strengthen the way we look at life
> And they give us a sense of belonging
> Our stories allow us to share our experiences
> And our ideas about the world
> > Burke Museum of Natural History and Culture (2016)

This chapter discusses the types of change which occur in languages when they become endangered. As most of them involve linguistic structures, there will be extensive use of linguistic terminology here; all terms are first introduced in **bold** and are explained in the Glossary. Some readers with less background in linguistics may find some of the material in this chapter fairly difficult and may wish to pass over it.

All languages change; the rate of change differs between languages and through time. Some non-endangered languages, such as Icelandic, change more slowly due to attitudinal factors which value and favour stability; others, such as English, change more rapidly. Dixon (1997) suggests that all languages go through long periods of equilibrium or stability, punctuated by periods of rapid change. Periods of change are often triggered by external factors, such as many of the sociocultural ones discussed in the preceding chapter. Endangered languages are normally undergoing major external influences, and so it is often the case that there is more ongoing change than in more stable or safe languages. This also means that internal divergence may be more rapid than in other situations: differences between the speech of older and younger individuals in the same community, change in usage through one's lifetime and particularly differences between different communities where there is little ongoing contact. This can lead to rapid dialect diversification, eventually leading to loss of mutual intelligibility and divisions within the group. Another outcome can be the development of new varieties of the endangered language, with radically different structures spoken by younger people, as in the case of Yolngu, Warlpiri and Gurindji in central and northern Australia. However, rapid change is not universal; there may also be structural stability in an endangered language or in some or many areas of its structure if local factors support this.

Tsunoda (2006: 77–97) illustrates the types of change seen in an endangered language using examples drawn mainly from Dyirbal in Australia, based on Schmidt (1985). There are various other overviews, such as Palosaari and Campbell (2011). In this chapter, we will illustrate this with examples drawn from our own original published and unpublished data on Gong as spoken in Thailand.

7.1 PHONOLOGY: THE SOUNDS

This section contains a number of phonetic symbols drawn from the International Phonetic Alphabet (IPA); for an explanation, see their website www.internationalphoneticassociation.org or any standard phonetics textbook, such as Ladefoged with Johnson (2015). One inaccurate stereotype about language endangerment is that sound systems tend to be simplified. Rather, what often happens is that there are two competing systems, so there may be two separate systems for fluent speakers of both endangered and replacing language, but more often blended systems or changed systems reflecting the structure of the dominant language among less fluent speakers of an endangered language.

Gong has a relatively large set of initial consonants, some medial consonants, a complex vowel system of ten vowels and three vowel sequences or **diphthongs** with many regularly distributed alternative pronunciations, and only three consonants which may occur at the end of the syllable, although most syllables have no final consonant. Each syllable also has a **tone** which is written here with two small raised numbers after the syllable; the number 5 represents the highest pitch in the speaker's range, and 1 represents the lowest; so $/^{35}/$ represents a tone rising from mid to high pitch within any speaker's pitch range. In Gong, these tones also change according to regular phonological patterns, a process usually known as **tone sandhi**. As in many languages of the world, the tones are a crucial component of the word, expressing important meaning differences; so, for example, the group's own name is /gɔŋ^{35}/ 'Gong'; /gɔŋ^{55}/ is 'high/tall', and /gɔŋ^{33}/ is 'horse'. Gong has voiced stop consonants /b/ /d/ /g/; Thai/Lao have /b/ and /d/ but no /g/. In principle, this consonant could be at risk during the process of endangerment, but, as it is so salient, including being in the group's name, it persists. However, in dialects which ceased to be spoken in the 1980s, even this /g/ was replaced by a consonant present in Thai, /w/, among their last few speakers.

Gong is still spoken in two villages, Kok Chiang in Dan Chang District of Suphanburi province and Khook Khwaay in Ban Rai District of Uthai Thani province, both in western central Thailand. It was also formerly spoken in various villages in Kanchanaburi province; see Bradley (1989a). In traditional Gong, as spoken by very old speakers in these two villages, the forms of vowels and diphthongs differ according to whether they are at the end of a syllable and have a vowel or diphthong said with the tongue slightly higher in the mouth, or with a final consonant and with a vowel or diphthong said with the tongue slightly lower in the mouth. Thus, every one of the ten vowels and three diphthongs has two slightly different alternative forms; the vowels in syllables with and without a final consonant are partly overlapping. In addition, the three non-low vowels and one diphthong produced with the tongue neither forwards nor **back** but rather **central** in the mouth have two further alternative forms: with the lips rounded where the syllable ends with a vowel, /ŋ/ or /ʔ/; and with the lips spread where the syllable ends with /k/. In native Gong words and assimilated loanwords, there are no vowels or diphthongs in syllables ending in a consonant which have the tongue maximally high in the mouth, and no front or back vowels or diphthongs in syllables ending in a vowel which have the tongue maximally low in the mouth; also no unrounded central vowels or diphthong other than before /k/. Thus, for example, the vowel /i/ is pronounced [i] in a vowel-final syllable and [I] (like the vowel in English *pit*) in a consonant-final syllable; and the central vowel /ɨ/ is pronounced [ɨ] in a vowel-final syllable, slightly lower [ɵ] in a syllable ending in /ŋ/ or /ʔ/, and unrounded [ɘ] in a syllable ending in /k/. For a more detailed discussion, see Bradley (2011b). Among younger Gong speakers, especially those for whom Lao and/or Thai is the dominant language, this system has broken down. Many Lao/Thai loanwords are used with high vowels in syllables with a final consonant, with low vowels in syllables with a final vowel and central unrounded vowels are used other than before /k/. This violates the original Gong pattern. Thus, paradoxically, the more fluent middle-aged speakers have the most complex vowel system with the entire Gong inventory of ten vowels and three diphthongs with a total of twenty-three realizations, but with a lot of variation in their pronunciation, and for Thai/Lao loanwords the entire Thai/Lao inventory of nine vowels, most of which overlap with a Gong vowel, and three other diphthongs. Less fluent speakers, and the orthography we devised for Gong, use a simplified system with all Gong words pronounced using the nine Thai vowels, one Thai diphthong partly similar to a Gong diphthong, and two of the three distinctive Gong diphthongs. One thing that is not present in traditional Gong is a long versus short vowel and diphthong contrast, as seen in Thai and Lao; although this is used in loanwords by the youngest speakers for whom Thai/Lao is dominant.

Traditional Gong syllables have a four-tone contrast, with a high-level tone, a mid-rising tone, a mid-level tone and a falling tone. There are two types of tone sandhi: one for noun forms with a falling tone in the last syllable of words containing more than one syllable, and one for verbs. The noun tone sandhi affects only the Gong falling tone. This is a low falling tone in a one-syllable word, but it changes to a high falling tone when it is the last syllable in a word with two or more syllables. For example, 'ten' is /sɛ^{21}/ and 'thirty' is /ʔoŋ^{33} sɛ^{21}/ 'two ten', pronounced [ʔoŋ^{33} sɛ^{53}]. Thai and Lao have a contrast between a high falling and a low falling tone in nouns, and recent loanwords are borrowed with these tones, disrupting the regular Gong pattern by introducing high falling tone in one-syllable nouns and low falling tone in the last syllable of polysyllabic nominal forms. For nearly all current speakers other than the oldest, this has led to a breakdown in the traditional pattern, and the innovative speakers simply assign either a consistently high falling or a consistently low falling tone to every Gong nominal form which traditionally had the falling tone.

The verb tone sandhi applies in a variety of environments, most frequently in verbs after the negation /ma^{33}/; here, the high-level and mid-level tones change to mid rising, the mid-rising tone changes to high level, and the low falling tone changes to low rising or mid rising. For example,

55 > 35	/ʔi^{55}/ 'die'	/ma^{33} ʔi^{35}/ 'not die'
33 > 35	/dɛŋ^{33}/ 'drink'	/ma^{33} dɛŋ^{35}/ 'not drink'
35 > 55	/ʔe^{35}/ 'know'	/ma^{33} ʔe^{55}/ 'not know'
21 > 13~35	/jo^{21}/ 'take'	/ma^{33} jo^{13}/ 'not take' ~
		/ma^{33} jo^{35}/

For all but elderly speakers, the sandhi form of verbs with the falling tone is mid rising; so, for most speakers, the high, mid and falling tones all merge to mid rising when sandhi occurs. There are also semispeakers in whose speech the verb tone sandhi process is variable or absent, and greater variation in sandhi for verbs with final stop consonants; see Bradley (1992b). Not surprisingly, these complex tone sandhi processes are strongly affected by the process of language endangerment; Thai and Lao have no such tone sandhi.

Consonants and consonant clusters absent from the replacing language may tend to disappear. For example, Gong as spoken in Kok Chiang village in Thailand had /ʔl/ (glottal stop plus /l/) as a consonant sequence, but the last speaker who used this died in 1984; it has been replaced by /ʔ/, which exists in Thai, the replacing language. For example, words such as the former /ʔlək⁵⁵ ʔlɛ³³/ 'fruit' are now pronounced /ʔək⁵⁵ ʔɛ³³/ by all remaining speakers. Similarly, although Thai has sequences of consonant plus medial /l/, the local Lao language spoken in the area does not; so words like /pli³³/ 'four' have now generally become /pi³³/ or sometimes an in-between variant [pji³³]. In this case, there are still a couple of living speakers who can recall which words used to have medial /l/, but do not now use them. This shows that speakers may change through their lifetime, adopting newer forms of the endangered language as the language changes.

The wide range of variation within an endangered language is exemplified within one large extended family, the descendants of the last Gong village headman and two Lao brothers from a nearby village who married his two daughters about sixty years ago. In their speech, the consonant /cʰ/ merges into the consonant /s/, as it does in Lao but not in Thai. However, the rest of the village keeps this distinction, although they also recognise the merged pattern of this family as valid. We initially spoke Gong with this merger; but later came to distinguish the two. The two mothers in these families must originally have distinguished them; but they came to follow the family pattern, reflecting **interference** from the sound system of Lao in their Gong, after many years of marriage. Over the same time, their two Lao husbands learned to speak Gong very well, apart from the absence of /cʰ/.

Another area of sound structure which may change is how syllables may combine consonants and vowels. In traditional Gong words, there were initial consonant clusters of any of /p pʰ b k kʰ ʔ/ plus medial /l/; as noted earlier, these are being lost as most speakers are now dominant in Lao, which lacks these clusters. Recent Thai loanwords add a number of other possible medial consonants such as /w/, as in the name of the village Khook Khwaay. The only consonants which can be at the end of a syllable in original Gong words are /k/ /ŋ/ and glottal stop /ʔ/; in older Lao or Thai loanwords, other final consonants are lost or replaced by one of these three, as in Gong /kʰik⁵⁵/ from Thai /kʰit⁵⁵/ (not from local Lao / kʰit²¹/) 'think', Gong /ceŋ³³/ from Thai/Lao /ci:n³³/ 'Chinese' and Gong /waʔ²¹/ from local Lao /wat²¹/ (not from Thai /wat⁵⁵/) 'Buddhist temple'. However, in recent Thai loanwords, additional Thai final consonants are used. This is also extended to personal names; many Gong people now have Thai or innovative Gong names with final consonants not found in native Gong words, like /caj^{53}/ with a final glide /j/. Some contrasts between long and short vowels also come in with recent Lao and Thai loanwords. Thus, the syllable structure of Gong as now spoken has adopted a number of characteristics of the Lao and Thai systems; this has also had a major impact on the vowel system, as we saw earlier.

Phonology can be one of the more complex areas of language structure, but it may tend to be simplified and regularized in advanced stages of language endangerment. The language contact and language learning literature suggests that learning native-like phonology, particularly phonetics, is difficult for adults; for a brief discussion of why this may be so, see Chapter 5. Thus, one might expect some ongoing **interference** from the phonology of an endangered language into the replacing language in early stages of the shift; at some point, semispeakers of the endangered language start to have better skills in the replacing language, and the interference reverses: the phonology of the dominant language may influence that of their endangered ingroup language, as in the case of restructuring of the tone and vowel systems in Gong. Where a language is being revived, as discussed in Chapter 9, complex phonological processes which are absent from the language spoken by the learners of the language being revived may cause problems.

7.2 MORPHOLOGY: WORD STRUCTURES

The definition of what is a word is primarily linguistic, based on structure, but also to some extent orthographic, based on whether written words are separated by spaces. Some languages have less complex word structures and others have more complex word structures, and writing conventions differ. All languages have basic **stems** with a core meaning; in many languages these can occur alone, in others they can or must have additional separate meaningful parts attached to them to be a full word. Nearly all languages can attach more or less additional material to the stem to form additional words.

One general phenomenon in language contact and shift is that morphology, particularly inflectional morphology, tends to be made more regular and often substantially reduced or even eliminated. For example, in Gong, two verbs have unpredictable and irregular changes in the stem, the verb 'eat' which has four stems, /so^{35}/, /se^{55}/, /si^{33}/ and

/sa^{33}/, and the verb 'go' which has two stems, /kɔ^{21}/ and /ka^{33}/. The Gong verb 'go' keeps the same initial consonant, but does not follow the regular verb tone sandhi process discussed earlier, and the vowel is different and irregular in the sandhi environment: /kɔ^{21}/ 'go' and / ma^{33} ka^{33}/ 'not go'. For 'eat', there are four different vowels in different environments, with the same initial consonant: /so^{35}/ 'eat' and / ma^{33} se^{55}/ 'not eat' with regular tone sandhi but an irregular vowel, and also /si^{33}/ in /si^{33} khe^{33}/ 'have eaten' and /sa^{33}/ in /maŋ^{33} sa^{33} la^{55}/ 'come and eat', both showing an irregular vowel and tone. This pattern is more or less regularized in the speech of semispeakers. Some semispeakers follow the conservative tone sandhi pattern for 'eat' but keep the same stem vowel, so they say /so^{35}/ 'eat' and /ma^{33} so^{55}/ 'not eat'. A few semispeakers generalize the conservative or innovative tone sandhi pattern to 'go', giving /kɔ^{21}/ and /kɔ^{13}/ or /kɔ^{35}/. There are also some semispeakers who retain irregular forms of 'eat' in some fixed phrases, like /maŋ^{33} sa^{33} la^{55}/ 'rice eat come' meaning 'come and eat' but regularize elsewhere. The least fluent semispeakers completely regularize to a single stem /kɔ^{21}/ 'go' and /so^{35}/ 'eat'.

Gong has very little inflectional morphology. This is a characteristic of many unrelated languages in the same area, but is also a likely outcome of long-term contact, and a frequent effect of language endangerment. As many related Tibeto-Burman languages outside this area do have very extensive inflectional morphology, it may well be that the ancestor language of Gong and closely related Tibeto-Burman languages such as Burmese lost this in a creoloid process (Trudgill, 2002) – not because Burmese is endangered, but because it is a language which has been replacing a number of indigenous languages of Burma since the arrival of the Burmans in Burma approximately 1,200 years ago, and was thus being learned by many people as a second language. There is a tendency for languages which have long been expanding to lose morphology; the history of English, Chinese and the development of Latin into the Romance languages provide other examples. Conversely, it may sometimes be the case that relatively complex morphology is found in smaller and more isolated languages, which may serve to reinforce the in-group and exclude outsiders by making the language difficult to learn. When a morphologically complex language becomes endangered, this may speed the process of language loss, especially if older speakers do not accept morphological change in the speech of younger people. On the other hand, it can also happen that a language becomes progressively more endangered while keeping all or most of its morphology, as in the case of East Sutherland Gaelic (Dorian, 1978, 1981, 2010b).

It often happens that a language in contact with another gets double patterns of morphology: its own original patterns plus patterns found in large numbers of borrowed words, which may then generalize within the language. For example, English has both its original Germanic **derivational** morphology and a large stratum of Romance derivational morphology borrowed through large numbers of French words and others direct from Latin, as well as some Greek derivational morphology. Original Germanic derivational suffixes producing new nouns include *-ing*, *-ness* and many others; highly frequent French and/or Latin suffixes which occur in many borrowed nouns and also produce new nouns include *-ment*, *-(a)tion* – likewise, Greek suffixes such as *-logy*, *-(o)nym*. This is also seen, for example, in the endangered Walser German variety spoken in north-eastern Italy (Denison, 1971) which has both its original German derivational morphology and a large component of morphology from Italian.

7.3 SYNTAX: SENTENCE STRUCTURE

Syntax is the combination of words into sentences. It is sometimes difficult to draw a line between morphology and syntax; the same function may be expressed by morphological processes within the word in some languages and by syntactic processes of sequences of words in others, or the two combined. Morphosyntax is the term for the two together; this is also what is traditionally called grammar.

In historical change in all languages, there is a tendency for complex structures and typologically unusual structures to be simplified or replaced by more analytic structures. This is particularly so in endangered languages, which may also be subject to influence from the structure of the replacing dominant language. In some cases, as for morphology, the outcome may be the use of two competing structural patterns: one traditional and seen in closely related languages, and one introduced from the pattern of the dominant language.

One clear example of this is the use of two **relative clause** structures in a number of Tibeto-Burman languages in South Asia. One is the typical pattern found in nearly all Sino-Tibetan languages: the relative clause precedes the noun it describes, then there is a relative marker, and then the noun: for example, Chinese *jintian lai de ren* 'today come Relative person' or 'the person who came today', unlike, for example, English where the relative clause follows the noun it describes. The other is the typical pattern of Indo-Aryan languages of northern South Asia, in which the relative clause contains a question nominal and the following head noun is preceded by a demonstrative. For example, in the Tibeto-Burman language Newari or Nepal Bhasa of central Nepal, the Tibeto-Burman strategy is exemplified by *wa-a-mha misA* 'come State Relative woman' or 'the woman who came' (O'Rourke, 2000: 84), and the Indo-Aryan strategy by *misA: gu-gu: pasal-e kitAb nyA-ta, wa pasa: thana du* 'woman which shop-in book buy-past, that shop here be' or 'The shop in which the woman bought a book is here' (O'Rourke, 2000: 87). As Newari becomes more endangered, with nearly all of its speakers now dominant in Nepali, the Indo-Aryan construction also seen in Nepali is becoming more frequent in Newari.

The basic sentence structure of Gong, like that of most other Tibeto-Burman languages and all closely related ones such as Burmese, is verb-final: Gong $/\eta a^{35}$ $ma\eta^{33}$ so^{35} $a^{33}/$ 'I rice eat (statement)', Burmese $/\eta a^{22}$ (or more politely $c\partial n\partial^{22}/c\partial ma^{44})$ $th\partial min^{41}$ sa^{41} $d\varepsilon^{22}/$ 'I rice eat (statement)', not verb-medial as in English 'I eat rice' or Thai $/p^{h}om^{15}$ kin^{33} $kha:w^{53}/$ 'I eat rice'. This is quite stable; even when a Gong sentence contains all or nearly all Thai loanword elements, it still remains verb-final, as in $/p^{h}e\eta^{33}$ $l\partial\eta^{55}$ $\hat{?}\partial^{33}/$ 'song sing (statement)' or 'Sing a song'; compare Thai $/r\partial:\eta^{55}$ $p^{h}le:\eta^{33}/$ sing song 'Sing a song.' Where the endangered language and the dominant language share similar syntactic features, it may be difficult to determine whether the dominant language has influenced the syntax of the endangered one, but here the distinction is clear.

In Gong, the formation of one type of question has changed among middle-aged and especially younger speakers. In traditional Gong and in all closely related languages such as Burmese, questions are indicated by a final element. For example, in Burmese a neutral yes/no question ends in $/la^{41}/$, a question expecting a yes answer ends in $/n\partial^{22}/$ and a substance question (containing a word which requires an answer other than yes/no, such as 'who', 'what' or 'when') ends in $/l\varepsilon^{41}/$. The Gong yes/no question marker is $/m\partial^{55}/$ and the substance question marker is $/we^{21}/$, and they are normally in sentence-final position: $/n\partial\eta^{21}$ $k\partial^{21}$ $m\partial^{55}/$ 'you go?' or 'Are you going?', $/\hat{?}o^{33}$ $k\partial^{21}$ $we^{21}/$ 'who go?' or 'Who is going?' and $/n\partial\eta^{21}$ $\hat{?}a^{33}$ $n\partial\eta^{33}$ $k\partial^{21}$ $we^{21}/$ 'you where go?' or 'Where are you going?' in the speech of the oldest fluent speakers. However, nearly all middle-aged and younger speakers have the substance question marker attached to the question word, as in $/\hat{?}o^{33}$ we^{53} $k\partial^{21}/$ 'who-? go' or 'Who is going?' and $/n\partial\eta^{21}$ $\hat{?}a^{33}$ $n\partial\eta^{33}$ we^{53} $k\partial^{21}/$ 'you where-? go' or 'Where are you going?'. This apparently started with 'who?' which has changed to $/\hat{?}o^{33}$ $we^{53}/$ for nearly all living speakers, perhaps to disambiguate, because $/\hat{?}o^{33}/$ is also the word for 'person', as in $/\hat{?}o^{33}$ $k\partial^{21}$ $m\partial^{55}/$ 'person go?' or 'Is a person/someone going?', and the **reduplicated** indefinite pronoun as in /ʔo^{33} ʔo^{35} ma^{33} ka^{33}/ 'person-person not go' or 'No one is going.' Since the question marker /we^{21}/ has become the last syllable in a noun word, it also undergoes the tone sandhi change from 21 to 53 tone for older speakers and is reassigned to high falling tone by younger speakers. This syntactic change may perhaps be related to the fact that Thai and Lao do not require a sentence-final question marker in substance questions.

Gong, like many languages in the South East Asian area, has a large array of **modal** and other elements which productively combine with the verb. In most related Tibeto-Burman languages, the vast preponderance of such elements come after the verb, in complex combinations and sequences. This is also true for various categories in Gong: modals, directionals, resultatives, **tense**/aspect marking and so on. However, there is also a smaller set of preverbal elements, more than ten of which are borrowed from Thai, including some borrowed a while ago and sometimes phonologically integrated into Gong. The pre-head elements that are not borrowed are the negative /ma^{33}/, the prohibitive /ta^{33}/, repetitive /wa^{35}/ and reciprocal /c^{h}ɔŋ^{21}/. The first two are preserved from Proto-Tibeto-Burman, the only two preverbal elements reconstructed there (Bradley, 1979a), the third is not attested in related languages and the fourth is related to the Burmese preverbal reduplicated reciprocal adverb /c^{h}in^{42} ɹin^{42}/, which can also attach to a noun in Burmese but not in Gong. One of the Thai preverbal modals often used in Gong is 'must', from Thai /tɔŋ^{53}/, borrowed as phonologically integrated /tɔŋ^{21}/ by older speakers or as unintegrated /tɔŋ^{53}/ by younger speakers, and always preverbal, as in /ŋa^{33} mɛʔ^{55} ʔa^{21} tɔŋ^{21} (or tɔŋ^{53}) ɲi^{21} wu^{21} ʔa^{33}/ 'I mother object must ask statement' or 'I must ask my mother'; the other borrowed Thai preverbal elements operate in the same way.

7.4 LEXICON: THE VOCABULARY

Lexicon or vocabulary is the area of most languages most susceptible to outside influence. In some cases, this enriches and expands the vocabulary; but for many endangered languages, vocabulary is replaced and original vocabulary disappears. Some languages like German tend to create more new compound words from internal resources; others, like English, tend to enrich the vocabulary with many loanwords. Thus, lexical change is far from unique to endangered languages. Some endangered languages traditionally tended to create new words from internal resources, but another change due to endangerment is that such internal coinage of new words may decrease or cease. This is not necessarily the case; Nakhota (also known by the Ojibwe exonym Assiniboine) has continued to use almost entirely internal resources for new lexicon, both by extending the meanings of existing words and by new coinage from internal resources (Collette, 2017). Conversely, an extreme case of massive borrowing of French nouns including associated morphological categories into the nearby Algonquian language Michif (also known as Métis) has misled some scholars into the belief that this is a mixed language (Gillon et al., 2018).

Of all areas of lexicon, nouns are the most frequently borrowed. This is both because new things and concepts come in with the word for them, and because nouns are an open class of words, to which additional words can be added, in all languages. The hierarchy of likely borrowings, and of losses and replacements in an endangered language, has nouns at the top, typically followed by verbs, adjectives (if these are a separate class from verbs) and adverbs. Borrowing into small closed sets of words like **deictics** or prepositions within a language is less likely. On the other hand, grammatical linking elements such as **conjunctions** and **discourse markers** and other highly frequent words such as 'yes' and 'no' are often borrowed. In Swahili, many Arabic loanwords are used in this way: *naam* 'yes', *la* 'no', *kabla* 'before', *baada* 'after' and *lakini* 'but', often with no remaining indigenous Bantu alternative, although for 'yes' and 'no' there are more frequent Bantu-derived alternatives *ndiyo* or *ndivyo* 'yes/it is the case' and *siyo* or *sivyo* 'no/it is not the case'; *siyo* and *sivyo* are however less frequent than the Arabic form *la* in the speech of the original coastal Swahili communities.

Even within small closed grammatical systems, change influenced by a dominant outside language may occur; for example, Lipo, which is more heavily influenced by Chinese than its close relative Lisu and endangered in many areas, has only two demonstratives in its deictic system, /he^{55}/ 'this' and /k^{h}ɯ^{55}/ 'that', semantically parallel to the Chinese deictic system but, unlike Lisu which has a quite different system of four main deictics, /t^{h}ø^{33}/ 'this', /go^{33}/ 'that (on same level)', /nø^{33}/ 'that (above)' and /dzø^{33}/ 'that (below)', with additional forms in most dialects (Bradley, 2003a, 2017); other related Ngwi languages also have complex deictic systems, like Lahu with five.

Loanwords into another language may be kept in their original pronunciation or adapted to conform to the phonology of the borrowing language, replacing sounds which are absent and removing combinations of sounds which do not occur in the borrowing language. Similarly, loanwords may either keep the original morphology of the source language, or they may have material from the borrowing language added to them, or both. These are the differences between phonologically and morphologically unintegrated and integrated loans. In early stages, where speakers of the endangered language have less familiarity with the dominant language and speak it less well, loans will tend to be integrated; in some cases, they may become almost unrecognisable due to the adaptation in pronunciation or due to later changes within the borrowing language, which usually also apply to loanwords within the language. As endangerment progresses and speakers become more familiar with the source language, unintegrated loans may also be borrowed.

In Gong, as in many languages, early loanwords are integrated; more recent ones are not. The old name for Thai, Siam, pronounced /saja:m/, is the source of Gong /ʔɛŋ⁵⁵/ with adjustments: /aja:/ replaced by /ɛ/ because there was no such sequence in Gong and the /j/ suggested a front vowel, and final /m/ replaced by /ŋ/ as there is no final /m/ in Gong; alternatively, this may have been borrowed before earlier final /m/ and /n/ merged into final /ŋ/ in Gong. There was a regular change in Gong which must have taken place since this word was borrowed a couple of hundred years ago; this changed all earlier /s/ into /ʔl/, which was then simplified over thirty years ago to /ʔ/. More recent loanwords do not show integration to such a degree, and the most recent are completely unintegrated, with their original Thai/Lao form.

A semantic category may be present in the traditional form of a language, but lost during endangerment. Virtually all Ngwi Tibeto-Burman languages have a separate verb/adjective cognate for 'to be long (of time)', distinct from the verb/adjective for 'to be long (length)'; see, for example, Lahu /mɔ³³/ 'to be long (of time)', /s̩³³/ 'to be long (length)'. However, Lisu usually uses a combination of the two, /mɯ³³ s̩³³/ long (time) + long(length) to mean 'long (time)'; and some Ngwi languages like Lipo lack such a distinction; Lipo uses /s̩³³/ 'long (length)' for both, again more like Chinese which has only *cháng* 'long (time or length)'.

All kinds of closed grammatical categories may also be susceptible to reduction during endangerment; for example, in traditional Gong, there are six distinct **numeral classifiers** used to categorize animals: /kʰlɛʔ⁵⁵/ for crustaceans and most small reptiles, /kʰɵʔ⁵⁵/ for birds and small mammals, /ma³⁵/ for fish, /kʰʉ ⁵⁵/ for most insects and some small reptiles, /kɔŋ³³/ for insects with large nests like bees and ants and /duŋ²¹/ for large animals including large snakes and reptiles. These must be used after the number when counting different types of animals; for example /tək⁵⁵ tək⁵⁵ thi³³ kʰlɛʔ⁵⁵/ 'monitor.lizard one (small.reptile)' or 'one monitor lizard', /ɲa³³ ʔa³³ ʔoŋ³³ ma³⁵/ 'fish three (fish)' or 'three fish', /ʔɔŋ³⁵ pi³³ duŋ²¹/ 'elephant four (large animal)' or 'four elephants'. However, five of these classifiers are eliminated in the speech of less fluent semispeakers, who generalize the most frequently occurring form, /duŋ⁵³/: /gɔŋ⁵⁵ tʰi³³ duŋ⁵³/ 'horse one (classifier)' or 'one horse'. This is more like Thai and Lao which use a single classifier for animals. Thus, the original Gong ethnotaxonomy of animals, as expressed in the classifier system, is lost.

A great deal of other valuable social, cultural and ecological knowledge is embodied in the lexical content and classification of a wide range of semantic fields of interrelated words: kinship terminology, colour and so on. Such systems are vulnerable to changes; the complex Burmese kinship term system for uncles and aunts based on which parent they are siblings to and whether they are older or younger than the parent, which applied systematically up to the late nineteenth century and persists to some extent in some rural areas, has now broken down in urban Burmese (Bradley, 1989b). Another fascinating area is metaphorical extension; for example, colours, body side directions and pictures of specific objects or animals are associated with political parties or type of parties: red, left and a picture of a hammer and sickle as the symbol of the communist party. This is culture-specific, and very susceptible to influence during language endangerment. In Gong, nearly every cultural metaphor is now derived from those found in Thai and Lao, and many taxonomies in the language, such as the kinship term system, are now parallel to those of Thai and Lao.

7.5 DISCOURSE AND GENRE: RUNNING SPEECH AND STYLES

Until late last century, few linguists were deeply involved in looking at the way language is structured over longer stretches of dialogue; this was considered more relevant to those interested in rhetoric. Most descriptive linguists used to stop at the level of the sentence, but this is no longer so; a large area of discourse analysis has developed over the last fifty years, building in part on older traditional analyses of rhetoric. While rhetoric is concerned with public speaking, which is one type of discourse, there are very many other types. They differ in whether they mainly or exclusively involve one person talking, a narrative; or whether two or more participants are talking, a conversation. They also differ greatly in their level of formality. Societies with a tradition of literacy have written versus spoken styles; there may also be subtypes of written and spoken styles. Part of the hollowing-out of traditional languages is a reduction in the range of styles and genres. In the case of Gong, there was no tradition of literacy; in the two villages where the language is still spoken, the range of styles has decreased rapidly over the last fifty years. Traditional religion and its oral art and local knowledge disappeared with the last practitioners and their replacement by Buddhist temples; traditional healing practices and associated oral performances disappeared as modern Thai health care spread into the area; traditional songs such as lullabies ceased to be sung; traditional oral historical narratives were not told, much less taught, to the next generation; and new majority genres came in. When electricity and Thai television arrived in one village in the late 1980s, leisure activities completely changed: television programmes in Thai were on all day, crowds of people going to the houses with televisions and total immersion in spoken Thai and Thai popular culture for people of all ages, with little use of spoken Gong while the television was on, morning to night. The novelty has worn off, but the effect on the persistence of Gong has been drastic. A few years before this in the mid-1980s, a school was opened in the village for the first time; until then, the few children who became literate in Thai had learned this in a Buddhist temple or a primary school in a Lao village an hour's walk away. Thus, knowledge of written Thai became widespread from the late 1980s; unfortunately, the orthography we developed for Gong with some local colleagues was not adopted in the community. When the school tried, they found that none of the children could speak the language, so they gave up. Furthermore, many Lao and Thai families moved into the village from the early 1990s, and are now the majority. Thus, Thai and Lao discourse patterns are now the norm, with extremely restricted use of the most basic spoken Gong in the home among the oldest people.

Code-switching is very widespread in bilingual communities. This is the alternating use of two different languages over varying stretches of speech by the same speakers within the same interaction. This is a very common resource; note that it requires all participants to have knowledge of both languages, and is thus a strong marker of in-group communication. The stretches of each language may be shorter or longer; the switches from one to the other may thus be more or less frequent. In many cases, there is a specific discourse or other trigger for each switch (Clyne, 1967; Gumperz, 1982). When code-switching is extremely frequent, some scholars call this code-mixing. Most scholars would not refer to code-switching when a single word or very short set phrase occurs in the other language; that would instead be called borrowing. Another important factor in code-switching and borrowing is whether each language retains its structure: phonology, morphosyntax and so on. Unintegrated code-switching and borrowing keeps forms in each language exactly as they would be in monolingual speech; each code-switch brings a completely different set of sounds, words and structures. Integrated code-switching and borrowing adapts the forms of one language into the sound, word and sentence patterns of the other language, in such cases called the matrix language. Where the two languages are closely related, it may sometimes be difficult to determine the matrix language and the exact location of and motivation for each code-switch. Multilingual code-switching among three or more languages in one interaction is much less common, but does occur.

It is not necessarily the case that there is code-switching during language endangerment; in Gong, for example, people either speak in Gong to other Gong, although this has decreased rapidly over the last fifty years, or in Lao to local Lao people, or in Thai to outsiders. As more Lao and Thai people move into the remaining two Gong villages, naturally this means that Gong is spoken less, as it is seen as inappropriate to speak Gong when anyone who does not speak it is present. This now includes all children, as Lao and/or Thai has become the language of socialization in the home. Even in the two remaining villages where the language is still spoken, parents stopped speaking Gong in the presence of their children in all homes about forty to fifty years ago. In other former Gong villages in Kanchanaburi province, this shift took place earlier.

A great deal of other subtle linguistic and social information is at risk during language endangerment; each society has its own patterns, which often differ. This includes whether to talk at all in a given situation, how much to talk, how to take turns in talking in a conversation, how long to pause within a turn or to wait before taking over a new turn, whether and how to give appropriate supportive short backchannel responses like 'I see' during someone else's turn, or whether overlap of talking, with two or more people talking at the same time, is normal. It also includes what to talk about in various situations: what are the neutral topics in a conversation between strangers, such as the weather in many English-speaking countries; what are taboo or undesirable topics that are normally not talked about, or only talked about between close friends and family; and so on. For example, illness and death are completely taboo topics in some societies, and normal neutral topics in others. Humour is also very closely bound with culture; in some cultures, injury may be highly amusing, and in others taboo; in some cultures, sexual joking is expected between some categories of people but not with some other categories. Some cultures value puns, proverbs, riddles, songs and other forms of verbal art; others use them less. Much of this richness of social knowledge and behaviour can disappear along with an endangered language, especially where the norms embedded in its social use differ from those of the dominant group. Distinctive Gong humour, verbal art and all kinds of social norms as expressed in language are now gone, although we have recorded and documented some of what remained of it in the late 1970s and 1980s.

7.6 CONCLUSION

If we compare rates of change in different areas of structure, we usually find that change in the lexicon, particularly the borrowing of nouns, is greatest. Conversely, some of the social use and discourse preferences may persist within a group even after the traditional language is no longer spoken, as among many Australian Aboriginal communities, where direct questions are inappropriate, and in some of them mention of dead people continues to be culturally taboo (Eades, 2013).

There is a great deal more variety in the effects of endangerment on phonology and morphosyntax. While complex structures of all kinds tend to be lost or replaced, some may persist. Change can be extremely rapid, particularly at the last stage of language shift among semispeakers, or where a new variety of the language is developing among younger speakers; or change can be relatively limited, with the last speakers using a relatively conservative speech variety. This depends on the language attitudes within the community, the social setting and the process of endangerment.

Where multiple languages persist in an area and many people are bilingual or multilingual, the languages may eventually become more similar; this leads to the development of linguistic areas, within which, languages share various phonological, morphological and syntactic characteristics. Where such similarities become very great, with extreme structural congruence and remaining differences mainly lexical, bilingualism and multilingualism are easier, but smaller languages may be lost rapidly when circumstances change, such as some north Burmish languages spoken by groups who are part of the Kachin social complex. For example, Bola is only spoken by one small clan in a very small area in Dehong prefecture, Yunnan, China; it is being replaced by closely related languages such as Lawngwaw or Maru as well as more distantly related Jinghpaw Lachin which is the common language of the Kachin culture complex. Nearly all speakers of north Burmish languages such as Lawngwaw/Maru, Zaiwa/Atsi, Leqi/Lashi and some varieties of Achang are multilingual in Jinghpaw and one or two north Burmish mother tongues from one or other of their parents (Bradley, 1996).

The long-term outcome of language endangerment and loss, and the shift of large populations from a variety of language backgrounds to speaking a dominant language, can be simplification of the dominant language in various areas of structure; consider English compared to Icelandic, Mandarin Chinese compared to Min Chinese varieties of Fujian, north-eastern Guangzhou and Taiwan. In an area where a particular other language or languages used to be spoken, there may be local differences in the dominant replacing language that are in part related to a substratum: persistent characteristics of the lost languages; such as the possible substratum effect of long-extinct Celtic Gaulish on relatively innovative French, as opposed to more conservative Romance languages such as Italian or Spanish.

CASE STUDY: HEBREW

Hebrew is the national language of the State of Israel, the language of the Jewish people. It is the only language that has been successfully renativized – that is, reintroduced after a long period of not being used as a spoken vernacular. It is a north-west Semitic language, in the eastern branch of the Afro-Asiatic language family.

Ancient Hebrew was spoken by Jews well over 3,000 years ago. After the Bar Kokhba rebellion against the Romans (132–135 AD) and the massacres that followed, most of the population of Judea perished or went into exile. The Hebrew language gradually lost domains of use, displaced by Aramaic, and eventually ceased to be spoken. It continued to be used as a written language of liturgy, literature and science but was not spoken as a mother tongue until the beginning of the twentieth century.

Modern Hebrew evolved first as a literary language in the eighteenth century. Many books were written in Hebrew during the Enlightenment period, secular, scientific and religious. Spoken Modern Hebrew, the language of contemporary Israel, was reintroduced towards the end of the nineteenth century, after about 1,700 years as a written language only. Following persecution in Europe, many Jews went to Palestine from the fourteenth to the nineteenth centuries. From 1882, successive waves of Zionist immigration brought many thousands of Jews to Palestine. The Zionist national movement, influenced by European nationalism, viewed the Hebrew language as essential to national revival. Here, we briefly discuss the situation in Palestine at the time. Following that, we describe the main aspects of the renativization of Hebrew. We use the term 'renativization', rather than the usual 'revival', which implies that Hebrew was a dead language prior to the last decades of the nineteenth century. Many scholars have made this point before (cf. Nahir, 1988; Spolsky & Cooper, 1991).

Prior to the Zionist immigration, some Jews had lived continuously in Palestine since the Roman-Judaean wars. These Jews, as well as some others who came over the centuries, were ultra-Orthodox and resided in the four holy cities of Jerusalem, Hebron, Tiberias and Safed. In the second half of the nineteenth century, as a result of increased persecution, many thousands of Jews immigrated to Palestine, then part of the Ottoman Empire.

The Jewish population of nineteenth-century Palestine was divided into Askenazim (i.e., Jews with Central or Eastern European background), Sephardim (descendants of Spanish and Portuguese Jews) and Jews from North Africa and the Middle East, sometimes called Mizrahi ('eastern'), but often included in the Sephardic group. The term 'Ashkenazi' comes from the old Hebrew word for Germany, *Ashkenaz.* The term 'Sephardi' comes from the Hebrew word for Spain, *Sfarad.* These communities had different languages, liturgy, dress and food.

The Ashkenazic Jews spoke Yiddish. The Sephardic Jews spoke Ladino, also known as Judeo-Spanish, Judezmo or Spanyolish. The Jews of Middle Eastern and North African origin spoke different varieties of Arabic. Yiddish developed from Middle German dialects as the main language of Ashkenazi Jews. It contains a large number of Hebrew and Slavic words, and is written in Hebrew script. Ladino is derived from Old Spanish. It also has many words from other old Romance languages of the Iberian Peninsula, Hebrew, Aramaic and Arabic. It used the Hebrew script, nowadays both the Hebrew and Roman alphabets are used. Other languages were also spoken: Russian, Romanian, Polish and so on.

In addition to Yiddish and Ladino, nearly all Jewish men and many women also knew Hebrew. Most of the writing of the Jewish community, such as contracts, wills and other legal documents, was in Hebrew. Spoken Hebrew was the lingua franca of the Jews, given that the Ashkenazic and Sephardic Jews had no other language in common. Hebrew was the high-status language, the language of classical Jewish texts, with a long uninterrupted tradition of religious, philosophical and literary writing. It was used daily in religious services, studying sacred texts and, more recently, reading secular literature and poetry.

From 1882 to 1903, the first wave of Zionist immigration brought about 35,000 Jews to Palestine. Most of them were from Romania and Russia, after pogroms which followed the assassination of Tsar Alexander II in 1881. These Zionist pioneers established Jewish rural settlements, the first of which were Rishon LeZion, Rosh Pinna, Zikhron Ya'akov and Petah Tikva. Many others followed. A second wave of Zionist immigration from 1904 to 1914 brought about 40,000 Jews to Palestine, mainly from Russia. A new suburb of Jaffa that they established is today's city of Tel Aviv. After the First World War, several more waves of immigration brought many thousands of Jews from different countries to Palestine. By 14 May 1948, with the proclamation of the State of Israel, the Jewish population was 650,000.

Zionism, the Jewish national revival movement, emerged in Eastern and Central Europe in reaction to increasing anti-Semitism. Its secular founders advocated a return to the land of Israel and the establishment of agricultural communities as a solution to the problems of the diaspora. Central to this endeavour was the renativization of the ancient national language, its re-establishment as the spoken language of the community.

The renativization of Hebrew is identified with Eliezer Ben-Yehuda (born Eliezer Yitzhak Perelman), a lexicographer, journalist and editor, a Zionist from Lithuania who arrived in Palestine in 1881. He was enthusiastic about the Hebrew language, imbued with the belief that not only was it possible for Hebrew to become again the spoken daily language of the community, but that it was necessary for the development of the nation in their ancient land. Ben-Yehuda led by personal example, changing his name to a Hebrew one, using Hebrew only at home despite being a native speaker of Yiddish, so that his children would learn Hebrew. His son Itamar Ben-Avi (born 1882) was the first speaker of Modern Hebrew as a first language.

Ben-Yehuda promoted the use of Hebrew in his public speaking and in his newspaper articles. He founded the newspaper *Hatsvi*, 'gazelle', which he published from 1884 to 1914. Ben-Yehuda also introduced the teaching of Hebrew and other subjects in Hebrew when he was a teacher in the Alliance School in Jerusalem, instead of Yiddish, which was usual at the time as the children's native language, as the language of instruction. In 1890, Ben-Yehuda founded the Hebrew Language Committee, which became the Hebrew Language Academy in 1953. It published many newly coined words, notes on grammar, orthography and punctuation, all necessary as Hebrew expanded into more domains, eventually becoming the language used in all facets of daily life. We give examples of new words coined by the academy later.

Ben-Yehuda's most important achievement as a lexicographer was his monumental *Dictionary of Ancient and New Hebrew* (Ben-Yehuda, 1908–59) with sixteen volumes and a preliminary volume edited by his son and wife.

Ben-Yehuda lived in Jerusalem, but, despite his great efforts and many publications promoting the use of Hebrew, the conservative religious Jews of Jerusalem were slow to adopt Hebrew as a spoken language. The actual process of renativization of Hebrew started in the new Zionist agricultural settlements.

Nahir (1988) describes the process in which the schools of the settlements played a central role. He suggests four sometimes-overlapping components in the transition to Hebrew. First, the children of the community were 'instilled with the desired linguistic attitudes'; second, they were presented with and acquired the linguistic model, Hebrew, as a second language; third, the children spoke Hebrew in school and also transferred it out of the schools; and, fourth, the children grew up, married and had their own children who spoke Hebrew as a first language. This process, carried out mostly by the schoolteachers of the rural Jewish settlements, was completed within a generation, by about 1915. By then, Hebrew was the community's major native language. Bachi (1956) reports that, according to the 1916 census, 40 per cent of Palestine's Jews spoke Hebrew as an 'only or first language'. Among the young, the percentage was much higher, 75 per cent in both the settlements and in Tel Aviv (Bachi, 1956, cited in Nahir, 1988: 289).

According to Nahir, the language choice in the new settlements was essentially between Yiddish, the native language of nearly all the settlers, and Hebrew. Unlike the urban centres in which the Sephardic Jews and the Ashkenazic Jews did not have a common language, there was no need for a lingua franca there. The motivation for the choice was mainly what Nahir (1988: 278) calls the National-Political Factor. The recent settlers came to Palestine motivated by national Zionist considerations, and the return to the ancient national language was a central part of the Zionist ideology. Yiddish, even though it was the pioneers' native language, had a lower status than Hebrew, it was considered 'vulgar', a 'jargon' unfit for science and higher culture. Above all, it was the language of the diaspora, associated with persecution and suffering which the settlers wanted to put behind them.

Hebrew, the ancient language of the Bible, the language of great literature, was promoted by community leaders and influential intellectuals, one of the first of whom was Ben-Yehuda. The pressure to return to the Hebrew language was quite intense in the community. Nahir suggests that the return was 'generally conceived of as a condition and a temporary substitute for national, if not political, revival' (Nahir, 1988: 283). Such attitudes towards Hebrew were enthusiastically adopted by the teachers in the settlements, who insisted that the school children speak Hebrew only. Nahir quotes an early report by a student who recalled how, in 1891, at the very beginning of the renativization process, he discovered the comparative status of Hebrew and Yiddish: '[the teacher] announced in the very first session "Hebrew in Hebrew", that is, forget Yiddish which we spoke at home, and listen to and speak his language, Hebrew' (Neiman, 1953: 22, cited in Nahir, 1988: 284).

The second component, leading to children acquiring Hebrew as a second language was carried out mostly by teachers in the settlements. Crucial to this process was the use of Hebrew as the medium of instruction, pioneered by Ben-Yehuda in 1883 in Jerusalem. The usual way at the time was the European way of teaching Jewish subjects in Yiddish, the children's native language. In 1888, David Yudelovitz, following Ben-Yehuda, introduced the 'Hebrew in Hebrew' method and also started using Hebrew to teach other subjects in his school in Rishon LeZion. Other schools followed in several other places.

A major problem for using Hebrew as a medium of instruction was the children's inability to speak Hebrew. Special kindergartens were established called 'preparatories', in which children would spend one or two years prior to elementary school in a Hebrew-only environment. Total exposure to spoken Hebrew was the sole aim of the kindergartens, no attempt was made to teach specific subjects. The 'preparatories' were a great success. They were opened in different settlements and towns.

Nahir considers the third component, the children transferring Hebrew as a second language out of the schools, as the most critical and unprecedented step of the transition to Hebrew. This step, however, was difficult to accomplish. In 1891, the Hebrew school graduates did not speak Hebrew outside of school (Smilanski, 1930: 9, cited in Nahir, 1988: 287). Gradually over the years, the situation changed; Nahir reports on the spread of Hebrew out of the schools, citing contemporary accounts. The acquisition of Hebrew proceeded from children to adults. Nahir reports on a letter to the editor in 1905: 'I saw my friend's daughter, two years and three months old, speak only Hebrew and sing beautiful songs. Yet she did not only learn how to speak Hebrew at school; she has also been teaching her parents whatever she knows' (Pirhi, 1905: 5, cited in Nahir, 1988: 288).

The fourth step, as newborn children of the graduates of the Hebrew schools acquire Hebrew as a native language, is the culmination of the renativization process. The graduates would have spoken Hebrew as a second language in and out of school for between one and two decades, they grew up, married and had children of their own who were exposed to Hebrew from birth. This new generation of speakers of Hebrew was born between 1905 and 1915, Hebrew was their native and often only language.

In the following pages, we describe some aspects of Hebrew writing, phonology, morphology, syntax and the lexicon. The transcription of the examples is that of the second author's native speech.

Hebrew is written from right to left. Like other Semitic languages, the twenty-two letters of the Hebrew alphabet indicate consonants only. The following pairs of words are written in exactly the same way. Without context, it is not possible to determine the intended meaning. Note that the first two words are unrelated, which is not the case in the second example.

(1) *zer*   *zar*
    bouquet   stranger
(2) *xavera*   *xevra*
    female friend   society

In Biblical Hebrew, the vowels are indicated by a system of **diacritics** called *nikkud* 'pointing'. Modern Hebrew is written without such diacritics; *nikkud* is only used in children's books, texts for learners of Hebrew and poetry.

Three letters represent two different sounds, a stop or a **fricative**: *b* or *v*, *k* or *x* and *p* or *f*. The stop pronunciation is indicated in Biblical Hebrew by a dot inside the letter called a *dagesh*. Modern Hebrew does not usually do that. So, for example, the first consonant of *bišul* 'cooking' and the second consonant of *levašel* 'to cook' are written the same way. Similarly, the third consonants of *melex* 'king' and *malka* 'queen' are spelled with the same letter, and so are the first and second consonants in *pitaron* 'solution' and *liftor* 'to solve', respectively.

Several sound distinctions made in ancient Hebrew are no longer made. The dental stop [t] is the only contemporary pronunciation of what used to be two distinct sounds, as indicated by two different letters, for example, in the words *matana* 'gift' and *matara* 'aim/goal'. Similarly the velar stop [k] is the only modern pronunciation in the words *kan* 'here' and *kar* 'cold', with the historical distinction, indicated by two different letters, neutralized. Another Biblical Hebrew distinction not made in current spoken language is that represented by the different spelling of the second consonant of the words *maxar* 'tomorrow' and *maxar* 'sell (past tense 3rd masc. sg.)', both pronounced as velar fricatives. The historical **pharyngeal** '(*'ayin*) is often not pronounced at all, or it is pronounced as a glottal stop. So, for example, the words for 'with' with a pharyngeal and 'if' with a glottal stop are both pronounced as *'im* or *im* in colloquial Hebrew. It should be noted that Israelis of North African and Middle Eastern origins sometimes pronounce the pharyngeals and *ḥ* in a distinct way.

Hebrew has complex and very productive morphology. Much of the inflectional morphology of Modern Hebrew is the same as in earlier periods, except for some neutralizations. The formation of new words also follows the historical ways of combining consonantal roots with *binyan* 'building' patterns for verbs and *miškal* 'weight' patterns for nouns and adjectives.

Hebrew nouns are either masculine or feminine. Animate feminine nouns have the stressed suffix *-a/-it* or unstressed *-et*, whereas masculine nouns are unmarked. For example, the word for a male friend is *xaver*, for a female friend *xavera*, the new Modern Hebrew word for a male dancer is *rakdan*, a female one *rakdanit*. A male director is *menahel*, a female *menahelet*. Most nouns ending in *-a* are feminine, but by no means all of them, for example, *aba* 'father' and *layla* 'night'. Also, there are many feminine nouns which do not end in *-a*, *-it* or *-et*, for example, *galut* 'diaspora' and *ayin* 'eye'. The plural of masculine nouns is formed with the suffix *-im*, the feminine plural is formed with *-ot*. There are, however, exceptions, for example, masculine *kir* 'wall', plural *kirot*, whereas feminine *šana* 'year', plural *šanim*. Hebrew also has a dual *-ayim*; this suffix is used for body parts and items of clothing which come in pairs, for example, *yadayim* 'hands', *eynayim* 'eyes' or *garbayim* 'socks'. It also occurs with words designating time periods, *yomayim* 'two days' versus *yamim* 'days'.

Hebrew adjectives have four forms: masculine singular and plural, and feminine singular and plural. Unlike nouns, they are very regular; masculine plural adjectives have the suffix *-im*, feminine singular adjectives usually have the suffix *-a*, and feminine plural adjectives have the suffix *-ot*. For example, the adjective 'good' has the four forms *tov*, *tova*, *tovim* and *tovot*. There is a large group of new adjectives derived from nouns which have masculine singular forms ending in *-i* and feminine singular forms ending in *-it*, *zmani/zmanit* 'temporary' and *xašmali/xašmalit* 'electrical'. There are also many new adjectives with *-i/-it* suffixes derived from loanwords, for example, *liberali/liberalit* 'liberal' or *psixologi/psixologit* 'psychological'.

In Hebrew, unlike English, an adjective modifying a noun follows the noun. It also agrees with the noun in number and gender, as well as in definiteness, which is indicated by the **bound prefix** *ha-* 'the' on nouns and adjectives. For example, with the masculine noun *bayit* 'house', we have the following forms: *bayit gadol* 'big house', *habayit hagadol* 'the big house', *batim gdolim* 'big houses' and *habatim hagdolim* 'the big houses'. The string *habayit gadol* is the full sentence 'The house is big', and *habatim gdolim* is the sentence 'The houses are big'. The other two possibilities, with the definite article on the adjective only, are ungrammatical.

The historical construct state *smixut* 'adjacency' is a sequence of two or more nominal elements of which the first is the head. The *smixut* is marked both morphologically and syntactically. The head noun appears in the bound construct form, whereas the second noun appears in the independent form described earlier. In many cases, the two forms are the same. Nearly all feminine singular nouns ending in *-a* have a construct form ending in *-at*, for example, *avoda* 'work', *avodat bayit* 'homework' (literally work-home); and *axila* 'eating', *axilat basar* 'eating (of) meat'. Some feminine nous ending in *-a* have a construct form in *-et*, as in *memšala* 'government', with the construct form *memšelet* as in *memšelet Israel* 'the government of Israel'.

The second regular paradigmatic alternation is that between masculine independent plural nouns with the suffix *-im* and their construct counterparts with *-ey*, for example, *batim* 'houses' and *batey even* 'stone houses'.

In addition to these regular alternations, there are many morphological and phonological changes in noun and adjective stems when suffixes are attached, including in construct state nominals. These are often complex and opaque. They range from vowel deletions, as in *bitaxon* 'security' with the construct form *bitxon-*, to idiosyncratic changes, as in *bayit* 'house' with the construct form *bet-*. In many cases where the vowels of the construct form differ from those of the independent form, native speakers tend to use the independent rather than construct form in colloquial speech, for example, *marak basar* 'meat soup' instead of the normative *mrak basar*.

In construct state nominals, unlike regular noun phrases, the definite article occurs only once, attached to the second noun. For example, the word for 'school' is the lexicalized construct state nominal *bet sefer*, literally 'house of book' and its definite version is *bet hasefer* 'the school'. The usual expression that one hears in spoken Hebrew is the prescriptively incorrect *habet sefer* 'school'. The tendency to put the definite article in front of the whole compound is strengthened by the use of abbreviations in writing, where it is easier to put the article in front.

Many of the *smixut* nominals are lexicalized, and there is no other word in the language for the given meaning, so speakers have to use the construct state nominal. There simply is no other word for 'school' other than *bet sefer*, for example. The situation is different with non-lexicalized compounds; the speakers can choose other expressions. In colloquial Hebrew there is a marked tendency to use more analytical means of expression, mostly but not only with *šel* 'of', especially for **possessives**. For example, *habayit šel hamore* 'the house of the teacher' replaces the construct state nominal *bet hamore*; *basar bišvil marak* 'meat for soup' for *bsar marak* 'soup meat' and *sefer im tmunot* 'book with pictures' for *sefer tmunot* 'picture book'.

In these examples, the bound head constituent was a noun. Adjectives can also occur in this position, for example, the feminine singular form of 'black' is *šxora*, which occurs in construct form in the compound adjective *šxorat se'ar* 'black-haired' when used to modify a feminine noun, as in *iša šxorat sear* 'a black-haired woman'. The corresponding masculine singular is *iš šxor sear* 'a black-haired man', with the adjective in construct form. In spoken Hebrew, construct state compounds with adjective heads are rarely used. These expressions are replaced by the analytical *iša/iš im se'ar šaxor* 'woman/man with black hair'.

The verb in Hebrew, as in other Semitic languages, consists of a triconsonantal root combined with a morphological pattern called *binyan* 'building'. The seven *binyan* conjugation patterns of contemporary Hebrew are the same as in Biblical Hebrew. The following example is the past tense paradigm for the verb *lamad* 'study/learn', with the root *l-m-d* in the first *binyan*, traditionally called *kal* or *pa'al*.

(3)	singular		plural	
	masculine	feminine	masculine	feminine
1st		lamad-eti	lamad-nu	
2nd	lamad-eta	lamad-et	lamad-etem	lamad-eten
3rd	lamad	lamd-a	lamd-u	

The citation form of the verb is the third person masculine singular past tense form which shows the characteristic morphological form of a given conjugation. Most roots can occur in more than one conjugation. For example, the root *l-m-d*, in addition to the *pa'al*, can also occur in the *pi'el* (*limed* 'teach') and *nif'al* (*nilmad* 'be studied/be learned') conjugations.

The main use of the seven *binyanim*, both now and in the past, is to create new verbs from nouns, adjectives and loanwords, as well as other verbs and new roots. The *pi'el* is particularly productive in this respect. For example, from the noun *šemen* 'oil' we have the new contemporary *šimen* 'to oil'; from *siman* 'a sign, a mark' the new modern verb *simen* 'to mark'. Similarly, from the adjective *xadaš* 'new', there is the verb *xideš* 'renew/restore', used since biblical times. From the loanword *telefon* 'telephone' Modern Hebrew created the verb *tilfen* 'to telephone', a fully integrated lexeme with all the suffixal forms; similarly, the verb *nitrel* 'to neutralize' from English 'neutral'. Other new *pi'el* verbs include *xišev* 'calculate', from the root *x-š-v* which in the *pa'al* means 'think'. There is also a large number of new verbs with quadriconsonantal roots like *tixnen* 'plan', *timren* 'manoeuvre' and *irgen* 'organize'.

Modern Hebrew verbs have a three-way tense system, which dates from Mishnaic times. This system is asymmetrical, the four Biblical participles function as the present tense, whereas the Biblical perfective and imperfective forms serve as past tense and future tense, respectively. Biblical Hebrew did not have tenses, it made an aspectual distinction between the perfective and imperfective. The participle, being morphologically nominal, inflects for gender and number only. The past and future forms are also inflected for person. The following four forms are the present tense of the verb *lamad* 'study/learn' in the *pa'al* conjugation.

(4)	singular	plural
masculine	*lomed*	*lomd-im*
feminine	*lomed-et*	*lomd-ot*

Modern Hebrew does not have regional dialects. It does, however, have differences between colloquial spoken language and written styles. We have already described some of these differences. Construct state compounds tend to be replaced in colloquial Hebrew by more analytic means of expression, except for lexicalized compounds. In formal and written Hebrew, construct state structures are common and often contain more than two nouns, as in *tmunat talmidey hamaxlaka* 'the picture of the students of the department'.

Moreover, more formal styles also have forms like *tmunato šel hatalmid* 'the student's picture' (literally, picture-his of the student) in which a pronominal version of the modifying noun is suffixed to the head noun. Such strings are frequent in newspapers in particular. They rarely occur in colloquial Hebrew.

New words are coined in Hebrew from the considerable morphological resources of the *binyan* patterns for verbs and the *miškal* patterns for nouns and adjectives, combined with consonantal roots and an array of **affixes**. We have given examples of new nouns, verbs and adjectives. To conclude this case study, we will show some new words proposed recently by the Hebrew Language Academy. Before that, however, we want to mention the first new word that Eliezer Ben-Yehuda coined. The word was *milon* 'dictionary', created from *mila* 'word' followed by the frequently occurring suffix *-on*.

The academy is proposing the new word *miršetet* 'Internet' from the word *rešet* 'net' combined with the feminine pattern, as in the word *mivrešet* 'brush' and many others. For 'the Internet of things', the academy suggests the construct state nominal *miršetet hadvarim* 'Internet of the things'. Another proposed compound is *koltey šemeš* 'solar collectors', with *koltey*, the masculine plural participle of the verb 'to absorb' in construct form and *šemeš* 'sun'. Another construct compound *ir halixa* (literally, city (for) walking) is proposed for 'walkable city'; both nouns exist in the language, but their combination has a new meaning.

The following new words proposed by the academy are formed by attaching a combination of suffixes to existing nouns. The abstract suffix *-ut* combines with noun stems to form many abstract nouns such as the Modern Hebrew *sifrut* 'literature' and the Mishnaic *šerut* 'service'. Another productive suffix is *-an*, as in the Mishnaic *ganan* 'gardener' and the modern word *'askan* 'activist'. These two suffixes can be combined to produce new abstract nouns like *gananut* 'gardening' and *'askanut* 'activism'. Parallel to these existing Modern Hebrew words, the academy proposes the new word *yesodanut* 'fundamentalism' from the noun *yesod* 'foundation' followed by the two suffixes. Another new abstract noun coined by the academy is *gilanut* 'ageism' from the word *gil* 'age' followed by the same sequence of suffixes. Time will tell whether these newly coined words will be accepted.

About a hundred years after the first modern generation of native speakers of Hebrew was born, there are now millions of Hebrew speakers. Many thousands of books, articles, plays and songs are written in Hebrew each year.

The unique success of the renativization of Hebrew was mainly due to the positive attitude to Hebrew, central to the new settlers' Zionist aspirations. The second factor was their deep knowledge of written Hebrew. Although the circumstances of each case will be different, a positive attitude and knowledge of its historical sources would be crucial to the success of any attempt to revive or revitalize an endangered language.

DISCUSSION QUESTIONS

For an endangered language that you are familiar with, discuss the specific aspects of the renativization of Hebrew that could apply to the reclamation of this language.

How would you go about coining new words in your language? Discuss with examples.

SUGGESTIONS FOR FURTHER READING

Bradley (1989a) provides an overview of the sociolinguistic status of Gong as of the late 1980s.

Spolsky and Cooper (1991) give an excellent overview of language use in Jerusalem.

Berman (1978) is a thorough outline of the structure of modern Hebrew.

8 Policy and Planning

La fortitficaziun dil rg fagess donn als idioms ch'ein las ragischs e las alas dil romontsch.

Reinforcing RG (Rumantsch Grischuns) would damage the idioms which are the roots and the wings of Rumantsch.

Pro Idioms Surselva (2016)

Universal Declaration of Linguistic Rights
Article 3

1. This Declaration considers the following to be inalienable personal rights which may be exercised in any situation
   - the right to be recognized as a member of a language community
   - the right to use one's own language both in private and in public
   - the right to the use of one's own name
   - the right to interrelate and associate with other members of one's language community of origin
   - the right to maintain and develop one's culture ...

World Conference on Linguistic Rights (1996)

Language policy and planning has a long history, but an explicit theoretical framework has only developed in the last fifty years. The process is regarded in a unitary way, and called language planning, while the decisions involved constitute language policy. Tollefson (1995), Hornberger (2008) and others discuss planning and implementing supportive policies for minority language education and cultural maintenance. Chapter 9 investigates planning related to reclaiming endangered languages; see also Hinton (2001a, 2011), Hinton et al. (2002), Lewis and Simons (2015b), among others. For a number of relevant case studies, see Hinton and Hale (2001), and Hinton, Huss and Roche (2018).

Policy and planning are not sufficient alone; maintaining everyday language use needs positive community attitudes and effective co-operation between government, community and relevant insider and outsider experts, not just symbolic efforts. Governments and outsider experts usually make policy, which is often implemented without consulting the end-users, the speakers of the languages. This kind of top-down approach is less effective than one which involves the community.

Government policies often reflect negative majority group attitudes towards minorities and their languages. They are nation-building activities to unify and strengthen the identity of the nation, often based on a single national language; countries which have more than one official language are the exception. Thus, language endangerment has been strongly promoted by nationalism and its language policy agenda in recent centuries.

The other model, a bottom-up approach, may develop organically from within a community, or it can be started and fostered by outside guidance. We believe that a bottom-up approach is much more likely to succeed in reclaiming an endangered language. Sometimes, governments have attempted top-down reclamation as a policy measure, as in the case of Ireland since 1922, promoting of Irish as the national language through education and prescriptive policies. This may also be effective once community attitudes come into line with government policy.

8.1 FRAMEWORKS FOR LANGUAGE PLANNING

Kloss (1969) introduced the terms Status Planning and Corpus Planning. Status Planning or language policy relates to decisions about the status and use that languages should have within a community. Corpus Planning or language planning relates to the form and structure of languages: graphization (creating or standardizing a written variety), standardization of its grammar and modernization of its lexicon. Status Planning is mainly the role of governments and educational authorities. Corpus Planning may also be carried out by central authorities, although ideally this work is done by linguistically sophisticated experts.

Another term introduced by Kloss is Ausbau (German 'building out'): the selection of a single variety of a language, often with high prestige and many urban speakers, also spoken or at least understood by many people whose own speech variety is different, to be the Dachsprache 'roof language' for a cluster of related varieties. Fishman (2006) adds the term Einbau (German 'building in') for a different policy, one which is much harder to implement successfully: taking components from several varieties and combining them into a new composite variety; the case study of Romantsch in this chapter is an example. Most language policy and planning is done top-down with Ausbau based on a selected Dachsprache, or occasionally by Einbau.

Another early mover in frameworks for language planning was Jernudd, with a model for application in developing countries, as outlined in Rubin and Jernudd (1971), which later developed into the language management approach of Neustupný, as outlined in Neustupný and Nevkapil (2003), focusing at the micro-level on language use in particular situations.

8.2 STAGES OF LANGUAGE PLANNING

The standard four-stage framework for language policy and planning was devised by Haugen (1966): Selection, Codification, Elaboration and Dissemination. Selection and Dissemination correspond to Status Planning, while Codification and Elaboration are part of Corpus Planning. Selection is the choice of languages and their standard varieties. Codification includes graphization and standardization of grammar and vocabulary. This may involve creation, modification or replacement of orthographies, similar decisions about grammar and vocabulary, preparation of standard grammars and authoritative monolingual and bilingual dictionaries. Elaboration is the expansion of use of the language and modernization through additional areas of new vocabulary or new genres of literary and other use. Dissemination is the educational, social and other implementation of the codified and elaborated varieties, also sometimes called Acquisition Planning, although that also has a narrower focus discussed later.

These models lack an essential component: evaluation; that is, the assessment of the success of policy and planning decisions, and, if necessary, changes. Another gap is the absence of prestige planning, the use of sociolinguistically effective implementation methods. They also do not explicitly consider linguistic human rights, such as the right of minorities to mother tongue education and access to government and national life.

A language policy is inherent in any political entity or institution, whether it is explicit or not. Every such entity has some official language or languages, even if this has not been proclaimed or legally instituted. These languages usually have a standard form. Sometimes the form changes gradually through time, but more often the written and formal spoken variety becomes fixed for a longer or shorter period, and thus gradually becomes archaic and less representative of current speech usage. This may sometimes lead to reform of the written variety, although such reforms are often contentious and tend to occur mainly after political changes. For much of recorded history, language policy has been a major tool of nationalism and building national identity, and language planning has often worked to unify nations around a single standard language at the expense of regional varieties and other local languages.

The basis of policy decisions can be explicit, as in the former USSR or the Peoples' Republic of China, where non-Russian and non-Han Chinese minority groups were recognised based in part on their language, and standard varieties of each language were selected based on being central, spoken by a large group, intelligible to other varieties and having an established sociocultural status, then codified in ways reflecting current political criteria. This meant use of Romanization in the eastern part of the USSR in the 1920s and its replacement by Cyrillic in the late 1930s, and in China in the 1950s the use of a Romanization based on the **pinyin** form codified for Chinese, then sometimes replacement by other scripts in the late 1970s or early 1980s. Languages like Tajik used a 1920s Romanization and a 1930s Cyrillic script in the USSR and a 1950s Chinese-based Romanization and a 1970s Arabic script in China; in Afghanistan, it continued to be written in Arabic script.

Micro-level language policy decisions are made every time one chooses to socialize children in a particular language, every time a teacher chooses a particular linguistic form, every time a government bureaucrat selects a language to address a member of the public and every time a government makes a proclamation. Political change may lead to linguistic policy changes, as in Greece or Burma, where democratization led to a shift in use away from the diglossic High, or in South Africa since 1994 and Nepal from 2006, where a number of local languages gained official recognition.

Institutions formulating policy may develop gradually, as in China where the Association for Writing Reform of the Communist Party, established in 1949, became the government Research Committee for Chinese Writing Reform in 1952, the Committee for Chinese Writing Reform in 1954, and, finally, the ministry-level State Language Commission in 1985. Policy bodies may also have their status and powers weakened, as in China, where the State Language Commission merged into the State Education Commission, now the Ministry of Education, in 2000.

There may also be separate official bodies responsible for minority language policy. For example, in China, the Nationality Affairs

Commission has a role at all levels, and has a number of general research institutes for all minorities and for specific local minorities at the national, provincial/autonomous region, prefectural and county level. It also has its own language research institutes and institutes collecting and editing traditional manuscripts in some areas; also a number of provincial and regional universities training teachers and others; for example, the Yunnan Minzu University currently trains teachers and other government workers in twelve languages, some of them endangered. These and many branches of the Academy of Social Sciences, various universities and the Religious Affairs Commission do a great deal of research on a wide range of languages; both developing and improving orthographies and documenting traditional culture. Education is one of the areas under local control in minority autonomous areas, and there is an amazing array of textbooks in the languages of many of the fifty-five officially recognised minorities, and in some cases for several of the diverse languages within a single minority group. These are mostly prepared and printed by various minority language publishing houses, mostly at the national and provincial level; these also publish translations of all laws and other official materials in each of the minority languages with a recognised orthography. The translations of these are mostly done by a separate government translation bureau, something which has existed in China for nearly 500 years.

Many minority groups in many countries, including some whose languages are endangered, have associations or committees that lead activities on their culture and language. These convene large gatherings to foster positive group identity, reinforce traditional culture, and discuss or promulgate language policy, especially concerning orthography. One of the main public displays in such meetings is the written version of the language on signage, and books reporting such activities are produced, as well as many other kinds of books; for example, the endangered Lepcha language of India and Bhutan has an active association based in Kalimpong, India. With increasing political recognition of minorities, these associations or committees may become part of the official government mechanisms in a country, as many did in Nepal after 2006 and some are now doing in Burma since 2015, planning and introducing language education in their languages.

Linguists have contributed extensively to formulating and implementing national language policies in recent years, most notably the Australian Joseph Lo Bianco, who prepared the official language policy for Australia (Lo Bianco, 1987), the first explicit language policy for any English-speaking country, led its implementation, and has also helped to draft and in some cases implement policies for many other countries, including New Zealand, South Africa, Sri Lanka, Thailand and Burma. Such policies all accord explicit recognition to all minority languages.

In **diglossia**, there is a language variety used in formal situations, especially writing, with high prestige. Another variety, often with a range of subvarieties, is used in informal situations and has low prestige; the original definition and examples are in Ferguson (1959). Once a language has a written form, this tends to be relatively stable, and so through time diglossia may develop naturally as the spoken varieties change and diverge; or the diglossic High can be created or reformed for nationalistic purposes, sometimes through Einbau, building in even more archaic elements where these are known, as in the case of Katharevousa Greek. In more unusual cases, the diglossic High may be a colonial language and the diglossic Low may be an unrelated indigenous language, as in the case of Paraguay with Spanish as High and Guaraní as Low. Like other speech varieties, diglossic High varieties can become endangered and may retreat into very restricted domains, such as religion, as in the case of the Bible variety of Greek in the Greek Orthodox Church, Latin in the Catholic Church until the 1960s, Coptic in the Coptic Orthodox Church in Egypt and elsewhere, Ge'ez in various churches in Ethiopia, and for millennia Hebrew in Judaism. After a period of initial diglossic use by the colonialists while they solidify their control, many colonial situations result in the endangerment and gradual loss of the indigenous diglossic Low varieties; Paraguay is very unusual in that its indigenous language has survived as a bilingual diglossic Low. Political and social change may also result in the endangerment of the diglossic High; in Greece, since 1976, the Katharevousa High is much less used, and in Burma since 2012, with the end of censorship and reduced government control of media, the literary High is also in retreat. However, education systems tend to perpetuate High varieties; knowledge and use is often seen as a sign of high status. Once the policy changes, especially if all domains of use disappear, a diglossic High can become endangered very rapidly and disappear into a purely literary archaic style.

8.3 EVALUATION, PRESTIGE AND OTHER PLANNING

As noted earlier, evaluation is a crucial component of language planning which is not explicitly discussed in most of the literature, but which is essential for a policy to succeed. This needs to be done repeatedly, with any changes implemented through ongoing policy and future planning. Evaluation should include measurement of acceptance and success of all activities; opportunities for community members and their leadership to provide feedback; and input from all other stakeholders, especially education, government and others. This does not mean embedding a policy and related planning activities in a multitude of formal tests and surveys, which may be culturally inappropriate and unhelpful, especially if they are conducted in the dominant language. Rather, the goal is successful outcomes, including improved attitudes and increased spoken and written use of the target language.

In the USSR from the mid-1920s, there was a strong push to develop new writing systems for a wide range of groups, mainly Turkic and other groups in Central Asia who had been using Arabic to write their languages. A Romanization was promulgated in 1928 following the same principles for all languages; one example was a 1930 Ket orthography discussed in the case study in Chapter 6. However, in the late 1930s, these scripts were banned and replaced by Cyrillic scripts, each of which used slightly different conventions for similar sounds. After 1990 when local choice again became possible, some newly independent nations in this area continued with their established Cyrillic scripts, some returned to Romanizations, some returned to Arabic scripts, and changes are still being made. For example, Kazakhstan proclaimed a new Romanization for Kazakh on 26 October 2017, to be fully implemented by 2025, replacing its Cyrillic script (which has five modified letters and one phonetic symbol) and using an apostrophe diacritic where necessary.

A second example of changes to top-down codification of orthographies following evaluation from within speech communities took place between 1958 and 1982 in China. Many new writing systems following the principles of Chinese **pinyin** Romanization were created in the late 1950s for some languages without traditional writing systems such as Bai and Hani, and for some languages that already had traditional orthographies: Christian missionary systems for Miao, Lahu and Lisu, Arabic scripts for Turkic and other languages of Xinjiang in western China, a traditional **logographic** script for Naxi and systems based on Chinese characters such as Zhuang. From the early 1980s, when local views were taken into account, Lisu, some Miao and most groups in Xinjiang returned to their original scripts; some groups continued to use both for different purposes. For the Lahu, the missionary script continued in Christian contexts and pinyin Lahu in government use. For the Naxi, although there are very few traditional shamans left who can read it, research and publication in the traditional Tomba logographic script continues, while the pinyin script is in limited use in education.

Prestige planning, as introduced by Tollefson (1991) and others, relates to the strategies for improving attitudes to minority languages, endangered and otherwise. Discourse planning is another term used for managing attitudes to languages and the way they are discussed and viewed in society. These were discussed extensively in Chapter 4.

Acquisition planning relates to the ways that languages are acquired – for example, in the home, in the community or in school. As we saw in Chapter 5, the most intimate family domains are crucial, but ongoing use and reinforcement in other domains is also essential, as discussed further in Chapter 9.

8.4 LANGUAGE POLICY AND HUMAN RIGHTS

A major current issue for language policy worldwide is linguistic human rights. The Universal Declaration of Linguistic Rights, part of which is quoted at the beginning of this chapter, was drafted and adopted at the World Conference on Linguistic Rights, 6–9 June 1996 in Barcelona; it has subsequently been endorsed by UNESCO. It includes the right to speech community membership and recognition, the right to use the language and to call the group and its language by their own preferred names, the right to associate with other members of the community across borders and the right to maintain traditional culture, among others.

The basic need is the recognition of the identity, language and culture of every group wanting such recognition, including both indigenous groups and immigrant groups, wherever they are. Such recognition should be available for every group and a matter of individual choice for each person and social network within the group. The right of continued association of immigrant groups with their places of origin is an issue for groups with a substantial diaspora population. The diaspora population can be a valuable economic, social and linguistic resource for the language in its original location; languages may be better preserved in the diaspora than in the original homeland.

In some places, group membership is administratively controlled: by the government registering citizens as members on their identity papers, as in China or Russia, by some in-group organization, such as a tribal council in North America, or based on specific criteria such as descent, personal identity and recognition by the rest of the group as a member, as for Aboriginal groups in Australia. This means that the first right, to be recognised as a member of a group, is not always respected; for example, Tohono O'odham people born in Mexico cannot normally register as members of the Tohono O'odham tribe in Arizona, although they share the same language, culture and close family ties.

The choice of name used to refer to a group may seem to be trivial; but it is not, particularly if the exonym used for a group and its language is regarded negatively by the group, or, as often happens, refers to more than one small group. It can be surprisingly difficult to get a majority group to change its terminology; old exonyms like Lapp, instead of the autonyms Saami or Sámi, can persist despite long-standing in-group wishes and changed government policies; they may also survive in administrative names, such as Lapland, the northern-most region of Finland.

Once names are enshrined in an official list, whether at the national level or elsewhere, changes may become even more problematic. For example, in India where extra resources and special advantages are provided for people who are members of officially scheduled (listed) tribal and caste groups, people must have the listed tribe or caste surname to access the advantages. Thus, the Lisu in India are listed under the official tribal name Yobin, a local pronunciation of the Jinghpaw name Yawyin, originally borrowed from Chinese *yeren* 'wild people', obviously in its origin a pejorative name, and all Lisu in India are registered with the family name Yobin. Lisu people have a range of clan names which they use as surnames in Burma, China and Thailand, and also when speaking or writing Lisu in India, but these are not used officially in India. The normal group autonym everywhere is Lisu, and this term is now officially used in Burma, China and Thailand in the national languages as well, although other terms such as Lisaw in Thailand and Burma and *yeren* in China were formerly in use.

Names can change fairly rapidly; the date when new names were created, such as Tangsa in 1948 in north-east India and Tangshang in 2003 in Burma, are well documented, but many other changes are not. Name changes also occur spontaneously within a group; the Katso of south central Yunnan changed their autonym to Khatso about twenty years ago.

One aspect of linguistic human rights which has been making pro-gress in recent years is early education through the mother tongue for minority groups, transitional to a national language. UNICEF and UNESCO have taken a leading role here; UNICEF strongly promotes initial mother tongue education for all children, while UNESCO supports a variety of initiatives to publicize and counteract language endangerment; both are well aware of and fully supportive of the desirability and benefits of bi- and multi-lingualism. Often, local leadership and many individual families are not fully supportive because they mistakenly think that immediate mainstreaming into education solely in the national language will provide better long-term educational outcomes and economic benefits; however, this is a recipe for educational failure and ongoing marginalization of a large portion of their own group.

As Fishman (2006) shows, Corpus Planning activities about the structure of languages may impact on their status: the ways endangered languages are recognised, viewed and used. For example, if the Corpus activities are centred on a national language, and other languages are treated as local varieties and written, if at all, in derivative orthographies based on the national standard, as in France, the related regional languages, as in the south-western part of France, will be deleteriously affected. Even languages which originally had their own orthography and traditions, like Provençal in south-eastern France, or unrelated languages spoken by minorities in France, like Celtic Bréton in Brittany in the north-east, Basque in the far south-west and German varieties in the north-east, may also be affected.

Since 2015, Burma has accorded some recognition to the more than a hundred languages of its 134 minority groups; Thailand has a similar policy which is not currently being implemented. Communist and some former communist countries such as Russia, China, Vietnam and Laos have minority policies derived from the 1920s Lenin model of recognising a large number of national minorities and in some cases giving them nominal autonomy and control of local education and cultural policy. The former USSR divided in late 1990 into its fifteen constituent republics, each ultimately based on a particular nationality: Russian in Russia and so on. Post-1991, Russia remains very ethnically diverse, with some 185 ethnic minorities; Russian is the national and official language.

The European Union (EU) has over sixty regional and minority languages, whose status is determined by national governments. Since 1992, with the EU Charter of Regional and Minority Languages (Hamans, 2008), there has been a Europe-wide policy for such languages, many of which are endangered due to earlier policies; but where the national government has not ratified the charter, or is not supportive, the charter is ineffective.

Bradley (2007b) discusses the policy at the time in the nations around the Pacific Rim. In some of these nations, recent changes have improved the language rights of minorities; notably Burma and Peru.

Over the last fifty years, and especially in the last twenty years, there has been a worldwide trend in this direction. In some cases, language status and rights are explicitly contained in constitutions and other laws, such as the 1982 Constitution of the Peoples' Republic of China and the 2008 Constitution of Burma; brief descriptions of these follow.

China's 1982 Constitution Article 4 states, among other things, 'The people of all nationalities have the freedom to use and develop their own spoken and written languages, and to preserve or reform their own cultures.' The 1984 Regional Autonomy Law is the basic law concerning the many autonomous regions, prefectures and counties established across the country where national minorities are concentrated, and provides for local control of some activities, notably education (Article 37) which should where possible be in the local language, and teaching materials and other publications in each language are to be supported by these autonomous areas. For the fifty-five groups recognised as national minorities, developments since the 1950s have been intermittent, with a major language policy and planning effort in the late 1950s, little progress in the 1960s and early 1970s, but major advances from the mid-1970s on. With local autonomy and some control of local education and cultural activities, national minority officials and the many researchers and workers in local institutions have strongly pursued their constitutional rights and worked hard for their languages. On the other hand, the classification of national minorities is now institutionalized and impossible to change, and many national minorities include a wide range of distinct linguistic groups speaking different languages; the most spectacular example is the Yi nationality, with perhaps eighty languages and four distinct traditional orthographic traditions (Bradley, 2001, 2011c). The policy has, if anything, tended to repress these internal differences within individual national minorities, by Ausbau and spreading 'standard' superposed varieties like the Shypnra local variety of Nosu in Sichuan.

Since independence in 1948, Burma has not exactly been a model in the treatment of its minorities, but at least the situation is improving for most of them. Burma's 1974 Constitution Article 21(b) provides freedom for all indigenous national races to use and develop language and follow cherished traditions and customs. The official list of 135 recognised national races was prepared shortly afterwards; it is now under revision to make it conform more closely to the wishes of the various national races. The 2008 Constitution Article 22(a) states that the central government will 'develop language, literature, fine arts and culture of the national races', and Article 354(d) gives the right 'to develop their language, literature and culture that they cherish'. The

2014 Education Law Article 42(b) tasks the Ministry of Education 'to help to open classes to develop the ethnic groups' languages, literature, culture, art, traditions and cultural heritage', and Article 43(b) allows the use of an ethnic language alongside Burmese in basic education. These major changes are in the process of being implemented in most areas of the country since 2016. The 2015 Ethnic Rights Law Article 2(a) states: 'The languages, literature, culture, art, traditions and historical heritage of the ethnic groups are to be respected'; and Article 3(a) states that 'The ethnic groups have the right to their languages, literature, culture, art, traditions and historical heritage' Such positive statements are not always fully reflected in local action, but there is positive movement for most groups, away from the situation after the 1948 constitution, when Burmese was the sole official language.

In his case study of the development of language policy in Colombia, Todd (2015) shows how the 2008 Protection Program for Ethno-linguistic Diversity of the Ministry of Culture and the 2010 Native Languages Law set out a strong policy framework for supporting the use and development of indigenous and creole languages, building on the recognition of the country's ethnic groups and their languages that was enunciated in the country's 1991 constitution. Many of those languages are endangered as a result of centuries of Spanish-language hegemony during colonialism and continuing after independence, with further challenges facing many of the communities due to Colombia's lengthy armed conflict. However, this programme was only fully implemented up to mid-2010 and was subsequently watered down, while there has only been minimal implementation of the legislation.

Similarly, the language policy developed for Thailand by the Royal Society from 2006 for mother tongue education and other support for the approximately seventy languages other than Thai which are now indigenous to Thailand was approved by two successive governments in 2010 and 2012, but is still awaiting approval by the current military government, in power since 2014.

Like these, many of the recent advances in language rights across the world have not been as successful in reality as on paper. While in-group activists may continue to pursue the expansion and development of their languages, enthusiasm within many groups is not strong, as there have been centuries of disadvantage and suppression leading to negative attitudes and language shift. The challenge is to reverse these trends, now that the relevant rights are being established and appropriate policies and institutional structures are coming into place.

8.5 LANGUAGE POLICY AND PLANNING FOR ENDANGERED LANGUAGES

When a language is endangered and does not already have a consensus standard form, it is particularly important to make the right choices in formulating policy and implementing planning. These include the selection issue: which variety of the language should be used as the basis; also various codification issues: how the language is to be written, if the community wants to write it; how the vocabulary should be documented; and what should be the preferred grammatical structures. Elaboration concerns both the creation and dissemination of language learning materials, dictionaries, grammars and other reading materials, and the expansion of the vocabulary. Dissemination through education lends prestige, but attitudes also need to be changed so language is transmitted and used in the home and family; use in other media, notably electronic media, is also important.

Selection of the standard and how much variety is to be recognised within it is a nontrivial and subtle issue. In some cases, there is an existing lingua franca variety or a literary language with historical status, so the choice is obvious. In other cases, one may wish to follow the usual Soviet nationalities policy model of the 1920s, also implemented in China in the 1950s, and select a variety which is centrally located, spoken by many members of the group, intelligible to other members of the group, and spoken in a more socioeconomically advanced part of the group's territory. It is desirable to be as inclusive as possible in accepting variation, both regional and between speakers of differing levels of fluency.

8.5.1 Orthography Development

An orthography must be based on a way of pronouncing a language, which may be problematic for some endangered languages where there is extensive variation and where semispeakers or younger speakers speak differently. In most languages, there are also regional dialect differences which may need to be considered and included or rejected. If a standard agreed pronunciation exists, or a prestige dialect is widely accepted as the norm, this is not a problem. Complex decisions are often required, preferably made by consensus among community members; they may seek advice from outside experts including linguists.

In many general studies on language endangerment, there are brief introductions to the principles of designing a new orthography from scratch; these include Grenoble and Whaley (2006: chapter 6) as well as Selfart (2006), Lüpke (2011) and many others. Many linguists who have attempted this process have also discussed their efforts, to give just two examples Sallabank (2002) and Ding (2005). This is also the topic of focused collections of studies such as Cahill and Rice (2014), and of a recently codified alphabet/orthography design workshop process.

Sometimes linguists do not reflect on whether literacy is necessary for maintaining an endangered language, nor on the effects of literacy on a community and its language, changing the cognitive nature of access to the language by mediating it with writing for those within the community as well as fossilizing oral traditions and endangering their ongoing transmission (Ong, 1982, 2002). Writing also makes information about the language and culture available to outsiders, which is an issue for many communities, as we have seen in Chapter 3. There is a well-reasoned discussion of this issue in Grenoble and Whaley (2006: 113ff.).

Furthermore, it is often the case that orthographies already exist; a writing system and its historicity are often an important factor in positive group and language identity. If there is an orthography which represents an accepted standard for the language adequately and is accepted in the community and by local authorities, there is no issue. Where there is more than one, each competing system will have its proponents and detractors; these may be based on different systems, **alphabetic** (e.g., Roman, Greek, Cyrillic, Arabic, **devanagari**, Tibetan) or other, and be in use in different sections of the community. Where the accepted system does not represent the sounds of the language adequately, or where it is imposed on varieties which are very different and thus require speakers to learn a different variety of their language along with literacy, this leads to problems. Also, if the writing does not follow national policy, there may be political issues. For example, in Thailand, government policy requires the use of Thai script for all minority languages, so many Malays in the south are learning literacy in Malay through Thai script.

In cases where there is existing orthographic controversy, it is wise not to become involved; even the choice of one system for disseminating results in the community may be problematic, as in the case of Lisu where we have produced dictionaries in two different orthographies for two similar dialects (Bradley, 1994; Bradley et al., 2006). Early on, one of the authors also attempted a very minor reform of the Lahu orthography (Bradley, 1979b), but this only provoked puzzlement and we no longer use or promote this. Some of these changes were subsequently adopted in the Lahu Si orthography, but this created a great deal of controversy, mainly among other Lahu, most of whom reject it completely.

If an existing well-established orthography does not represent the sounds of the language accurately and completely, it may be necessary to allow its use to continue; educated speakers will be attached to it, and attempts at reform will divide the community. If impetus for reform comes from within the community and is very widely accepted, it may be helpful to change such scripts to represent the sounds better, but only after extensive consultation and community agreement.

When creating new scripts, it is desirable to choose a locally relevant alphabet so that there can be maximum synergy in learning to write the endangered language and the national language. This will facilitate transfer of learning between writing the two languages, may be helpful in integrating minority groups into the nations where they live, help majority-group teachers and other outsiders to recognise and use the local language, and make the preparation of material easier as the same computer and other resources can be used for both.

An Orthography Design Workshop, also called alphabet design workshop in the literature which mainly discusses creating Romanizations, is an efficient way of creating a new writing system; see Easton and Wroge (2012) for a step-by-step outline. Similar procedures have been followed by many communities and linguists for a long time, as we did with the Bisu in Thailand in 1977. This method is quicker and more effective than allowing an orthography to emerge and evolve slowly. The workshop assembles stakeholders with language knowledge and interests from within a community: teachers, leaders, other authority figures and one or more outside linguist facilitators working together over a number of weeks or months. The linguist facilitators should ideally be known to the community and familiar with the language. The workshop participants discuss and attempt to implement various ways of representing the language, initially making the fundamental choice about which writing system to base the new script on, and, once that is decided, using symbols and conventions from that source script to represent the language – usually starting with consonants, continuing with vowels and, if necessary, also dealing with suprasegmentals such as stress and tone. After working for a few days to produce an initial proposed system, the workshop breaks up and the local participants attempt to write down various short texts individually. After some time (a week or so) the workshop reconvenes and participants read out their texts, look at each other's attempts to write them and discuss problems they encountered. This normally leads to some revisions, which are then tested by the workshop members by writing down more texts; then, the workshop reconvenes. This is repeated until the workshop comes to a consensus on the draft orthography. It may then be desirable to have some kind of celebratory announcement, where the workshop participants present their results to the community, asking for their views. Once the community is satisfied, the members of the workshop start to use the writing system within their normal work; for example, by introducing it to the school, to written versions of village announcements or in religious settings.

Some communities want their writing system to be very different from the national language, and sometimes a community activist will invent a distinctive script. Some of these, like the Cherokee syllabary, have succeeded and become the normal writing system for the language (Unger, 2005). Outsider missionaries tend to use the script associated with their religion: Romanization, Arabic, Greek, Cyrillic or devanagari. There are also regional preferences for new scripts, like devanagari in South Asia, pinyin Romanization in China and scripts of national languages in various other countries.

If possible, new orthographies should avoid the use of **diacritics**, extra symbols adjacent to normal letters. These may cause problems in the production and transmission of language materials, but, more importantly, there is a strong tendency for literate speakers to omit diacritics, very often or even entirely. Bradley (2006) is a case study of the main orthography for Lisu and problems in its use in email, SMS and other new domains. This orthography distinguishes the six Lisu tones, but in practice speakers omit a very high proportion of the tone marks, which are written with extra punctuation marks after each syllable, even in very formal writing. In the other main Lisu writing system, based on Chinese pinyin, the tones are indicated by an extra consonant at the end of each syllable; in this orthography, omission of tones is much less frequent because no inconvenient diacritics are required.

In some cases, there may be an established outside lingua franca. Speakers of endangered languages who have substantial knowledge of such a language may wish their orthography to follow similar principles to the orthography of that language; thus, for example, the Bisu in Burma have chosen to have a script based on that of Lahu, the language of the local Lahu missionaries who converted them to Christianity.

The same endangered language may be spoken in several countries where different national languages and orthographies are in use. In recent years, contact between Bisu in Thailand, Burma and China has been re-established after a long separation, after the writing of the poem that opens Chapter 2. Unfortunately there is now no way for this group to use one writing system; the Bisu Thai-based script from Thailand is not suitable for use in Burma or China. If such a trans-national group is in contact, it is highly desirable for their script to be the same across national borders, as the Mien/Yao have achieved through direct contact and compromise between the Mien in Thailand, China and the United States (Purnell, 1987).

The development of a Bisu orthography using Thai letters since 1977 (see the case study in Chapter 2) was an early example of an Orthography Design Workshop and is an example of maximizing transfer between the endangered language and the local language of education. It is also in accord with government policy; see Person (2018) for more information. The only Bisu consonants not already present in Thai are /g/ /ts/ /tsʰ/ /ʃ/; all the vowels can easily be represented in Thai script, although the vowel length contrast in Thai does not exist in Bisu. Bisu has a simple three-tone system, high, mid and low, which is again less complex than the Thai tone system. Two letters are combined to represent the consonants /ts/ and /tsʰ/; we initially suggested combining the Thai letters for /t/ or /tʰ/ plus one of the Thai letters for /s/, but the speakers came up with the elegant solution of writing these as /t/ or /tʰ/ plus /r/, a sequence of consonants that does not occur in Bisu. For /g/ and /ʃ/, in 1977 we proposed using very rare consonants which are only found in a few Pali loanwords in Thai, and this worked well. Recently, a Thai linguist wanted to implement a general policy used in various orthographies created by his colleagues to represent /g/ using Thai /k/ plus a subscript dot; the Bisu have not acted on this suggestion. In general, the use of diacritics that do not already exist in a writing system is not a good idea unless absolutely necessary. Because the Thai contrast of vowel length does not exist in Bisu, there has been a lot of variation in writing Bisu vowels using Thai long or short forms. Due to changes in the tones of Thai since the standardization of its writing system, the same tone diacritic in Thai can represent different tones depending on the type of consonant at the beginning of the syllable. However, in Bisu we decided to write the high tone consistently with one Thai tone diacritic, the low tone consistently with another Thai tone diacritic and to leave the more frequent mid tone unmarked. While this means that Bisu children learning literacy in Bisu and Thai have to learn to use the same tone diacritics differently, it avoids introducing unnecessary complexity into the Bisu writing system. Younger Bisu speakers have mostly lost the contrast between voiceless and voiced nasals and /l/, and the Bisu have made the realistic decision not to distinguish them in writing, even though older speakers still do.

8.5.2 Dictionaries

A dictionary is both an important symbol of the value of its language for the speech community and preferably a practical tool for their use. It is also a key component in any language reclamation process, and reflects the endpoint of a major effort of language corpus planning and codification. This is why it is extremely important to make dictionaries suitable for community use.

Many dictionaries are monolingual; the most extensive are adult-level mother tongue dictionaries, but there are also simplified mother tongue dictionaries for children, and second-language learner dictionaries including pronunciation, simple definitions, clear explanation and examples of the use of function words and of extended meanings; learner dictionaries may also be bilingual, and some contain a longer or shorter grammatical sketch. Linguists usually prepare bilingual or multilingual dictionaries, sometimes with solely academic aims and full of linguistic terminology. The inclusion of etymologies and historical citations, as in the *Oxford English Dictionary*, makes a dictionary much larger. **Lexicography**, the preparation of dictionaries, is a major subfield of linguistics; for further discussion see Svensén (2009).

In an endangered language dictionary, a compromise between these various purposes is desirable. Some users may be mother tongue speakers, others will be semispeakers with varying degrees of knowledge or child learners from within the community with little or no knowledge of the language. Thus, a learner-oriented bilingual dictionary in the language and the language which is replacing it is probably the most appropriate. As, in some cases, only one dictionary of a language will ever be produced, it should be as comprehensive as possible, much more so than a normal learner dictionary. For some case studies of dictionary preparation for endangered languages, see Frawley et al. (2002).

Community usage should determine how to represent the language orthographically. In some communities with more than one orthography, preferences are determined by external factors. Religion is one: Muslims often prefer Arabic-based scripts; sometimes Catholics and Protestants within a language group have different Romanized scripts. Geography is another: transnational groups may use different orthographies in different countries. History is a third: there may be earlier and more recent versions of a script. Newly developed internally based scripts, such as the Cherokee syllabary and some Karen and Hmong scripts, also need to be considered for use in the dictionary if that is what the community prefers; for some examples, see Unseth (2008).

Related to questions of orthography, there is the issue of alphabetical order; this should preferably follow local norms, whatever those are; for example, starting with **velars** in most indigenous South and South East Asian alphabets. For languages with **syllabic** scripts, the order of syllables is usually also fixed as with Japanese *kana* or the Cherokee syllabary, so there is no issue. For logographic scripts like Chinese characters, order may be problematic; local preferences should be followed.

Most dictionaries of endangered languages will be bilingual or multilingual; monolingual dictionaries are more normal for dominant languages, although, once literacy is fully established, an endangered language community may also want a monolingual dictionary. Another issue is the other language(s) to include: the local national language, several local national languages for transnational minority groups, some outside language(s) of wider communication. Another is which direction(s) the dictionary should be in, minority language to dominant language(s), dominant language to minority language, or both ways. When preparing a dictionary, thought should be given to making it easy to reverse: from X to English (which is what most linguists tend to do first) into English to X (which may be what a community wants). With most types of dictionary software, this is possible; but it is a great deal of work to reverse a dictionary prepared in a word processing format like Word.

Each entry starts with the form of the word in the local orthography; where this does not unambiguously indicate the pronunciation, that is also essential. It is rather unlikely that local wishes for the representation of pronunciation and the usual desire of linguists to use IPA or some similar system will coincide; careful discussion and planning is needed here. Another related issue is how much dialect difference to include; where this is not consistent, it may be useful to give multiple pronunciation alternatives, and identify which is which. Shortened rapid speech pronunciations or other stylistic alternatives which should be included.

Linguists normally include grammatical information about the **form class** of each word; if this is included, there should be a brief introduction in the language explaining and exemplifying the terms used. In fuller dictionaries, entries are enriched by example sentences showing the word in context; this makes them much longer but also more useful, and may help to give cultural context.

In a monolingual dictionary, definitions normally use shorter and more basic words; in a bilingual dictionary, the complexity of the language in the definitions will differ depending on the target users;

for maximum accessibility these should also use relatively simple language; don't define 'brother' as 'elder or younger male sibling'. Some dictionaries include **etymology**, where earlier stages of a language are known; this may include related words in other languages, or the results of historical comparison between languages. For most purposes, etymology is unnecessary in a community-oriented dictionary. Conversely, in endangered languages, it is very frequently the case that many words, especially nouns, are borrowed; the dictionary needs to show the source language, and note any ways in which the word behaves differently – for example, does it sometimes or always keep the word structure patterns of the source language, even when used within the endangered language – like English irregular plurals such as 'child'/'children' or 'knife'/'knives'.

A key question is whether to separate **homophonous** entries or to include all same-sounding words as subentries within one large entry. It is better to separate, especially when the entries are of grammatically different types or when the meanings are unrelated. The order of such multiple homophonous entries needs to be consistent – for example, nouns first, then verbs, then other form classes; and within each form class roughly according to frequency. Another is whether to put all compound words and expressions containing a word together with the relevant entry, or to put them where alphabetical order implies; it may be helpful to keep all the words containing the same component together, and so to have compound words in more than one place, not just where they appear alphabetically.

In some orthographies, there are consistent conventions for spaces between words; in others, each syllable is separate; and, in others, there are no spaces. In some languages there can be ambiguity about word boundaries which fluent speakers can deal with due to the extra information from the context; but semispeakers, learners and outsiders need more information. A dictionary will need to be consistent, and should indicate the components of compound words so that syllable boundaries are clearly marked, and should use some convention to indicate these boundaries; one widely used possibility is a hyphen, another is an apostrophe, and, in some linguistic analyses, a period/full stop is used: is 'startup' 'star' plus 'tup', or 'start' plus 'up'? This can be represented as 'star-tup' versus 'start-up' or similarly.

Dictionaries can be of widely differing size and scope. Some include extensive cultural data, detailed botanical, zoological and other environmental information and other types of special knowledge. Words from a wide range of speech styles, including ritual, song, archaic language and child language may be included; if so, they should be consistently marked as such to keep them distinct from everyday speech material. Loanwords should be included, preferably with indication of the source language. Where the loanwords are from the language which is also the source of the orthography, difficult choices may need to be made about how to spell loanwords: as they are written in the source language, or as they are pronounced in the language – consistency is important here.

A bilingual dictionary for an endangered language community needs at least two introductions: one for the community, in the language, explaining the structure of the entries and any linguistic terminology that has been included, and if necessary the orthography used; and one in the other language, giving some relevant information about the community and a brief outline of its structure and orthography. It may also be helpful to have one or more pre-introductions by important in-group individuals.

There should be careful consideration about the means of delivery. A large hard-copy version published by an academic publisher in a developed country will be expensive, difficult to transport and probably have copyright constraints and a limited print run. An entirely electronic version does not pass the community shelf test: a dictionary, preferably large, is something to sit on a prominent shelf and feel proud about. Lower-cost hard-copy production near the community is important if a dictionary is actually to be used. Distribution of these copies also needs planning; a dictionary is no use sitting in boxes. For this purpose, as for many other purposes, local community organizations need to be involved; book sales, including to outsiders, may even be a source of income for them. Electronic delivery may be very useful in communities in developed countries with reliable Internet access, but is less practical in the places where most endangered languages are still spoken. Open access is best, ideally something interactive which speakers can correct and add to with appropriate moderation.

A superb example of a dictionary of an endangered language prepared entirely by a community member over many years, with extensive assistance from many others within the community, is Tamsang (1980). This has a brief introduction explaining the traditional Lepcha script, which is unique and used only for Lepcha, 1,025 pages with about 300,000 entries in Lepcha script, pronunciation, brief English gloss, form class and a longer explanation in English. Sadly, many such efforts do not achieve the circulation and use that they deserve.

There are also some communities who do not want a dictionary, or who want to restrict access to their dictionary to the in-group. For a discussion of one such instance, see Hill (2002); for a case in which community plans changed during a dictionary project, see Stebbins (2003). We should not assume that what we want or what we think the community should want is what they want – discussion and consensus are essential.

8.5.3 Grammars and Other Materials

As for a dictionary, the first issue is the target user of a grammar or other materials. If intended for the community, the grammar needs to be free of linguistic jargon and full of real examples. As in other areas of linguistic work for communities, prescriptivism should be avoided; don't say that something should or can be said only one way when in fact people say it more than one way. If there is a consensus standard which can be followed, that makes life easier, but, where there are substantial dialect differences, these may need to be discussed; in a dictionary it is easy enough to list alternative forms and identify their dialect, but in a grammar the issues may be more subtle.

A monolingual grammar in the language is not very likely to be useful to the community in an advanced language endangerment situation, and is not accessible to outsiders, although this is the norm for pedagogical grammars in many languages. The norm in academic work is a grammar in a dominant world language, and where the community already uses one such language (English, Spanish, Chinese, French, Portuguese, Hindi or whatever) and this is the language of local advanced education, this is the obvious choice. Other national languages may also be appropriate in some cases; it is particularly important that the grammar and other materials should be in a language known to outsiders such as teachers, health workers and others coming into the community.

In a few communities there is an indigenous grammatical tradition; often this is influenced by a particular traditional grammar: Latin in Europe or Sanskrit in South Asia. Such grammars may try to impose inappropriate categories; there are even instances where such external categories get added to the indigenous system, whether in an independent genre such as the Nissaya style of Burmese used for glossing Pali texts (Okell, 1967) or even entering the language, as in the case of the literary diglossic High style of Burmese, with, for example, a nominative **case** marker almost certainly due to Pali influence (Okell & Allott, 2001: 245).

Linguists are not experts in writing pedagogical grammars; conversely, most old-fashioned pedagogical grammars are very formulaic and follow a traditional step-by-step pattern with lots of **paradigms,** which is why education systems in many parts of the world have stopped using them. The ideal grammar is systematic, complete, full of cross-references and sentence examples and with a minimum of opaque linguistic terminology, and includes some short sample texts. In many languages, linguistic terminology does not exist or is very limited and inconsistent; it is not helpful to invent new terms, even if these are explained.

In addition to dictionaries and grammars, which can serve a major symbolic role within a community as well as being useful to the more advanced members of the community, there is a need for a wide range of practical materials to disseminate and elaborate the language. These include a variety of types of teaching materials: primers for initial literacy aimed at children, possibly separate primers for adult literacy, other materials for early readers, both children and adults, including culturally appropriate materials such as traditional stories, songs, proverbs and riddles, and more advanced traditional materials such as genealogies, transcribed oral history, religious and other epic poetry. A variety of basic health, agricultural and other materials containing useful knowledge can also be produced in minority languages to make this kind of information more accessible.

Experts in preparing curriculum materials recommend the initial use of alphabet charts with a letter and a picture of a common noun beginning with that letter – 'a' for 'ant', 'b' for 'bee', 'c' for 'cat', 'd' for 'dog'. Learners often chant out the alphabet while they learn the letters and practise writing them. For many alphabets of the world, there is a standard list of nouns associated with the letters; in other cases, these will need to be invented. The next step is graded 'big books' which have a large picture of something and a small amount of text in large print at the bottom of the page. These may initially be just pictures of animals and other objects, building up to short sentences: 'The cat sat on the mat.' Communities can work together to draw the relevant pictures and produce big books with locally relevant content. Once some reading ability is established, learners can progress to intermediate-level materials; such materials do not exist for many languages and may need to be created or simplified from fully traditional adult-level materials. Language experts from within communities often want to produce very advanced traditional materials, and should be encouraged and assisted to do so, because this will preserve these traditions; however, such materials may be frustratingly complex for early learners, particularly if they are in archaic language or contain complex and unfamiliar structures, and will need explanation and adaptation for pedagogical use.

Another genre which may be useful in raising the profile of a group and making more outsiders aware of its existence and its language is phrasebooks, whether targeting tourists or majority group members who work in a community. These can include interesting cultural information and help tourists to have positive experiences with the group while also benefitting their economy; see, for example, Bradley et al. (1991, first, second, and third editions) which has brief phrasebooks on six larger minority languages of Thailand and surrounding countries, and briefer materials on four others including three endangered languages. They may target specific needs in depth, such as health care situations, or be more general.

Where available, electronic media have become a very valuable resource for language vitality and reclamation, with many websites containing a wealth of downloadable material as well as interactive platforms such as Facebook, chat rooms and SMS. There is a wide range of other community-produced audio-only or audio and video recorded materials on cassette, CD or directly on the Internet via iTunes or websites, including a lot of music, some of which is karaoke with the words of songs appearing on the screen, but also various other genres; for some examples from south-western China, see the online journal *Asian Highlands Perspectives* (https://independent.academia.edu/Asian HighlandsPerspectivesJOURNAL). For a number of examples of how this happens among the youth of the Yup'ik community in Alaska, see Wyman (2013: especially 212–27). In addition to making language reclamation more relevant for young people, such platforms are an extremely valuable source of data on current informal speech styles.

How materials may differ when prepared for reclamation purposes in a community whose language is endangered will depend on the current level of knowledge and use of the language in the community. If there is already literacy in some other language, especially if many learners have limited ability in the endangered language, material can be given in the replacing language alongside the target language. If there is a national curriculum, versions of the beginning-level textbooks may be produced in the endangered language, both to assist monolingual children to make the transition to the main language of education and for children who do not speak their traditional language who can learn it in school. If initial mother tongue education is implemented, materials not just for language study, but also for other topics such as arithmetic and science are needed. Where possible, it may be desirable for most materials to be monolingual in the endangered language, both for the prestige of the language and to motivate and maximize learning. This may require some elaboration of vocabulary, preferably in close consultation with the community. If much of this vocabulary is borrowed from the replacing language, it may detract from the autonomy and prestige of the endangered language, but it will facilitate learning and maximize transfer.

8.6 CONCLUSION

Careful attention to language policy and planning issues is an important component of any widespread language development activity. Many countries have started to have more open and pluralistic language policies, and to give greater recognition and status to their indigenous and immigrant minority languages. Often, the implementation lags behind the policy, and in some cases the policy changes have come very late for many endangered languages. Even if official policies are not supportive, communities can and should undertake planning and other measures to reclaim their languages, including Corpus-related codification and elaboration decisions and actions and as much dissemination as the official language status policy allows.

CASE STUDY: RUMANTSCH

Rumantsch, Romontsch or Romantsch (hereafter Rumantsch) is a cluster of five main varieties spoken in the Canton of Graubünden (German 'grey leagues'), Grisons (French 'grey ones'), Grigioni (Italian 'big grey men') or Grischuns (Rumantsch 'grey ones') in south-eastern Switzerland. It is 'a language which the Swiss claim to be proud of, but do little to sustain' (Posner, 1996: 193). It is usually said to be related to Ladin and Friulian as spoken further east in north-eastern Italy; together, these languages form the Rhaeto-Romance subgroup of Romance within Indo-European, named from the Roman province of Raetia, of which modern Graubünden was the south-western corner.

In Switzerland, there has been close contact with Germanic languages, most notably Alemanic Swiss German, since about AD 250; in Italy, the strong contact influence on Ladin and Friulian and to a lesser degree the Engadine varieties of Rumantsch has been from Italian and its dialects. All Rumantsch speakers are now bilingual in Swiss German; the classic study by Uriel Weinreich, one of the first modern investigations of the process of language endangerment, Weinreich (1951, 1953), is a study of the contact between Sutsilvan Rumantsch (the most endangered variety) and German.

Since a referendum in 1938 added it to Article 116 of the constitution, Rumantsch has been the fourth national language of Switzerland, in addition to the three national and official languages, French, German and Italian; in 1996 after another referendum, it became the fourth official language. Baur (1996) traces its history and development.

The Canton of Graubünden is officially trilingual, but now mainly German-speaking, with a small and decreasing Italian minority in the south, and about 25 per cent of the population identifying as Rumantsch, although fewer actually speak a variety of the language. The capital of the canton, Chur (German) or Cuira (Rumantsch), was the seat of a semi-independent bishopric from AD 537 until the Reformation, which helped to maintain Rumantsch, although this did not include the Engadine area. However, the city of Chur has had a German-speaking elite for about 1,500 years, and has been mainly German-speaking for about 500 years; the northern part of the Canton has long been entirely German-speaking, and some valleys in the south-east had an influx of Walser German speakers many centuries ago; movement of Swiss German speakers into Rumantsch areas continues.

The five varieties of Rumantsch are, from west to east, Romontsch Sursilvan (in Oberwald, south-west of Chur), Rumantsch Sutsilvan (in Nidwald, south of Chur), Rumantsch Surmeir (in Oberhalbstein and Unterhalbstein, south-east of Chur, with some local subvarieties), Puter ('upper', in Upper Engadine) and Vallader ('lower', in Lower Engadine). A distinct subgroup within Vallader is the Müstair Valley subvariety in the south-east. This subvariety, and to a lesser extent the other Puter and Vallader varieties, show some influences from Italian, not surprising since they were ruled by an Italian bishopric until the early seventeenth century. The name of the language in Puter and Vallader varieties is Ladin, the same name as the very different Rhaeto-Romance language further east in eastern Bolzano province and elsewhere nearby in Italy, which is not mutually intelligible; the other three varieties use Romontsch or Rumantsch as their autonyms. In addition to these traditional varieties, there is a new literary variety, Rumantsch Grischun (RG, or, in German, Bündnerromanisch), created by the Romance philologist Heinrich Schmid (1982) based on a comparison of the five varieties and the creation of a single new variety derived from combining them; its creation facilitated the elevation of Rumantsch to an official language status by providing a single convenient literary standard.

There is considerable intelligibility among the varieties of Rumantsch, although some speakers deny this; for a quantified study, see Gloor et al. (1996: 37–43). Table 8.3 below shows the approximate speaker populations of the five varieties; the exact figures are uncertain and disputed. For example, the village studied in Weinreich (1951), Feldis (German) or Veulden (Rumantsch), had 176 inhabitants, 73 per cent Rumantsch mother tongue speakers, or 128 people, in 1941 and 140 inhabitants, 14 per cent or twenty Rumantsch-speaking people, in 2000. In 1941, some local Germans could speak Rumantsch; this is no longer so. According to the local tourism website, in 2013, a third of local people could speak Sutsilvan; even if this is so, the decline has been rapid.

Since the first Swiss census in 1803, the proportion of Rumantsch speakers in Switzerland overall and in Graubünden has been declining, but an absolute decline in speaker numbers is more recent. The 1803 census found 36,600 of 73,000 people, or over half, in the canton of Graubünden to be speakers; the 1941 census reported a total of 46,456 speakers across Switzerland, 1.1 per cent of the overall population and 31.3 per cent of the population of Graubünden at the time. See Table 8.1 for the progressive population statistics since then; self-reporting of mother tongue as collected up to 1980 may be exaggerated. Census statistics suggest an increase in absolute terms, but slower than the overall rate of population increase and with more of the speakers living outside their traditional communities. This includes about 10 per cent of the population of Chur, where the proportion of the population speaking Rumantsch was stable at about 11 per cent from 1880 to 1980, but has since been declining; the proportion of speakers elsewhere in Switzerland outside Graubünden has increased even more, as Table 8.1 implies, from 13.5 per cent in 1941 to about a

Table 8.1 *Rumantsch-speaking population of Switzerland*

Census	Population of Switzerland	Rumantsch-speaking in Switzerlad		Rumantsch-speaking in Graubünden	
		Number	Percentage of population	Number	Percentage of population
1941	4,265,703	46,456	1.1	40,187	31.3
1950	4,714,992	48,862	1.0	40,019	29.2
1960	5,429,061	49,823	0.9	38,414	26.1
1970	6,269,783	50,339	0.8	37,878	23.4
1980	6,365,960	51,128	0.8	36,017	21.9
1990	6,873,687	55,707	0.8	36,722	21.1
2000	7,288,010	49,134	0.7	33,707	18.0

third now; so well over 40 per cent of the speaker population now lives outside traditional areas. These and most other statistics are drawn from Furer Roverdo (2005). The shift away from Rumantsch is also illustrated by a slow decline in the number of communes officially classified as Rumantsch-speaking, as some shift to German, although sixty-three of 116 remain officially Rumantsch-speaking and eighteen others partly Rumantsch-speaking.

From the 1990 census on, Switzerland changed the census question from mother tongue to best-known language, family language, work language and school language, thus giving people four opportunities to report different domains of use of Rumantsch. In the censuses of 1990 and 2000, speaker totals given in Table 8.1 show 'family language' data and are not comparable with earlier data. Table 8.2 gives complete data on the four language questions in these two censuses, revealing a decline from 1990 to 2000 in reporting Rumantsch as best language and in family use, reflecting a decreasing vitality; but an increase in work and school use, reflecting greater institutional support.

The data on use in school suggests high use among the portion of the school age population in traditional Rumantsch-speaking areas; up to 97.2 per cent in schools in the Müstair Vallader area, 92.2 per cent in the core Sursilvan area, 82.7 per cent in the core Surmeir area and so on (Furer Roverdo, 2005: 49); there is also one Rumantsch school in Chur. The 2010 census was not based on an enumeration by universal questionnaire; it is derived from a sample survey supplemented by local and other government statistics, so it is completely incomparable.

A 2012 census bureau survey indicated that 40,804 people or 15.2 per cent of the population of the canton aged fifteen years and over-reported Rumantsch as their main language. Relevant language information in 2014 census bureau surveys based on yet another set of questions gives a total of 42,410 Rumantsch main language speakers aged nine or over, representing 0.5 per cent of the total population of the country over nine. The age distribution of Romantsch main language speakers in 2014 was skewed to older speakers, 26.3 per cent sixty-five and over versus a nationwide proportion of 17.2 per cent, with only 13 per cent under fifteen versus a nationwide 15.1 per cent. For more information, see www.bfs.admin.ch.

Advocates of Rumantsch usually claim higher numbers of speakers: 100,000 or even more. They base their claims on the fact that the pre-2000 census data did not allow for bilingualism, while all Rumantsch speakers are bilingual and may instead have reported on their other language, usually German; or they add the totals for 'best language' and 'family language' from the 1990 and 2000 census data, although

Table 8.2 *Rumantsch use, 1990 and 2000, Switzerland and Graubünden*

Census	Best		Family		Work		School	
	Number	Percentage of population	Number	Percentage of population	Number	Percentage of population	Number	Percentage of population
1990 all Switzerland	39,632	0.58	55,707	0.83	17,753	0.55	5,331	0.60
1990 Graubünden	27,679	17.07	36,722	21.70	13,178	16.27	4,731	22.46
2000 all Switzerland	35,095	0.48	49,134	0.74	20,327	0.59	6,411	0.63
2000 Graubünden	27,038	14.45	33,707	19.45	15,715	17.26	5,940	23.33

Table 8.3 *Rumantsch varieties*

Variety	Introduction of writing in these varieties	Speakers	Endangerment
Sursilvan	1611, 1615	17,897	Vulnerable
Sutsilvan	1601 (1944)	1,111	Severely endangered
Surmeir	1755	3,038	Definitely endangered
Puter	1560	5,497	Definitely endangered
Vallader	1534	6,448	Vulnerable

these two groups overlap. However, under-reporting in the census seems unlikely, given the strong positive group identity and institutional support for the language; if anything, over-reporting seems more likely.

Table 8.3 shows the earliest use of writing for the five main varieties, their speaker populations from the 2000 census, and their level of endangerment; UNESCO (2009) assesses Rumantsch as a whole as definitely endangered, but this is an exaggeration for Sursilvan and Vallader, which are regularly used in core areas, and an underestimate for Sutsilvan. A sixth variety, Jauer, is closest to Vallader and is spoken in Val Müstair, the easternmost and lowest-altitude part of the canton; it has no separate orthography, relying on Vallader or formerly on Italian for literacy; Jauer speaker numbers are included in Vallader in Table 8.3.

Sursilvan has two orthographies: one used by Protestants since 1611 and one for Catholics since 1615. Sursilvan was also used as a literary standard for Sutsilvan until 1944 when a new standard for Sutsilvan was implemented; the older Sutsilvan orthography had limited use. There are also orthographies for Ladin Vallader, with the earliest orthography, for Ladin Puter, the second oldest, and for Surmeir (one variety). All the orthographies use alphabetic symbols; some follow spelling conventions more like German, others more like Italian. Despite the creation of the new standard for RG in 1982, work continues to be published in most of the literary varieties; notably three newspapers: *Gasetta Romantscha* in Catholic Sursilvan (1857–1996), *Casa Paterna/La Pùnt* (1920–1996) in Protestant Sursilvan and Sutsilvan and *Fögl Ladin* in Vallader and Puter (1941–1996); these three newspapers were all combined into the new five day per week newspaper *La Quotidiana* from early 1996, which also contains a page in Surmeir, *La Vousch da Surmeir*, as well as general content in RG. There was a monthly Surmeir page, *La Pagina di Surmeir*, in *Gasetta Romantscha* from 1946, which became a separate newspaper in 1949 and was also incorporated into *La Quotidiana* in 1996. The *Engadiner Post*, normally in German, has a page in Engadine Rumantsch three times per week. RG is a case of Einbau, the creation of a new compromise standard variety. It is now used in various public written domains: official cantonal documents, information pages in the cantonal telephone book, forms and leaflets of the cantonal bank, public signage such as on government offices, roads and in the local narrow-gauge railway, in various canton-wide commercial advertising and, as we have seen, in a five day per week newspaper since 1996. A cantonal referendum in 2001 approved the use of RG as the sole official variety, but activists who favour maintaining the traditional Rumantsch varieties say this was due to support from the German-speaking majority in the canton. The cantonal radio and television network Radio Televisiun Svizra Rumantscha broadcasts partly in RG. There is a federal government subsidy and a cantonal government subsidy for the maintenance and development of Rumantsch including RG and other varieties, and new school textbooks started to use RG since 2001, with plans to stop printing textbooks in other varieties from 2005, and to make RG the sole school variety from 2010. However, this was only implemented in the schools of forty communes between 2007 and 2009, not in forty-one others. In 2011, the cantonal government decided to abandon the compulsory shift to RG in school; all but about ten schools, in Surmeir and in Trin, have now returned to the local variety for newly enrolling students. Older students who started school in RG continue to use RG in school, while younger students in the same schools are learning local speech and some RG in addition. New textbooks are again being prepared for local varieties.

Some of the choices made during Einbau, and the difficulties which these have created for speakers of all existing varieties, are illustrated with some vocabulary differences shown in Table 8.4.

As Table 8.4 shows, the RG word is usually taken from the more frequent form, replacing the unusual spellings such as 'tg' for /tʃ/ with 'ch' ('dog', 'horse'), sometimes using Rumantsch lexical items rather than Italian-like forms ('breakfast', see Italian *collazione*), but other times preferring more Italian-like forms ('eat', see Italian *mangiare*), sometimes preferring phonologically simpler forms ('horse' final consonant), sometimes creating new forms ('breakfast' first syllable). The outcome is RG forms most of which occur in some variety or varieties, but not together outside RG.

Much of the work of implementing the new standard RG has been carried out by the Lia Rumantscha (Rumantsch League), originally

Table 8.4 *Rumantsch vocabulary*

Gloss	Sursilvan	Sutsilvan	Surmeir	Vallader	Jauer	Puter	RG
breakfast	solver	anzolver	ansolver/ culaztgung	püschain/ culazchun	püschegn	culazchun/ cruschina	ensolver
dog	tgaun	tgàn	tgang	chan	chaun	chaun	chaun
to eat	magliar	maliear	magler	mangiar	maingar	manger	mangier
foot	pei	pe	pe	pè	pè	pè	pe
horse	cavagl	tgavagl	tgaval	chavagl	chavai	chavagl	chaval
month	meins	mains	meis	mais	mais	mais	mais
summer	stad	stad	stad	stà	stà	sted	stad

205

established in 1919 under the Sursilvan name Ligia Romontscha and based in Chur. This body is led and staffed entirely by Rumantsch speakers. There is also a great deal of material published in and on the various Rumantsch varieties by many authors, mainly from within the community: dictionaries, grammars, school textbooks, children's books and literature. Rumantsch may have the highest proportion of published authors among its speakers of any language in the world.

There is great controversy about the imposition of the new RG standard, as there was concerning several earlier attempts over the last 200 years. Since 2011, a grassroots movement Pro Idioms with two local branches, one in the Engadine and one in Sursilva, has successfully pushed for the reinstatement of greater public use of the traditional varieties; their website, www.proidioms.ch, has many relevant publications in German and two varieties of Rumantsch available, mostly very negative about RG; see, for example, Pro Idioms Surselva (2016), quoted in part at the beginning of the chapter. In any case, people continue to speak their own local variety in daily life, although a few official spoken domains such as cantonal broadcast media and some schools have moved towards use of the new standard. This is extremely confusing for many children where RG is used in schools; they may be hearing one variety in the home and community, but then must use another variety, generally viewed as artificial, in school; nor is it easy for teachers, who are usually mother tongue speakers of a local variety and have only recently started to teach RG. In some areas, older siblings are still using RG in school, while younger siblings in the same school have reverted to learning their local variety first.

For recent data on attitudes to RG among young people in a Sursilvan community, see Tessarolo and Pedrotti (2009: 77–81); briefly, it is regarded of very low prestige, familiarity, usefulness and other positive characteristics, and very high on negative characteristics; local Sursilvan and German both show the reverse profile: high positive and low negative evaluations. Many older adults share the same views. Another study suggests positive views between the traditional Rumantsch varieties (Gloor et al., 1996: 43–4).

RG is an attempt to implement a single literary diglossic High variety, parallel to the High German diglossic High used in Switzerland alongside the various local Alemanic Swiss German diglossic Low varieties. However, High German has a long historical foundation, established prestige and long-term use for religious purposes; and it was based on an Ausbau process, building on a pre-existing spoken and written variety. Conversely, RG has no historical basis, no prestige other than what has been officially attributed to it since 1982, no literary tradition, no constituency of speakers for whom it is a normal everyday language and was created by an outsider linguist by Einbau without community consultation. RG is a new and artificial competing literary High; it was created and imposed alongside existing spoken varieties all struggling against endangerment, and nearly all with existing literary forms used in various domains, notably religion and literature.

DISCUSSION QUESTIONS

Find another example like Rumantsch where top-down language policy creates problems; discuss the difficulties caused by unpopular and unrealistic top-down policies.

Should the dictionary you are preparing include all taboo words including body parts and other types of insults? Discuss.

The local teacher, who is not a member of the in-group speech community and does not speak the local language, asks for your help to introduce the local endangered language in the school; what should you do?

SUGGESTIONS FOR FURTHER READING

Weinreich (1951) is a very detailed study of language shift in Switzerland; not just on Rumantsch, but also on the French/German linguistic border and for Italian.

Fishman (2001) is a ground-breaking and reflective study about how to undertake policy and planning measures to implement a reversal of language shift.

9 Language Reclamation

Miyurna! Naa marni purrutyi	Ladies and gentlemen, are you all good?
Ngai nari _____	My name is _____
Ngai wangkanthi	I say
"Marni naa pudni Kaurna yarta-ana,	"It's good you all came to Kaurna country,
iranti yarta."	exclusively indigenous land."
Ngaityu yakanantalya, yungantalya.	My dear brothers and sisters (thank you).

Kaurna Warra Pintyanthi (Amery et al., 2013)

This chapter discusses various subtypes of language reclamation: **revitalization**, **revival**, **renativization**, nativization and heritage. A further possibility is **denativization**, as seen for Rumantsch in Chapter 8; this is a top-down language unification strategy, imposing an artificial standard. Sadly, heritage activities, including limited language use, is the likely future for N‖ng (Chapter 3) and many other languages around the world. Language reclamation work in a community depends crucially on the current situation of the endangered language; concerning levels and stages of endangerment, see Chapter 2. See Chapter 8 concerning the four components of language planning (Selection, Codification, Elaboration and Dissemination) for reclamation, and the required actions, such as work on orthography, pronunciation, structural and interactional patterns and vocabulary.

For language reclamation as a whole, Fishman (1991) prefers the term Reversing Language Shift, correctly indicating that reclamation is a process of reversal of endangerment. Bentahila and Davies (1993) use the term revival for all types of reclamation, with examples that would here be classified as revitalization (Welsh or Irish), revival (Cornish) and renativization (Hebrew); they also make the point that most reclamation work involves some change to the language: transformation rather than solely restoration. Another widespread term for language reclamation is language maintenance, which suggests a steady state; this is often used to refer to various subtypes of language reclamation as well as work to maintain languages which are less endangered. In practice, most language maintenance work is done in reaction to perceived threats to the continued use of the language. Hinton (2011) and other scholars use the term revitalization as a cover term instead of reclamation, but this is slightly misleading as not all reclamation processes aim for full revitalization, and not all are starting from the basis of a language with living speakers to provide a model. The dangers of language engineering can be seen in the recent experience of Rumantsch: denativization through the creation of a new standard which is no one's dialect, under the guise of official revitalization. A similar issue with competing standards arose for Cornish during its revival, although this is now resolved.

The literature does not always distinguish the subtypes of language reclamation, and the same terms are used in quite different ways in related disciplines. In ecology, reclamation refers to various kinds of remediation of ecological damage; land reclamation means creating new land where there used to be water by bringing soil or landfill. In anthropology, revitalization is a term widely used to refer to indigenously developed, often religious movements for renewal and change: not reclaiming a language, but innovating a subsystem of culture. This kind of movement is sometimes called a revival if it has a mainly religious orientation, and messianic if there is a charismatic leader; note that it necessarily involves cultural change, although insiders often view it as a return to cultural roots. In political science, nativization sometimes refers to giving control over political or other resources to indigenous groups ('natives') instead of colonial outsiders. Many other disciplines make different uses of the same terms.

Where a language is not yet extinct, it is essential to involve remaining speakers in revitalization efforts. For an extinct or sleeping language without living speakers, a revival strategy must be employed, as in the case of Kaurna or Cornish; this relies on the availability of materials which the community regards as authentic, the Selection of the variety to be used and the Codification and Elaboration of materials for practical use. If a language is out of everyday use but persists in the community for some purposes, such as liturgical use, it will need some Codification and a lot of Elaboration to enrich the language for daily domains in renativization, as for Hebrew. Once nativization has taken place within a community, the choice is whether to develop the resulting contact language into wider use. For all types of reclamation, it is very important to have agreement on the form of the language selected: the spoken and written forms, a positive attitude to the effort (Chapter 4), the resources needed and realistic goals.

For nativization of contact languages and their expansion into wider use, Selection, Codification and Elaboration are needed as the contact language gains written and more spoken domains. The community attitude may initially be negative, especially where the prestige lexical source language is also used in the community, as in Haiti, Papua New Guinea and other postcolonial settings. Without nativization, a pidgin will disappear when the contact which led to its development ends, like pidgin Arabic spoken by Romanian guest workers in Saddam's Iraq (Avram, 2010), pidgin Japanese, Korean and Vietnamese spoken there by English-speaking soldiers during and after wars (Norman, 1955), Tây Bôi or French as spoken by Vietnamese servants during French rule in Vietnam and many other known or unrecorded instances through human history. There are many excellent studies of the wide range of pidgins, creoles and other contact languages. Once a language is nativized, then it may expand or become endangered; if it becomes endangered, it may perhaps be revitalized in some circumstances, like Patuá (see the case study in Chapter 10), but is probably less likely to be revived after a long period of endangerment. Creoles often disappear through a process of decreolization leaving some residue. For some discussion of these issues, see Garrett (2012) among many other sources. For a contrary view in which the development of creoles via pidgins is regarded as only one subtype of contact language nativization, and contact languages may contain complex structures from various source languages because they arise in bilingual or multilingual contact communities, see Ansaldo (2017).

Heritage is the symbolic use of a language for community identity, in the form of public activities and displays involving language and culture. Often these are reinforced in schools through some language learning: greetings, words for culturally important activities and so on. Symbolic heritage activities are often present in communities whose languages are still in use to some degree; where the languages are no longer actively spoken, heritage activities can preserve at least some identity and pride.

Denativization is essentially the creation of a new artificial standard from parts of existing spoken varieties. This is intended to unify those varieties by a top-down planning process, without giving priority to one existing variety. One successful example is Lisu: a committee of Christian missionaries and Lisu colleagues created a new literary standard from 1914 onwards. The spread of this new variety, initially used mainly for Christian literature, has now extended into all written genres, some formal spoken domains and interdialect oral use, as discussed in Section 9.3. Other examples include Rumantsch (see the case study in Chapter 8).

9.1 TYPOLOGIES OF RECLAMATION

The terminology adopted here distinguishes between the subtypes of reclamation as if each were unitary, but each is a continuum: in revitalization, depending on the level of persistence of the language within the community; in revival, depending on how long the language has been sleeping, how much group identity persists and how much language information is available; within nativization, depending on the degree of decreolization; within renativization, depending on the degree of prior standardization, available materials and the range of domains of surviving use; and within denativization, depending on how close to Ausbau of an existing dialect the newly constructed standard is.

Within the Graded Intergenerational Disruption Scale (GIDS) model, Fishman (1991: 466) calls reclamation reversing language shift, which he says in principle starts from the bottom-up. Fishman (2001) calls Levels 8–5 attaining **diglossia**; he calls Level 4a and upwards transcending diglossia; it should be noted that this is not the usual use of this term discussed in Chapter 8. He distinguishes within his Level 4 according to whether there is local control of curriculum and teaching staff, as seen in Table 9.1.

Lewis and Simons (2010: 117) illustrate stages of reclamation within extended GIDS (EGIDS), as in Table 9.2; this is also viewed as starting from the bottom-up, working towards intergenerational transmission.

Walsh (2009) points out that, in a revival, where the language is no longer spoken in a community, these models do not apply, and revival often proceeds in ways that do not follow these hierarchies and with goals that need not include full reintroduction of the language in all kinds of everyday use. Revitalization and renativization also often proceed in ways that do not follow a step-by-step process from the bottom-up; they start with GIDS Level 6 or EGIDS Level 6b by using the language to socialize children in the home, or even Level 4 by promoting writing; the first spoken domain may be the classroom.

In many societies, there is great interest in maintaining or reviving traditional cultural practices, some of which only indirectly involve language: dance, instrumental music, cooking and eating, clothing and personal artefacts, building and household decoration, agricultural

Table 9.1 *Severity of intergenerational dislocation GIDS*

Level 4a	Public schools for children, offering some instruction in the language, but substantially under majority curricular and staffing control
Level 4b	Schools in lieu of compulsory education and substantially under community curriculum and staffing control
Level 5	Schools for literacy acquisition, for the old and for the young, and not in lieu of compulsory education
Level 6	The intergenerational and demographically concentrated home–family–neighbourhood–community; the basis of mother tongue transmission
Level 7	Cultural interaction in the language primarily involving the community-based older generation
Level 8	Reconstructing the language and adult acquisition

Fishman (2001).

Table 9.2 *Revitalization EGIDS*

6a Vigorous	The language is used orally by all generations and is being learned at home by all children as their first language
6b Re-established	Some members of a third generation of children are acquiring the language in the home with the result that an unbroken chain of intergenerational transmission has been re-established among all living generations
7 Revitalized	A second generation of children are acquiring the language from their parents, who also acquired the language in the home. Language transmission takes place in home and community
8a Reawakened	Children are acquiring the language in community and some home settings and are increasingly able to use the language orally for some day-to-day communication needs
9 Reintroduced	Adults of the parent generation are reconstructing and reintroducing their language for everyday social interaction
10 Rediscovered	Adults are rediscovering their language for symbolic and identificational purposes

Lewis and Simons (2010).

and handicraft processes and so on. Reclamation materials and activities need to cater for these interests. Conversely, it is important to make the reclaimed language relevant for modern society, as Perley (2012b) and Wyman (2013) discuss: Internet use, music lyrics and other contemporary activities. The Internet is also a major resource for reclamation and dissemination of all kinds of knowledge; see, Buszard-Welcher (2001) for an early discussion of this, which has become a major resource, with Internet companies like Rosetta Stone and Google supporting community reclamation efforts.

9.1.1 Revitalization

In most types of revitalization, the older generation and the younger generation interact directly, without necessarily involving the middle generation(s) who do not know the language, or whose knowledge of the language is not regarded by the community as sufficient or appropriate for transmission. There are several widespread strategies for this. One is the **Language Nest** model, as first applied to the revitalization of Māori in New Zealand from 1982 under its Māori name *te Kōhanga Reo* (King, 2001): bring older-generation fluent speakers into a school setting with pre-primary- or early primary-aged children who have not learned the language in the home. Another is Hinton's **master–apprentice** scheme initiated in 1992 (Hinton, 1994, 2001b; Hinton et al., 2002, Hinton, Florey et al., 2018a), which links one grandparent-generation fluent speaker and one young adult with a desire to learn their background language but little or no prior experience of it; this produces one new young speaker, who can then disseminate knowledge further. A third much more widely applied method is heritage language classes, most often for adults of various ages, sometimes taught by enthusiastic amateurs who may have little more knowledge of the language than the rest of the class. In such contexts, the Formulaic Method developed by Amery (2016) and discussed in the Kaurna case study may be a useful beginning point. Most often, attempts are made to reintegrate an endangered language directly into the normal school curriculum: as a heritage activity, learning some cultural knowledge and lexicon; with formal language study aimed at speaking knowledge and some literacy; or in addition as the medium of learning for some subject areas other than language. Tsunoda (2006: 200–14) gives a number of further examples of subtypes of education-oriented reclamation methods.

In an endangered language, initial child language acquisition in the family may have skipped one or more generations. Many revitalization efforts involve adult second-language learning, not mother tongue acquisition in the family during childhood, although the Language

Nest model at least gives an early start. One of the most intensive and systematic attempts to improve language abilities in the missing middle generation is discussed in Olthuis et al. (2013) for Aanaar Saami in northern Finland. This involved language study in a classroom setting to improve the language skills of a cohort of adult professionals, who could then use the language in their normal work, both with older members of the community more fluent in the language, and with the generation of children learning the language mainly through school or from their grandparents.

The only kind of reclamation which attempts to produce new transmission from adults to children is when a committed family chooses to use a language within the family; this also happens in cases of revival and renativization. In such cases, there can be a question about the authenticity of the resulting speech form if the adults providing the model did not themselves learn the language as children; see Section 9.4.

Note that most revitalization strategies are aimed at the in-group and some exclude outsiders, although some may rely initially on outsider linguists, educators and authorities. We believe that an outsider linguist who has benefitted from working with a community has an obligation to assist that community in any reclamation, but not to attempt to control such efforts, as outlined in Chapter 3.

Several case studies in other chapters of this volume illustrate revitalization, which is both the most widespread of the three types of reclamation and the most likely to succeed, although not guaranteed to do so; see, for example, Bisu in Chapter 2 and Patuá in Chapter 10.

9.1.2 Revival

Revival is a special case where old materials, usually written, provide the crucial data. Such materials are usually not prepared by linguists, and may be problematic and not comprehensive. Even where there are descriptive linguistic materials, these often neglect conversations: a serious gap for revival of everyday spoken interaction. To fill such gaps, there can be borrowing from nearby closely related languages, as in the case of Wembawemba in Australia, use of hypothetical historically reconstructed words or patterns, and new compounding from known resources, among other strategies.

The task in revival is much harder, because there is no authoritative spoken model. Usually the range of genres of material is limited, sometimes with little material of any kind. From the perspective of a part of a community who no longer speak the language, what is revitalization elsewhere can instead be revival. With an external model available, there is no problem about a model; however, that model may be a different dialect, which brings another kind of problem, as Dorian has noted for her East Sutherland Gaelic speakers, whose speech is very different from standard literary Scots Gaelic (Dorian, 1978, 1981, 2001, 2010b).

Below is a case study of the Revival of the Kaurna language of Adelaide, Australia; this has been underway for several decades, and has started to bear fruit. Similar efforts have been underway for much longer with Cornish, and are also underway for some North American languages, see, for example, Yamane (2001), and in many other Australian Aboriginal settings, see Hobson et al. (2010), which includes the Gumbaynggir example discussed in Walsh (2010) among many others.

9.1.3 Renativization

Where a language has continued in use in a community in restricted domains, such as religion, there may at some point be a desire to return to use of this language in more domains. For Hebrew, as we saw in the case study in Chapter 7, ongoing liturgical and scholarly use of Biblical and post-Biblical Hebrew within the Jewish community facilitated its renativization starting in the late nineteenth century, assisting the political process leading to an independent Jewish state in 1948. One key question here is authenticity: is modern spoken Hebrew the same language as Biblical Hebrew? Also, given that the language was used in a traditional society, went out of use as an everyday spoken language as it was displaced by Aramaic, and was mainly used in religious domains for a long time, many areas of vocabulary are unavailable. See Chapter 7 for more discussion of the linguistic consequences, which affect the sound and grammatical systems as well as the vocabulary of renativized Hebrew.

9.1.4 Nativization

This volume is not the place to discuss nativization in depth; there is a vast literature on the types and examples of contact situations which lead to the development of **pidgins**, some of which are nativized; also on the development of **creoles** or contact languages, with or without pidgin antecedents. Creoles can also move with populations from one place to another, and then undergo further separate evolution. One very frequently encountered process of creole endangerment is decreolization during ongoing contact with the prestige lexical source language. Many scholars believe that the Afro-American variety of English is one long-term example. Naturally, where a creole or contact language becomes endangered, the community may react with attempts to revitalize it; but, as creoles often have relatively low status, even among their speakers, this is fairly unusual. It does happen sometimes, as in the case of Patuá, Macao Portuguese creole, which originated from Kristang, Malacca Portuguese creole (see the case study in Chapter 10).

The ultimate source creole, spoken in former Portuguese settlements on the west coast of India, is critically endangered; the immediate source creole, Kristang, is also being revitalized in Malaysia, although it remains endangered. Since 2007, there is a small community voluntary school in Melaka which uses a Malay-based spelling, various materials from linguists including Baxter and support from older speakers. The spelling was devised with the leaders of a local administrative committee, but all these leaders have now passed away and the spelling is resisted by Portuguese-oriented traditionalists, supported by a Portuguese-funded NGO, who prefer the traditional Portuguese spelling. There are also some activists at the University of Malaya and the National University of Singapore who are themselves actively studying, learning and using Kristang, so there is some hope.

9.1.5 Heritage

Sometimes a community does not want full spoken language use, but does wish to express its identity and background through heritage activities including limited language use: words, short phrases, songs and street and shop signs. Other external non-verbal symbols of identity, such as traditional clothing, architecture, decorative motifs, tools and artefacts also form part of this. As Thieberger (2002) points out, this is also a valid choice and should be respected; it may also be an initial stage on the way towards more extensive language reclamation activities. Heritage activities often take the form of festivals with music, dance, sport and food, or special folkloristic performances. These may also be directed at outsider tourists, as are clothing, handicrafts, special foods, herbal medicines and other folkloristic products. Such heritage activities often develop into substantial sources of community income and pride, even if they are only partly traditional. For example, the traditional Kristang *intrudu* (Lent) festival with masquerade, water-throwing and roaming musicians, has been revived – but there is limited language content in the festival.

9.1.6 Denativization

This is usually a process imposed on a community from outside, providing a newly created 'standard' through Einbau; for example, Rumantsch in Switzerland (see the case study in Chapter 8) where the government wanted a single 'standard' variety to unify a diverse range of written and spoken varieties, or literary Lisu. As the newly created variety has no mother tongue speakers, it may be difficult to develop its use, as has happened in Switzerland with Rumantsch. On the other hand, some such attempts around the world have succeeded. For Lisu, this was due to motivation from the association of the new standard with Christianity and a desire among converts to use it. Denativization is not necessarily a response to endangerment, and it is different from the other four types of reclamation as its origin is top-down.

9.1.7 Stages of Reclamation

Language shift is normally at different stages for different individuals, families and communities, and so reclamation strategies need to cater for differing needs and build on available strengths. A language may be learned by children in some communities or families but not others; the speakers who can communicate can be used as a resource for others who are further along the continuum of shift. The same language may need different types and levels of revitalization in some locations and revival or heritage activities in others. Different communities may also have different desires as to what they wish to aim for in reclamation.

It is also likely that there will be more than one view within any community about what kind of reclamation is appropriate, and that such views will change through time, with support for language reclamation ebbing and flowing. This can lead to competition and even conflict. One example is the competing revival efforts for Cornish since the seminal work of Henry Jenner, which led to the creation of two main orthographies and pronunciations from 1929 (Nance, Unified Cornish) and 1986 (George, Kernewek Kemmyn 'common Cornish'), as well as two others, Gendall's Modern Cornish and Williams's modified Unified Cornish. The activists involved in the revival were divided between these various systems, with considerable conflict. Dissatisfaction with this counterproductive situation and policy changes for minority languages in Europe led to the formation of the Cornish Language Partnership in 2005, which produced a unified standard written form of Cornish in 2008.

Reclamation, like many other human activities, is cyclical and requires great energy and motivation in order to succeed. One problem with such efforts is that they may start as and remain elite activities.

9.2 MOTIVATION

Motivation is the main problem in language reclamation. Although many people feel and express positive attitudes that 'we ought to' work towards language reclamation, far fewer will actually participate or more crucially get their children to participate. Many who start with enthusiasm will give up when too much time, effort or expense are required. Children may also be deterred if the reclamation efforts take them away from other recreational activities, are poorly designed or are not useful in actually communicating with their grandparents.

An outsider cannot single-handedly create momentum for language reclamation; this must come from within the community. By working with, training and motivating local people, showing them that their language is a rich and interesting part of their cultural heritage, and providing ideas about how to proceed, the outsider can move some in-group members towards reclamation. There are usually some people who have interest in aspects of language and culture, and may need encouragement, guidance and assistance. Leaders' attitudes are very important, but need to be matched by similar attitudes and motivation within some of the group for reclamation to succeed. The ultimate aim is to build resilience into the community's use of the language; both equipping it for ongoing use in a complex world and helping people to return to a positive attitude about the language.

In any reclamation effort, it is crucial to avoid raising unrealistic expectations. Initial enthusiasm and widespread involvement are key resources; people need to see that progress is being made and goals are being achieved. Thus, the goals must be realistic and the methods must be appropriate and well-designed, as discussed in Chapter 8. See also Section 9.5 for more discussion. It is crucial to maintain unity of purpose and agreement on the form of language to be reclaimed, how this is to be implemented and the degree to which it is to be reclaimed.

9.3 METHODS

There is no one method to carry out language reclamation; the language capacities and needs of communities differ. It is important to know the situation of the language in the attitudinal, setting and linguistic factors discussed in Chapters 4–7, and to be certain that policy and planning issues discussed in Chapter 8 are carefully addressed so it is clear what is possible and realistic. The people within the group who have motivation, skills and knowledge to work in the reclamation process must be found, trained and supported; local leaders need to authorize and support the process.

Hinton (2001a) speaks from extensive experience about the need for careful planning of reclamation, under the guidance and control of the community and with practical targets; and for regular and frank evaluation and adjustment of methods and goals. This may mean that the process starts slowly while consensus is being achieved. Projects should not try to move too fast; a failed reclamation project may be worse than no project at all, as it discourages future attempts.

Reclamation requires materials, which must sometimes be created or collected and usually need revision and dissemination. Use of an orthography representing an agreed variety of the language is normally essential, except for those few communities who reject writing. Where this orthography is new, materials for adult literacy and primers for children are needed. If there is nothing interesting or useful to read in the language beyond this, people may become discouraged and their reading and writing skills will not progress. School textbooks in the language, including textbooks for language learning at progressively higher levels and textbooks for subject material are needed if these are also to be learned through the language. Other material for early literate people to read, such as simple stories and current events, are often neglected. Community insiders may be particularly enthusiastic about traditional materials: songs, proverbs, rituals, stories and genealogies; they may wish to have these among the earliest printed materials, even though they are sometimes in archaic or poetic style. Christian communities want the Bible, hymns and other relevant materials, even though these are very complex for beginning readers. Other kinds of practical materials, such as information about agriculture, animal husbandry, health and medicine, should also be made available once literacy is established.

A brief case study on the development of writing, literacy and materials among the Lisu, a group of over a million people in China, Burma, Thailand and India, illustrates how the development of materials may progress. In 1914, a group of Christian missionaries devised an orthography, revised and implemented in 1916. This is a unique Romanization which uses only upper-case letters, upright and inverted; a Unicode version was recognised in 2008. The orthography represents a compromise dialect similar to the central dialect but with some northern dialect features introduced from the 1930s onwards, when northern dialect speakers began to convert to Christianity; the writing system is flexible enough to write any dialect, and Lisu writers often criticize each other for using too much of their own dialect instead of the standard written language. The first publication was a 1916 literacy primer with mainly Christian content, revised and reprinted many times since, then Bible portions from 1921, a New Testament in 1938 and Bible in 1968. Since then, several revised versions of the New Testament have been produced, and there is a lot of other Christian materials of many kinds. Extensive development of school textbooks started in China in the 1950s and especially since the 1980s, with several hundred Lisu books published by the nationalities publishing houses of Yunnan province and Dehong prefecture. Apart from several textbook series for Lisu language study up to the end of primary school, these include many volumes of traditional Lisu songs, stories and proverbs, some with Chinese translations; we have also published some Lisu songs in Lisu and English (Bradley et al., 2000, 2008). Now there are Lisu authors writing new Lisu prose: history and fiction. There is a daily newspaper in Lisu in Nujiang prefecture in China, and there have been various magazines in Lisu published in Burma; parts of these are original Lisu material, but much is translated from other languages. There are also many books translated from English or Chinese on religious, agricultural, medical, political and other topics. Literacy in the Christian Lisu script is mainly associated with Christianity; about half of the Lisu, especially in Burma and India but also in China and Thailand, are Christian.

There is also a Lisu script based on the principles of Chinese pinyin, which was created in the mid-1950s and approved for use in China since 1958, which non-Christian Lisu still sometimes use; but the governments of the two Lisu autonomous areas, Nujiang prefecture and Weixi county, chose to return to official use of the Christian script in 1983. Literacy in Lisu is taught in churches across the four countries where the Lisu live, and in the first few years of some primary schools in Lisu autonomous areas of China and also in northern Burma. Several other smaller groups in China such as the Nusu and Anong, who were converted by Lisu Christians and live in areas where Lisu is the dominant language, also use Lisu as a liturgical language and a local lingua franca, with many literate in Lisu. For more details, see Bradley (1994, 2003b, 2006), Bradley and Bradley (1999), and Bradley et al. (1991, 2006). Despite a century of literacy, few Lisu can read texts as complex as the Bible.

Tact and patience may be required if there are existing materials which have problems: a writing system which does not distinguish all sounds of the language or established translations which are problematic. It may be necessary to use nonideal orthographies and materials because the community prefers them. Eventually, community members may want revisions, but it is not the job of an outsider to instigate these. For an unwritten language, choices about orthography and standard must be made by community members, in accord with local government policies, and carefully and consistently implemented in all materials (Chapter 8).

It is important not to rely entirely on school-based learning and not to focus too heavily on literacy. Most endangered languages are currently mainly oral. Even in a school setting, oral skills can be the main focus of attention. While many of the usual reclamation strategies are school-based, it is also important to put the language to use in its real context. This can include camps and excursions with elders who speak the language and can teach traditional knowledge – finding water, food and other plants, hunting animals, tracking, sacred places and stories associated with them. Performances and festivals are another type of community event with cultural as well as language content, where the language content can be reclaimed. Once they have some language knowledge from a school setting, children can learn from their grandparents, who may be delighted to use their endangered language with their descendants again. The final stage is restarting normal child language acquisition from early childhood; for this, the parent generation needs to have the necessary language skills.

One issue for many language reclamation projects, like many other local-level activities, is finding resources and funding; also training, recognition and accreditation for participants. Some local communities control their own buildings and other facilities and can use them as they wish; others may need to rely on a local school or other organization. Funding can be a problem, although most small-scale reclamation processes do not require much money. There may be various kinds of government funds that are available; the outside fieldworker can help in finding and applying for them and helping with any other paperwork required. In some societies, it is normal for people to contribute a small amount of money towards local activities; if so, they may be willing to support the initial stages of a reclamation process.

Training and qualifications are sometimes an issue in processes that involve schools or governments; elders with language and culture knowledge are very unlikely to have formal teacher training, so some administrative flexibility is essential. There may be a need for orientation and training for such participants in the reclamation process, in an unthreatening and culturally appropriate way respecting their knowledge. A fieldworker with an academic background may need training and preparation to participate in reclamation. Similarly, an enthusiastic insider may also benefit from some prior orientation – for example, about teaching and learning strategies: not relying on memorization and not teaching students long lists of nouns. In most reclamation processes, the goal is achieving the ability to communicate in the endangered language, so oral skills in everyday interaction need to come first.

Having started a reclamation process with appropriate leadership, contributors, materials, resources and in-group participation, progress needs evaluation and agreement on how to progress to other stages. A reclamation that has only a Language Nest, where the students move on to a normal school which does not reinforce their learning and continue to live in families who do not use the language, may eventually be seen as a failure, as it does not lead to renewal of language use in the community. Thus, it is important for reclamation processes to continue to develop until they have reached a level that the community finds sufficient for their desires.

It often happens that some individuals and families move far ahead of others in their reclamation; these people should be seen as models rather than fanatics, so that others will emulate them. Recognition of such skills can be formalized, as in the case of the revived Cornish community recognising people who achieve certain levels of proficiency as bards. Such people will become leaders in the reclamation process.

Hinton and Hale (2001) compiled short case studies of various types of reclamation activities, mainly in North America, but also in Hawaii, Wales and New Zealand. Hornberger (2008) provides a model for introducing an endangered mother tongue into the education system and case studies from four continents showing what does and does not work. Grenoble and Whaley (1998) provide a step-by-step outline of the issues and methods in language reclamation, with useful case studies from North America, Latin America, Hawaii and Siberia. In this volume, we have chosen case studies which illustrate the principles and implementation of reclamation, mainly in other areas of the world: Asia, Australia, the Middle East and elsewhere in Europe and Africa. The literature in this area is rapidly expanding, as language reclamation is becoming increasingly widespread around the world, and so new reclamation projects can now build on widespread experience.

9.4 AUTHENTICITY

A reclaimed language is unlikely to take over all domains of language use within a community. Hebrew is a near-exception, although some traditional Jewish languages of the diaspora still persist in the family and community among immigrants to Israel; however, most of them are endangered and becoming more so. As Fishman (2001: 463–5) says, the aim should be to regain some informal diglossic Low domains in the speech and writing of people of all ages, while also maintaining or gaining full knowledge of any necessary outside diglossic High. It is often difficult for multiple dialects to be reclaimed; where policy decisions to level out dialect differences into a standard form of the language have been made without sufficient consultation, this can be a matter of controversy. Speakers may see the language as not representative of their traditional dialect, and as artificial if it represents a composite Einbau variety like Rumantsch.

The authenticity of the reclaimed language may be questioned by insiders and by outsiders. Outsiders, seeing many loanwords and spelling conventions which follow a local dominant pattern, may view the reclaimed language as a 'broken' version of the dominant language; this is especially so for nativized creoles. Adult speakers within the community may see the version of the language which is chosen for reclamation, if it represents younger semispeakers' usage, as excessively simplified 'baby talk'. Conversely, if the version chosen is so archaic that only the oldest people (if anyone) still speak that way, it may be seen as 'too hard'; prescriptive attitudes of any kind are unhelpful, although understandable. This is why extensive input from the community at the standardization stage is essential, as discussed in Chapter 8, and it is good if puristic attitudes can be avoided, as we saw among the Bisu in Chapter 2.

9.5 GOALS

The goal of language reclamation is to expand the use of a traditional language within its community. The maximal target is that the language should again be transmitted to children in the home by parents and other family members, but this is not the only goal and is not normally the first goal where a language is already critically endangered or sleeping.

Fishman (2001: 474–7) gives a three-way typology of language reclamation: 'shoot for the moon', 'the right step at the right time' and 'anything is better than nothing'. The first he describes as 'reaching too high and losing it all': unrealistic goals for a 'total multi-front struggle', which many language activists attempt. The third he believes to be insufficient, 'a retiring and isolating self-enfeeblement', but especially in revival efforts, many communities are happy with a return to some limited symbolic heritage use of their language, which *is* clearly better than nothing (see Section 9.1.5). The middle represents a long continuum, ideally of gradual movement in the direction of greater use of the endangered language. This is what Fishman advocates; in particular, he views intergenerational transmission as crucial, so the choice by as many as possible parents and grandparents to socialize children in an endangered language is the ultimate goal.

Lewis (2011) introduces a Sustainable Use Model for language maintenance at various levels related to EGIDS. He proposes five essential FAMED conditions: Functions, Acquisition, Motivation, Environment and Distinct niche. Acquisition issues are discussed further in Chapter 5; Motivation, language attitudes and identity are the main topic of Chapter 4; Environment relates both to policy issues discussed in Chapter 8, and to attitude issues discussed in Chapter 4; and both Function and Distinct niche are language domain issues discussed in Chapter 5. It is certainly true that all or at least most of these conditions need to be present for reclamation to succeed.

Language reclamation is never an easy task, but it is feasible when approached in a realistic way using appropriate materials and methods. It is the only way that much of humanity's linguistic heritage will survive this century. Dorian (2011) gives a positive appraisal of such efforts, observing that they are increasing around the world. There is also greater awareness of the need for language reclamation in the general community, educational systems, governments, leading international institutions such as UNESCO and UNICEF, academic areas such as anthropology and linguistics, and, critically, within the small communities whose languages are endangered.

CASE STUDY: KAURNA

Kaurna is the indigenous Australian Aboriginal language of the plains in and around Adelaide in south Australia, a member of the Pama-Nyungan language family. The community retains a Kaurna identity and a connection with their land and history. In the 1840s, when Kaurna was generally spoken, two German Lutheran missionaries, Christian Teichelmann and Clamor Schürmann, documented the language, representing a large corpus of words and sentences in a non-scientific and somewhat inconsistent alphabetic transcription; various other travellers also collected more limited data, mainly word-lists, with two collected from Kaurna speakers living far away in western Australia and Tasmania. After a precipitous drop in use in the second half of the nineteenth century, the language ceased to be actively spoken in 1929. Therefore, it is not normally listed in some inventories of endangered languages, other than in Moseley (2007), as it was already sleeping before 1950. It has recently been added to the *Ethnologue* (Simons & Fennig, 2017) as reawakening.

Since 1989, working very closely with community elders, the Australian linguist Rob Amery and more recently other colleagues at the University of Adelaide have been using data from all the nineteenth century materials to revive the language and prepare a wide range of teaching materials including books such as a spelling primer, vocabulary, songs and funeral protocols, as well as a recently-published learner's guide (Amery et al., 2013). For a series of discussions of this process, see Amery (2000, 2016, 2018) and Amery and Kanya Buckskin (2012).

Australian linguists have developed techniques for working out the likely phonology of words in Aboriginal languages represented only in old non-scientific transcriptions, based on the widespread structural similarity of phonology across the continent and by comparing cognate lexical material in related languages (Blake, 2002); these procedures have been applied for Kaurna. The initial revival materials developed from 1989 on were very carefully tied to the original nineteenth-century sources. However, a 2010 spelling reform introduced more consistency in Kaurna writing and removed redundant information, such as any distinction between voiceless and voiced stops like 'p' and 'b'; this contrast is absent from nearly all Australian languages, but is often distinguished by untrained outsiders. The spelling reform also introduces a clear orthographic distinction between the three 'r' sounds and between **interdental**, **alveolar** and **retroflex** sounds.

Now, one of the most frequently occurring Kaurna speech events is a 'welcome to country' – a brief statement at the beginning of a meeting or event mainly for non-Aboriginal people, in which a Kaurna community member welcomes the group to Kaurna country, the Adelaide Plains area; the standard example from the community's website is seen at the beginning of this chapter. Across much of Australia, such welcomes are done in English, but for the last two decades most Kaurna and a few outsiders do their welcome in Kaurna.

A valuable strategy developed by Amery and his Kaurna colleagues is Amery's Formulaic Method (Amery, 2016: 237–40). This starts with use of one-word sentences appropriate in many circumstances, including responses such as *Marni* 'Good', question words such as *Ngana* 'Who?', simple commands such as *Tika* 'Sit down!' and culturally important concepts, with staged introduction of progressively longer and more complex well-formed sentences that are frequently used, and can be used in contexts where the dominant language, English, still predominates.

Another substantial step towards reclamation of Kaurna started in 2010, when the first child who is acquiring Kaurna in the home from early childhood was born; this family now has three children, all learning Kaurna in the home. A TV documentary about this and other aspects of the revival of Kaurna was aired on national public television in Australia on 13 October 2013, www.abc.net.au/tv/programs/buckskin/. This traces the story of Jack Kanya Buckskin, father of the first Kaurna child language learners since the late nineteenth century and a very active teacher of Kaurna language at many schools, including, since 2008, the Kaurna Plains School, which is an Aboriginal school in northern Adelaide where many Kaurna revival activities for people of all ages have been based. He is now at Tauondi College, developing a Technical and Further Education (i.e., vocational) Certificate III course on Kaurna to follow on from a TAFE Certificate IV course already implemented.

Recent developments include many other steps forwards: a 2012 government grant to support language work now extended to 2022, various 2013 radio programmes in Kaurna, completion of formal qualifications in language study by nine adult Kaurna in early 2013, with two continuing to the TAFE Certificate IV, and a Kaurna Language Learning Series Youtube channel, http://bit.ly/kaurna. In September 2013, the University of Adelaide committed to ongoing teaching and research on the Kaurna language, and a community-based organization Kaurna Warra Karrpanthi 'supporting Kaurna language' was established in October 2013. This sleeping language is returning to regular use in many domains, with community, government and academic support. There have also been setbacks, with the passing in 2017 of some of the most active community leaders, but the revival continues. For a more detailed overview, see Amery (2018).

DISCUSSION QUESTIONS

How might a formerly sleeping revived language differ from the traditional language from which it is derived? What kinds of problems would one expect in the revival of a sleeping language, and how might they be overcome?

The community where you do research is divided into two factions who use different orthographies, and one faction asks you for help in designing language reclamation materials. What should you do?

The leaders of a group whose critically endangered language is spoken only by a few very old people, has not previously been documented and has no agreed orthography ask for help in a language reclamation effort. What should be done?

SUGGESTIONS FOR FURTHER READING

Amery (2016) is a description of the procedures used in reconstituting Kaurna from old materials and the achievements during twenty-five years of its revival; for up-to-date information, see the author's website www.adelaide.edu.au/directory/robert.amery and the Kaurna community website Kaurna Warra Pintyanthi www.adelaide.edu.au/kwp.

McCarty (2013) discusses efforts towards Navaho language reclamation over the last thirty years, and similar work in many other indigenous communities in North America, with particular attention to community participation.

Hinton, Florey et al. (2018) contains a large number of relevant case studies and overviews of language reclamation methodology and its implementation across a wide range of communities.

10   Methodology

The young lady in the window

Patuá	Portuguese	English
Nhonha na janela	A moça na janela	The young lady in the window
Co fula mogarim	Com uma flor de jasmim	With a jasmine flower
Sua mae tancarera	Sua mãe é uma Chinesa pescadora	Her mother is a Chinese fisherwoman
Seu pai canarim	Seu pai é um Indiano Português	Her father is a Portuguese Indian

Busuu.com (2011)

We will discuss three main types of data collection: the questionnaire approach, the use of other types of structured elicitation methods, and the participant observer approach. Finally, we will consider sampling: how many people should participate in a study?

As we saw in Chapter 3, a community will often be suspicious of a researcher who does not attempt to learn the language. One must have adequate initial ability in another language known within the community. Part of the preparation for fieldwork is reading all available materials on the target group, as well as the area and other nearby groups, and whatever has been done on the group's own language. Fieldwork will be much more effective if the language is learned fairly well during the process; this is not a short-term task. Unfortunately, most scholarly linguistic materials are not designed for learning conversational skills; but there may be materials aimed at tourists or incoming local government workers; see, for example, Bradley et al. (1991, first, second and third editions) for a brief introduction to five minority languages of mainland South East Asia and southern China.

We have not yet discussed what to call the community members who provide data. In psychology and some social sciences, they are usually called 'subjects' or 'participants'; in older linguistic sources, they are called 'informants', but the implication that they are passive rather than active in the process and the negative connotations of these terms have led to their replacement by the term 'consultant'. The main 'consultant' becomes a colleague in the analytic process, and as was suggested in Chapter 3, such people should be trained and equipped to work both within your survey and separately as they think appropriate. In publications, it is often appropriate to include the names of consultants who provided data and/or helped in its analysis as co-authors, if they wish to be named.

It may be useful to read some of the tourist or expatriate worker literature about the area where you will be working; these will answer many of your general questions about culturally appropriate behaviour in the area, although not for the small group with which you are working.

Unless you are a medical doctor, you should not be providing medical advice or medication to people in your community; you can help them to get medical advice and treatment when possible. You should be prepared; do a higher-level first aid course, take medical advice about any inoculations or medications you should have and do not assume that these will be available locally. If transport is likely to be an issue, be aware that not all countries recognise international driving licenses, and road behaviour may be quite different.

Most places in the world now have mobile phone coverage, but your smartphone is less robust than a simpler device, and cannot replace a laptop; make sure your phone is unlocked and can use a local SIM, or, even better, buy locally.

10.1 QUESTIONNAIRES

There are many questionnaires for eliciting information about endangered languages around the world in a consistent format; this may miss some local issues, may inadvertently contain culturally problematic questions, and is rather procrustean. They include the eight-question Linguistic Society of America survey (Yamamoto, 1996: 161); the Krauss questionnaire in Krauss (2000, 2007a), UNESCO (2003a) and implemented in Brenzinger (2007a) and UNESCO (2009); the UNESCO ETXEA survey (Martí et al., 2005: 284–8; Cunningham et al., 2006) and the SIL International questionnaire developed in Lewis (2008) and Lewis and Simons (2010) and implemented in recent editions of the *Ethnologue*. A very short questionnaire was implemented in the ELCat project www.endangeredlanguages.com, and a European-based questionnaire is used in EuLaViBar (European Language Vitality Barometer of the ELDIA project, www.eldia-project.org), as briefly discussed in Section 2.6; there are various others in use elsewhere, in various languages.

More specific locally appropriate questionnaires are found in Moser (1992) and Kayambazinthu (1995) which focus on domains of language use in two African settings. Suastra (1995) investigates language use in Bali; Russell (2001) looks at language shift in an East Malaysian community and Easton (2007) focuses on orthography development in Papua New Guinea. Pelkey (2011) and Yang (2010) both survey the language situation in particular language clusters in south-western China, and Thamrin (2015) is primarily concerned with attitudes to language in a community in western Indonesia (see the case study in Chapter 4). All also collected extensive other information on important cultural practices: traditional feasting in East Malaysia, clothing and dance in south-western China, or knowledge and use of speech levels in Indonesia. All of these are postgraduate theses; a thesis normally includes the questionnaire used to collect the data, often omitted in later publications.

Another kind of questionnaire is aimed at collecting data on culturally appropriate behaviour, using either open or multiple-choice answers. Questions ask people what they would do in a series of particular scenarios. This can reveal interesting and sometimes unexpected cross-cultural differences; see, for example, Bradley and Bradley (1984: 240–55).

In all societies, an interview using a questionnaire is somewhat unfamiliar and unnatural. In many traditional societies, being asked a long series of questions only happens in threatening situations involving outside authorities. Some of the concepts built into a standard or predesigned questionnaire may be unknown or culturally problematic. Ideally, a locally appropriate questionnaire should be designed with a cultural insider or someone who already has considerable familiarity with the society. The questionnaire provides a clear structure for the data; but good design is crucial for accuracy, relevance and value.

In linguistic anthropology, rapport in a fieldwork situation or for that matter between insiders has been extensively discussed; see Blommaert (2007) and related studies. Rapport is scalar; various social and other factors are relevant, producing some degree of social distance between the fieldworker and the community members. The parallel in Labovian variationist sociolinguistics and in Hymes' ethnography of communication is situational factors. Unlike previous models which accept this as inevitable in fieldwork, the Rapport model suggests that a fieldwork situation can be made more natural by shifting scale and establishing rapport. However, one must not assume or claim that one has reached complete rapport and is collecting fully natural data. There is always some degree of observer effect: the presence of an outsider affects how people behave.

The kinds of issues to discuss are outlined in earlier chapters: Chapter 4 on attitudes, Chapter 5 on language knowledge and use and Chapter 6 on other non-linguistic factors. In every questionnaire, local sociocultural norms, government rules and personal privacy must always be respected. If a questionnaire is too long or contains inappropriate questions, community members may be unwilling to complete it; this is particularly crucial in small communities where word gets around that you are asking problematic questions and/or taking a lot of time, so others may not agree to participate; see the discussion of sampling in Section 10.4. It is advisable to trial a questionnaire with a few main consultants, discuss and amend it before starting a full survey. Obviously, interviewees must be treated with respect and rewarded in an appropriate way, as discussed in Chapter 3.

Another problem in questionnaire data is that people may tell you what they think they should, or what they think you want to hear. There is also the usual sociolinguistic problem of inaccurate **self-reporting**. If you ask people whether they think their language is important, they are very likely to agree; thus, you get over-reporting of positive attitudes to their language. Conversely, if you ask older people whether younger people speak correctly, under-reporting is likely: older people usually think younger people speak badly. Questions which tend to push people towards a particular answer or **push-polling** is normally to be avoided at all costs.

In a questionnaire or interview, data from yes/no questions and **forced-choice** multiple choice questions is easy to process, but much less revealing than open-ended questions. In the next section, we discuss a number of other types of data-collection instruments, starting with some that are heavily structured and may have similar flaws.

10.2 OTHER STRUCTURED RESEARCH TOOLS

You may not wish to use all of the methods described in this section, but they can all be useful and revealing.

10.2.1 Wordlists/Phrase Lists

Most initial linguistic research starts from a wordlist. These are usually elicited in isolation through an external language, and are prone to problems. In one widely used wordlist in China, most of the entries for one language are shifted one column to the right. Even the very widely used initial 200- and later 100-word lists (including ninety-two from the 200 word list) originally devised by the linguist Morris Swadesh in the 1950s contain ambiguous items ('bark' – of a tree or of a dog?) and items unusable in some parts of the world ('snow'). The original claims about the possibility of using these lists to measure degree of genetic relationship ('lexicostatistics') and date the separation of languages ('glottochronology') are now discredited, but the lists remain in use for various purposes.

There are many longer lists devised and used in particular parts of the world, for use with languages of particular genetic families. SIL International has a list of 400 items, supplemented locally with a few additions in each part of the world. We suggest you find out what language family the language to be investigated belongs to, find a suitable list designed for that family and that linguistic area, discuss whether the list is appropriate with knowledgeable scholars and use it; a longer list also has the potential to provide enough information to start working out the phonology of the language, which is impossible with a shorter list. For example, Bradley (1979a, 1979b) devised an 866-item comparative wordlist for investigating Tibeto-Burman languages in southern China and mainland South East Asia, which is still in use with some additions in a 1,000-word version (Yang, 2010; Pelkey, 2011).

For elicitation purposes, wordlists should be grouped into semantic fields (animals, body parts, kin terms, houses, natural features, colours, motion verbs and so on) which make them mnemonically easier to collect. A long list which is alphabetical in some external language is difficult to collect; each word is a separate translation task for the consultant.

There is no similar standard list of phrases to collect; tourist phrasebooks follow a fairly strict template, with a standard list of frequently used phrases. The problem with translated phrases is that they may contain cultural bias, and the sentences may be in an unnatural translationese. A Chinese-specific list of 132 suggested sentences to elicit is found in ChiLin (1972: 278–85); there are similar lists of sentences in most parts of the world, but these are much less widely used than standard wordlists.

10.2.2 Culturally Structured Semantic Fields: Ethnotaxonomy

Humans organize things into categories; this includes many areas of human activity and the external world. Investigating and clarifying the structure of these taxonomic systems provides a good initial insight into an important area of a society, and can form a substantial research project in itself. For a general overview, see Ellen (2006).

One type of taxonomy which has long been an anthropological staple is kinship. Kinship terms and categories are best collected both by direct elicitation and discussion, by observation of actual address and reference usage, and in genealogies; the goal is a complete framework with reference and address forms for all socially relevant categories, both consanguineal and affinal. If your training in this area is not sufficient, there are classic work such as Murdock (1949) and detailed studies of a particular group in the area where you plan to work, such as Spiro (1977) on Burmese kinship. The universally relevant factors are generation, gender and marriage; relative age, birth order and other locally relevant factors are also often present. Speakers often have difficulty explaining the semantic basis for groupings or extensions of kin terms; this is better just observed where possible. Could you clearly explain why the gender of a cousin is not expressed in the kinship terminology of English, and whether this means that the gender of your cousins does not matter or is unknown to you? Other important social groupings include some which are kinship-based such as family and lineage, as discussed in Chapter 6. It is important to discuss these areas with your consultants. Naturally, some people are interested and knowledgeable; others may not be. In some societies, genealogies are universal, long and historically revealing; in others absent. There may also be taboos associated with kinship and social rules concerning relationships between people in certain kin categories. These should all form part of the discussion on kin and family structure which you have with your consultants, and you can also observe how this taxonomy is reflected in behaviour.

In preliminary work in ethnobotany and ethnozoology, the first stage is to walk around with people observing plants and animals, eliciting their names and videorecording brief accounts of what they are useful for, demonstrations of how they are prepared for use and any other cultural notes. As in kinship, some consultants are excellent at doing this, others are less interested. Sometimes males are more familiar with animals and females are more familiar with plants. Plant and animal knowledge related to traditional medicine may be private knowledge of medical specialists, and difficult to collect.

To do a formal taxonomic study, scientific identifications of the plants and animals is essential; properly prepared samples need to be collected for a botanist or zoologist to identify. A suitable set of scientifically well-documented pictorial stimulus materials from the area where the language is spoken can also be used to collect data. There are many excellent and fully illustrated local field handbooks for birds – if anything, with too much detail – and sometimes others for other local fauna and flora, although these are often less comprehensive. Note that if you assemble your own pictorial stimulus material, pay attention to keeping all pictures at the same scale – not gigantic ants and tiny elephants. As for kinship, it is also important to observe everyday usage of plants and animals from these taxonomies.

The taxonomy of colour has been a well-researched topic since the classic work of Berlin and Kay (1969). Standard colour chips can be used to collect data, but this is somewhat abstract. Objects have a colour: some types of objects have special colour terms or use terms in special ways (such as for human hair in English); some colour terms are derived from the names of objects which have that colour. There is usually a taxonomy with a small set of basic terms; it is important to observe how the terms are used and extended in society (e.g., 'red' > angry or politically left-wing) and how new compound and other terms are created.

There are many other interesting taxonomies: other perceptual mechanisms such as smell or taste and many other areas of culture such as disease, weather and religion. If you find an interesting taxonomy, and your consultants want to talk about it, this is worth pursuing.

10.2.3 Narrative and Conversation

Both extended narrative (mainly one person talking) and conversation (several people talking together) should be recorded, transcribed and used as the primary data about the language – not isolated words or sentences that you elicit. These also have embedded cultural information. Conversation can be difficult to transcribe; you should do so soon afterwards with the help of a consultant.

Some widely used tools for collecting narratives are series of pictures – for example, the frog story (a pet frog gets lost, a boy and his dog look for it; Berman & Slobin [1994] based on Mayer [1969]) and the pear story (boys steal pears from an orchard; Chafe [1980]; www.pearstories.org). These stories are culturally bound and may not work equally well in all societies. Similar structured pictorial representations for collecting information about representation of space and time also exist; see http://fieldmanuals.mpi.nl.

Other narratives will include those which your consultants want to tell you and want preserved for their community:

1) individual life stories – biography and family history
2) procedural narrative – explaining how to do things

3) oral history – often there are previously recorded materials available

4) oral literature – songs, stories, proverbs and riddles, and so on

If the language is written, some of these genres may already exist in a handwritten form or even in print.

Procedural narrative is particularly important for cultural activities which are in the process of disappearing; videorecord a person who knows how to make a basket in the traditional way, a person who is particularly good at making animal traps or a person who can explain traditional religious practices.

Conversation happens all the time; often in poor recording conditions. Special events like religious activities, community events and so on are particularly noisy and hard to record, but may be valuable for their content, provided permission to record is given. It is always good to record more conversation than one intends to use, so that the best-recorded and more interesting conversations can be used. One should also carry a notebook at all times to make additional observations, which can later be discussed with a recorder going.

10.2.4 Recorded Stimulus Tools

One type of recorded stimulus is known in sociolinguistics as a Subjective Reaction Test: a set of selected passages with speakers reflecting differing formality, linguistic conservatism, fluency or accent. Listeners rate the speaker of each passage on a number of scales, some relating to status (intelligence, social status, etc.) and some relating to solidarity (friendliness, honesty, etc.). Each rating is on a five-point Likert scale. Naturally, this kind of study needs to be carefully devised; it requires carefully selected recorded passages from speakers unfamiliar to the listeners illustrating linguistic features discussed in Chapter 7. This is an excellent indirect way to investigate judgements about attitudes and change within an endangered language. In a very small community, such a study may not be possible, as the speakers will be recognisable. For more discussion of such studies, see Labov (1966) who invented them and used them in a socially stratified community; Lambert and Tucker (1969) who applied them in bilingual communities, where it is known as a matched guise test; and Giles and Powesland (1975) who developed and extended their use in social psychology of language. Such indirect measures are typically more accurate than self-reporting or from structured questionnaires such as the Multigroup Ethnic Identity Measure (Phinney, 1992) or the Subjective Vitality Questionnaire (Johnson et al., 1983), although those may be useful if adapted appropriately.

Another important procedure for use in language endangerment situations, as well as elsewhere, is intelligibility testing. The standard method, called a Recorded Text Test, plays a number of short narratives recorded in carefully chosen locations to ten listeners in each of these and other locations, and asks ten questions about the content of the passages. Provided that there is no prior familiarity with speech differences between the stimulus locations and the locations tested, this provides a matrix of mean intelligibility ranging down from 100 per cent (at the source location) for each passage; high **standard deviation** in the rates of intelligibility may indicate contact. Some sources describing this process are Casad (1974, 1991), Blair (1990) and O'Leary (1994). Some examples of implementation include Yang (2009) and Pelkey (2011).

10.2.5 Interview and Group Discussion

Questionnaires can give stilted and limited data. So do interviews which stick closely to a list of questions; but freely flowing interviews in which people talk mainly about what they choose can be more natural. Interviewing people in groups of two or three friends can also be a good strategy; then they may have a normal conversation. Once the essential information required in the interview is collected, the good interviewer fades into the background.

Political scientists and sociologists use focus group discussion, in which a selected diverse group of different ages, genders and backgrounds is asked to talk about something; they may be given some questions to discuss, some issues to resolve or just a general topic. This will provide useful information about people's attitudes and views and a great deal of conversational data. Unlike family and public conversation, recording conditions can be much better in interview and focus group data.

10.2.6 Mapping and Dialectology

There are various standard language atlases which locate and classify the languages of the world, both endangered and safe. These may be a useful first step in identifying a target language for study and the surrounding languages with which it is in contact. For the entire world, see Asher and Moseley (2007). Concerning the languages of the Pacific and South East Asia, see Wurm and Hattori (1981/1983). For China, see Wurm et al. (1987/1991), and on languages of wider communication see Wurm et al. (1996). Other local and regional atlases also provide detailed coverage elsewhere. Endangered languages spoken by small communities are often absent from such large-scale works; see also the atlases which focus on endangered languages: Wurm (1996, 2001), Moseley (2007) and UNESCO (2009).

Part of a comprehensive study of a language community is locating all the speakers of a language; speakers in one community will usually know about other nearby communities, and place names should also be collected. Often the same place will have different names in different languages; meanings of place names should also be collected. Local etymologies of these place names may also be revealing; for example, where these names reflect former populations speaking other languages, as in much of the north-eastern United States.

Perceptual dialectology was developed by Dennis R. Preston (Preston, 1999, 2011; Preston & Long, 2002). Community members are asked to draw lines on a map to indicate dialect differences, judge how different the dialects are on a scale and make various social evaluations of the dialects. Recorded dialect samples can be played to see how well they can be located on a map; interviews also discuss dialect differences. This technique provides valuable information and examples about sociolinguistic stereotypes.

It is not necessary to attempt every type of study listed in Section 10.2; these are some possibilities. Your research interests and the interests of members of the community may suggest which can be the most productive.

10.3 PARTICIPANT OBSERVATION

This is the traditional anthropological approach: live in a community for extended periods of time, become embedded in the community, learn its language and observe, participate in and document its activities across the full year cycle and any longer cycles if possible. For example, in February 2014, one of the authors participated for the second time in a traditional Nisu festival held in one village in China once every twelve years. Such longer cycles are beyond the scope of a normal student project, but can at least be discussed with community members if not observed. Shorter stints of participant observer fieldwork are also possible; then you need to choose the right times of year to see culturally significant activities.

There are many fieldwork manuals for anthropology and linguistics that go into more detail on methodology. Some recent ones are Bowern (2008), Chelliah and de Reuse (2011), Robben and Sluka (2012), Schilling (2013), and Podesva and Sharma (2013). One particularly reflective and interesting collection about applying this methodology with the Nosu in China is Bamo et al. (2007), which shows both the outsider perspective of the foreign anthropologist and the insider perspective of the in-group co-worker in revealing detail; this includes some comments on how the insiders initially perceived the outsider somewhat negatively, and how their research co-operation later deepened.

10.4 SAMPLING

In a community whose language is endangered, one must be particularly careful about the choice of speakers. There are communities with one remaining older fluent speaker, but in most cases there will be a range of speakers of different ages. Older speakers often disparage the knowledge and speech of younger speakers and suggest that it is not worth working with them, but one must determine the range of semispeaker and passive ability.

If the community is small, it may be possible to include everyone; in a larger group, one should start with a complete survey of one village, then collect data elsewhere. In a rolling survey, people from the first village are asked where else the language is spoken, and the chain is followed outwards. In some cases, these chains of contact between villages are regularly reinforced by marriage, which may be at a long distance. For example, we recently visited the isolated Lisu village Longtanqing in Lufeng county in central Yunnan, which gets wives and sends daughters as brides to Lisu villages over 200 km to the north in Huaping county in Yunnan and Miyi county in Sichuan.

Community members who have moved away can usually be found starting from the village; in a city, this is difficult. Displaced speakers of endangered languages often live in urban centres far away, even overseas; the Endangered Language Alliance (www.elalliance.org) is utilizing this resource in New York City. In cities, fieldwork is much more convenient, but many kinds of data are impossible to collect. Sometimes languages persist only among such displaced speakers (Evans, 2001; van Engelenhoven, 2002).

Recruiting of consultants may need to be done in consultation with local authorities, who may also need to agree to terms of work and payment; see also Chapter 3. You will find that different people have different skills; some may be very helpful in transcribing and explaining things, others may be gifted for giving examples and analysis in phonology, syntax or semantics, while others will be fluent and knowledgeable but unable to explain or discuss things. Ideally, you need multiple people to work with, and should not commit yourself to one or two consultants at an early stage.

Your main consultants can assist you in recruiting people for other work; they should be chosen for language ability and to give a representative sample of gender, age and so on. Outsiders who have lived in a community for a long time, although they may not be suitable as sources of primary linguistic data, will have useful insights about cultural and linguistic differences between the in-group and the majority. When you travel, you should first ask whether there are kinship or other connections elsewhere. You may need to go through local authorities in each place, but personal contacts are also useful.

Sample size and structure depend on the type of work being done; for recorded stimuli (Section 10.2.4) and intelligibility testing (Section 10.2.6), the required number of participants is larger, but in all cases both genders and a range of ages should be represented. Where more than one location is being studied, the sample should include people of both genders and a range of ages and language abilities from each place.

10.5 EQUIPMENT

You will need lots of field notebooks and pens/pencils, sturdy but high-quality audio, video and still camera and laptop, and the means to keep them clean, dry and working if the community has no electricity. You will also need a base outside the community, to store archived notebooks, audio, video and still materials; perhaps also a local colleague or organization outside the community to store further backups.

Some funding bodies have specific requirements about equipment; most suggest you should use a good external microphone, not the built-in microphone of your laptop or recorder. A still camera or tablet with a built-in global positioning system is useful for exact locations of people, villages, plants and whatever else you photograph.

Suggestions about specific equipment will date very quickly; in the last few decades, several audio recording standards and data storage device types have come and gone. You will find some communities still using cassette tapes; these can be digitized and archived, but the sound quality may be low. If the information on a cassette is unique or useful and acoustic analysis is not a priority, this is fine; you may wish to bring a cassette digitizer which can also play cassettes if necessary. Be sure that your laptop can cope with various CD formats, such as VCD, in case the community has materials that you want to copy. If possible, don't rely on just one audio, video or still camera device, always read the instruction manuals, scan them and keep the scans accessible.

Concerning software, again specific recommendations will date quickly; see Chapter 11 for some current suggestions about transcription software, and follow the guidelines of your own institution and any body to whom you should give copies – the local community, a national research body, a local and/or your own university, a funding body or some archive.

There are websites with detailed suggestions about specific equipment and software. Some currently maintained resources are www .emeld.org/school/toolroom/index.html.

Most people love to hear and see themselves and others; you will need small external speakers which run from your audio recorder or laptop, and video recorder and camera with large inbuilt screens. Edited copies of audio and video materials can be provided to your consultants on whatever media your community uses. This is a good way to give back to the community, unless there are any local constraints.

10.6 CONCLUSION

Fieldwork is not for everyone; it is not just a quick and cheerful excursion to the exotic other. If you cannot cope, get help – in the community, from local colleagues, medical help or other authorities. Field security, for you personally and for your equipment, is an issue in some communities, particularly for lone female researchers. Take local advice about this, and don't put yourself at risk. If this means going accompanied, do so; listen to any local advice.

In some cases, displaced communities can be studied in urban settings; this is not exotic, but can be nearly as effective for collecting some kinds of linguistic and other data.

Fieldwork is a great experience, but don't feel that you are a failure if it does not work for you. Even if you cannot do extended participant observer research, you can probably collect enough data with structured methods discussed in Sections 10.1 and 10.2 to do something valuable for that language and community. It is really life-affirming to become part of a community, even if just for a while, to do something for them, and to bring back extensive information ensuring that knowledge about an endangered language and its cultural context is preserved – ideally not just in academic publications and archives, but also in the community.

CASE STUDY: PATUÁ

Patuá, the Portuguese-based creole of the former Portuguese colony of Macao, returned to China in 1999, is a critically endangered creole. First colonized in 1557 as a new town on coastal islands, Macao was mainly settled from other Portuguese Asian outposts, including various ports on the west coast of India, Goa as well as Ceylon/Sri Lanka, and especially from the beginning of 1641 from Malacca in what is now Malaysia, and in 1667 from Macassar in what is now eastern Indonesia, as well as slaves from Portuguese African colonies. After the Dutch conquest of Malacca in 1641 and Macassar in 1667 there was some further flow to Macao. The lexical input to the creole was primarily Portuguese, with a substantial Malay element from Malacca and later Macassar, and to a lesser extent Dravidian and Indo-Aryan from southern South Asia. The preexisting Kristang creole of Malacca, settled by the Portuguese from 1511, was probably brought to Macao in 1557, with subsequent decreolization during continuous contact with standard Portuguese. During over 450 years in a Cantonese-speaking Chinese environment, surrounded by a 90 per cent or greater Cantonese-speaking majority for nearly four centuries, Patuá also acquired a lot of Cantonese lexicon. There was ongoing literacy in standard Portuguese as used by administrators, some priests and other metropolitan Portuguese inhabitants and especially through public education from the early twentieth century, and substantial knowledge of spoken Portuguese. There has long been bilingualism in Cantonese as spoken by the vast majority of the population, but Patuá continued to be a local diglossic Low and now serves as a symbol of local identity, although it is critically endangered as a first language. Since the mid-nineteenth century, knowledge of English also became widespread in the community, especially among those who moved to Hong Kong and other ports on the coast of China or worked with British companies in Macao.

One key feature in the continuing survival of the community and its language is that they are Catholic, and traditionally married within the Catholic community; initially, many spouses were brought from other Portuguese outposts, notably Malacca. Over the last century, this preference for in-group marriage has greatly decreased, and there is more intermarriage with Cantonese speakers (de Pina-Cabral, 2002).

The language goes by various names: *Patuá* 'dialect' is the most usual term; the adjective for this is *Maquista*, also spelled Makista, which is also used as a term for the language. It is also called *Lingu Nhônha* or *Lingu Nhom* 'language of young women/young men'; *Papiâ Cristiâm di Macau* 'Christian speech of Macao'; *Papiaçâm* 'speech'; *Macaense*

'Macanese' and more emotive terms such as *Maquista chapado* 'pure Maquista', *doci Papiâçâm* 'sweet speech', *doci Papiâçâm di Macau* 'sweet speech of Macao' and *doci lingu di Macau* 'sweet language of Macao'. Some English-language sources call it Maccanese, Macanese or Macao Creole Portuguese. The language is well-documented, with two dictionaries (Senna Fernandes & Baxter, 2001, 2004) and various other studies such as Baxter (2009), Pinharanda-Nunes (2011, 2012a, 2012b, 2014) and others. Kristang, the somewhat less endangered Portuguese creole of Malacca from which Patuá is derived, is also well-documented, with a grammar (Baxter, 1988) and a dictionary (Baxter & de Silva, 2004).

After 1841, there was substantial migration of Patuá speakers to Hong Kong and other treaty ports in China, and from the midtwentieth century movement to the United States, Canada and Australia. Prior to Macao's return to China in December 1999, many of the remaining Patuá-speaking community moved to Portugal where they are gradually integrating into the general Portuguese-speaking community. A residual group of about 10,000 ethnic Macanese stayed in Macao, with perhaps as many as 50,000 elsewhere in the world. Local sources claim about fifty fluent speakers in Macao, mainly females over fifty, as well as semispeakers and passive understanders. The lawyer Miguel Senna Fernandes, who is in his fifties, is a leader in efforts to energize and revitalize the language. Patuá also competes with English, which has been the trade language of China coastal trade since the 1840s and has become a diglossic High in Macao, as well as the language of contact with the very large migrant population in Englishspeaking countries. After 1950, and especially since 1999, Mandarin as the national language of China has also become increasingly important in the community; most Macanese people of Portuguese descent now use Cantonese or English for most purposes, Mandarin occasionally if they know any, and Patuá only rarely if at all, mainly in the home and in-group settings. Older people with Portuguese education also know and use standard Portuguese, but this is less widespread among younger people.

In his extensive study of sociopolitical change in Macao, the anthropologist de Pina-Cabral (2002: 32–9) suggests that the main shift away from spoken Patuá started in the mid-nineteenth century, when Macao became a normal Portuguese colony rather than just a trading post under Chinese sufferance, more of the local Macanese population started to go to Portuguese schools, and Portuguese identity became more clearly advantageous in the context of European dominance in trade with China after the Opium Wars. Language shift away from Patuá to Portuguese and decreolization of Patuá would have been at their most rapid during the century after 1850, at the same time as knowledge of English was spreading.

Although the main tourist attraction is casinos, Maquista food and culture are also a drawcard for the huge numbers of Chinese visitors coming to Macao. The local Portuguese-language and English-language print and broadcast media give extensive coverage to Patuá language and Maquista culture. The local university has a Department of Portuguese with several staff and research students who do excellent work on Patuá. Public written display (street signs, shop signs, restaurant menus) is in standard Portuguese, which was always used as the diglossic written and formal spoken High, was the official language up to 1999, remains one of three official languages of the Macao Special Administrative region of China and has long been taught in schools; it is only relatively recently that Patuá has been written at all.

Written Patuá literature existed since the late nineteenth century, but has increased since 1950; much of it is nostalgic accounts of traditional life in Macao. There were various short stories and novels in standard Portuguese with short dialogues and vocabulary in Patuá written by Henrique de Senna Fernandes, the late father of Miguel Senna Fernandes, from 1950; his two novels of 1986 and 1992 were also made into films (Brookshaw, 2011a). A volume of poetry in Patuá, *Poema na lingu Maquista* by the late Jose dos Santos Ferreira, was published in 1992 (dos Santos Ferreira, 1996); he also wrote many songs and stories in Patuá. For nearly twenty years, there have been annual plays in Patuá, written and produced by Miguel Senna Fernandes, as part of an annual Maquista festival. In recent years, these plays also include short film segments in Patuá.

Another important area of folkloristic activity is music. Since 1935, the band Tuna Macaense has been performing songs in Patuá. All current core band members are in their fifties or older, but their vocalists and audience include many younger community members. In addition to original material in Patuá, they also perform adaptations of modern mainstream Portuguese styles such as fado, as well as material with younger vocalists in Patuá or other languages; see, for example, *Macau Terra Minha* 'Macao my land' www.youtube.com/watch?v=05HySd6-KhA for a song with a Portuguese title, sung in Mandarin, with subtitles in traditional Chinese characters (not simplified characters now used in China). It is introduced by the Macanese band leader in Cantonese; the young singer briefly speaks English before and after the song. In the video of the song *Macau sâm assi – doci papiaçâm di Macau* 'This is Macau, sweet speech of Macao' by José dos Santos Ferreira, www.youtube.com/watch?v=JmPYVbKWF70, there is dialogue in Patuá between two older ladies in a Maquista restaurant about the annual Maquista play, with traditional Chinese, standard Portuguese and English subtitles, followed by a young vocalist who sings in Patuá with Patuá, traditional Chinese, Portuguese and English subtitles, with beautiful vision of the traditional Maquista attractions of Macao. Both these songs reflect the positive attitude of the community about their identity, which has been facilitated by the departure of the Portuguese government with its constant reinforcement of standard Portuguese as a diglossic High.

There are various community websites: the Macao Association, established in 1996, www.admac.org; a private genealogical website run by Henrique d'Assumpção, www.macanesefamilies.com, which is aimed at documenting and preserving family links within the community, including migrants. Senna Fernandes and Baxter (2001: 213–30) give a list of widespread personal names; there is a strong tendency for Macanese people to have Portuguese baptismal given names and a variety of Portuguese surnames, as well as a Chinese name among those who are still in Macao. A cultural history website Projecto Memoria Macaense maintained by Rogério P. D. Luz, http://rpdluz.tripod.com/projectomemoriamacaense/index.html, includes a large section on Maquista food, as do some of the literary works about life in Macao (Brookshaw, 2011b).

All the following linguistic examples for Patuá are drawn from Baxter (2009) or Senna Fernandes and Baxter (2001). In some cases, Patuá is more conservative than standard Portuguese, as in the pronunciation of *ch*, as in *tacho* 'frying pan', Patuá 'frying pan; also name of a typical Maquista dish'; here modern Portuguese uses /ʃ/ as in English 'sh' in 'ship', but Patuá still has /tʃ/ as in English 'ch' in 'church'. In other cases, both have innovated, as in the vowel sound of *ei* as in *leite* 'milk', originally /ei/ as in English 'bait', but Patuá /e/ as in 'bet', modern Portuguese /ai/ as in 'bite'. Patuá also simplifies; for example, by omitting *r* and *l* at the end of words as in 'to speak', Portuguese *falar*, Patuá *fala* and before or after another consonant as in 'thank you', Portuguese *obrigado*, Patuá *obigado*, or Portuguese *soldado*, Patuá *sodado* 'soldier'. Patuá has a final velar nasal /ŋ/ (like English 'ng' in 'sing') where final -*m* is written, but Portuguese now has nasalized vowels as in 'good' *bom*, pronounced as /boŋ/ in Patuá and /bõ/ in Portuguese. Most Portuguese *lh* as in *filho* 'son' are simplified to Patuá *l*. Patuá shares these and other sound characteristics with Kristang, the creole Portuguese of Malacca.

Despite centuries of contact and now-universal bilingualism, Patuá borrowings eliminate the tones. However, recent Cantonese loans do introduce some additional sounds, such as initial /h/ which is present in written Portuguese and Patuá, but not pronounced. On the other hand, although all the input languages other than Portuguese distinguish 'm', 'n' and 'ng' at the end of a word, Patuá, like Portuguese, usually does not, except in some recent Cantonese and English loans.

In its grammar, Patuá has many differences from Portuguese; for example, the frequent omission of the articles *o/a/os/as* (like English 'the') and *um/uma* 'a/an', frequent absence of marking of plural by an -*s* multiple times (on the article, on a possessive, on a noun and on an adjective), absence of verb endings marking the number and person of the subject, absence of the verb 'be'. Nouns are sometimes made plural by repetition as in Malay: Portuguese *filhos*, Patuá *filo-filo* 'sons'. All such characteristics are variable, due to centuries of decreolization in contact with standard Portuguese. Examples of most of these grammatical features can be seen in the poem at the beginning of this chapter.

The most salient differences are in vocabulary, which, as noted earlier, comes in part from Malay as well as from Konkani (the Indo-Aryan language of Goa), Tamil (the Dravidian language of south-eastern India and northern Ceylon/Sri Lanka), other languages of southern South Asia, especially from Cantonese, and most recently from English. Senna Fernandes and Baxter (2001: 43–207) give many examples, with etymologies. For example, Malay *gondong* gives Patuá *gondôm* 'bubble'; from Tamil *nellu*, Patuá has *nele* 'rice with crust'; from Cantonese *ham^4 sap^1 lou^2*, Patuá *hám-sâp-lou* 'lascivious'; and from English 'honeydew (melon)', Patuá *anidiu*. Among the few words from Konkani are *ladú* 'type of Maquista dessert'. There are also many Patuá words without clear etymologies, like *chacha* 'grandmother, elderly woman'. Loanwords are usually completely integrated and often have Portuguese/Patuá suffixes, as in *pacfanista* from Cantonese *pak^9 fan^2* 'white powder/heroin' plus the Patuá/Portuguese suffix -*ista* together meaning 'heroin addict'. Other combinations using resources of more than one language also occur: Malay stem *cucok* 'trouble' plus the English suffix '-maker' as in Patuá *chuchumeka* 'troublemaker'. In many cases, the Patuá words of Portuguese origin have different or additional meanings, like Portuguese *ver* 'see', Patuá *ve* 'see' and also 'look, appear to be'; *tacho* is another example, as seen earlier.

Despite its current critically endangered status, of which the community is very well aware, Patuá serves as an important symbol of local identity and many people are involved in efforts to document and revitalize it, and to use it in additional literary and other public domains.

DISCUSSION QUESTIONS

You find an excellent consultant who has extensive plant knowledge, but you have no botanical training and little knowledge of plants. What should you do?

There has been extensive prior anthropological research in the field situation which you plan to study, but in the field you find that much of the published data appears to be incorrect, and community members strongly deny that the society ever was the way the earlier anthropologist claimed. How should you disseminate these findings?

For whatever reason, you have a restricted time in the field; how can you overcome this problem? Should you attempt to do a small amount of each type of data collection discussed in this chapter, or concentrate on one or a few methods?

SUGGESTIONS FOR FURTHER READING

Blair (1990) introduces a number of the techniques discussed in Section 10.2. Preston (2011) summarizes perceptual dialectology and related techniques discussed in Section 10.2.6.

11 Conclusion

TOOVLÁŠ UPIS OLMOOŠ	A FORMER ACQUAINTANCE
lah ovddii náál.	Indeed, you are like before.
Jieh tun lah ennuvgin muttum	You haven't changed so much
kyevtlov ivveest.	in about twenty years.
Mut lii-uv tuts	But have you gone through
kielâ muttum?	a language change?
Mon kielânsun	In what language
tuu kolgâččij tiervâttid?	should I greet you?

Matti Morottaja (1983) in Aanaar Saami, translated by
Olthuis et al. (2013: v)

Working with a group to maintain their language can be mutually beneficial, with positive community and scholarly outcomes. We have seen in Chapter 3 how to behave in an ethical way in the community, in Chapter 4, how community attitudes and identity function and change, in Chapter 5, how language learning and use is crucial, in Chapter 6, some of the non-linguistic factors which may be important, in Chapter 7, some likely linguistic outcomes of the process, in Chapter 8, various policy and planning settings and activities to reinforce a language, in Chapter 9, strategies which have worked in language reclamation efforts and, in Chapter 10, techniques for carrying out socially grounded scholarly research.

From the community perspective, the underlying aim for an endangered language is resilience for the group's language and culture; this requires the implementation of resilience linguistics techniques, as outlined in Bradley (2010) and discussed in Chapter 4. Languages, like ecosystems, go through four main stages: growth, conservation, release and reorganization; the factors that work together in change and their outcomes are the topic of this book. Once the threshold into release is crossed and a language becomes endangered, a different state may evolve, as we are now seeing in thousands of languages. We need to strive for adaptive responses that promote reorganization to new stable states with an ongoing role for traditional languages and cultures within their communities.

The goal is to maintain what the group wants and is able. Where it is difficult to maintain ongoing language and culture transmission, we should use new reclamation strategies together with the community. We should also develop resources in case a later generation wishes to reclaim their language and culture. These are also our ethical and scholarly obligations. Otherwise, the knowledge embedded in the endangered language and its culture risks being lost forever.

11.1 WHAT CAN A LINGUIST DO ABOUT LANGUAGE ENDANGERMENT?

One crucial element in language persistence is in-group attitudes and identity (Chapter 4). By doing research, we may help to change the balance, giving the language more prestige as well as more resources; but the community's own attitudes are crucial. As Chapter 3 outlines, we should involve and train local people in research skills and help them to become advocates for their language and provide a focus for positive identity, positive attitude change and long-term community development. In-group researchers may also need relevant advanced training to make their work successful.

Chapter 8 suggests ways to facilitate the development of an appropriate orthography and provide materials for local use such as dictionaries and learning materials. We should document the sociolinguistic context in terms of language attitudes, language knowledge and use, processes of linguistic change and the external setting, as discussed in Chapters 4–7, using the methodologies outlined in Chapter 10, based on the principles set out in Chapter 3.

It is extremely important for an outside researcher not to be proprietorial about the language; the community owns it and its orthography, lexicon and texts, and should be in control. In-group researchers have an especially difficult path to tread. They have kin and other networks to assist their initial access and make their work more authoritative, and can permanently improve the prospects for the language, but there may be pitfalls, as Perley (2011) found in his Maliseet community. Other researchers, including those with skills in other discipline areas, should be sought out, welcomed and assisted. In-group researchers may need mentoring and support; local and national experts should also be involved as much as possible.

Outsider researchers may sometimes encounter resentment and resistance from within the group. It is also very likely that there will be negative attitudes, from within and from the local majority, and negative policies, as shown in Chapter 4 and 8; otherwise, why would the language be endangered? Such issues need sensitive handling through explicit consultation and feedback and through more general consciousness raising.

Local and national majority groups should be better informed about their minorities; this is a public relations exercise where sympathetic journalists, local NGOs and government officials can be helpful. Governments and other bureaucracies may be more willing to listen to a high-prestige outsider than a low-prestige local minority group member. As an outsider, you may be an effective advocate for all kinds of local needs and desires, but not without bringing people along with you; literally as well as metaphorically.

When the time is ripe for reclamation of a language, there are various strategies presented in Chapter 9 which may be useful. It is crucial not to raise unrealistic expectations, which can lead to disappointment which may be detrimental for the language and the community.

11.2 DOCUMENTATION AND LANGUAGE MAINTENANCE

Documentary linguistics is a new name coined in the late 1990s for a comprehensive approach to descriptive linguistics; it refers to the preparation of a grammar, dictionary and texts for a language. These three are the Boasian trilogy, named after the Franz Boas, who published the trio for some North American indigenous languages and trained the leaders of American anthropology in the next generation to do likewise. The innovations of documentary linguistics are the digital archiving of recordings and transcriptions of texts using standard annotation software such as **ELAN**, **FLEx** and formerly Toolbox, also software for dictionaries and so on. There are also some apps for use on smartphones, such as Aikuma (Bird et al., 2014; Bird, 2018) which allows material to be recorded and transcribed using Android devices. Tools of this type are developing so rapidly that any listing provided here will be out of date almost immediately; for some others, see Hermes et al. (2016).

Good documentation is no guarantee for the survival of a language, but it makes its maintenance or reclamation possible. A solely linguistic documentation is inadequate for community purposes; it lacks both practical language learning materials and information on important cultural topics which are unfamiliar to most linguists, although they tend to be more central for anthropologists. Documentary linguistic materials are usually in inaccessible style and form, and use technology inappropriate for most communities. Only some communities have computers and web access; and none apart from our in-group co-workers know our jargon and phonetic symbols, nor are they interested in theoretical debates illuminated by data from their language and culture.

A full documentation of local knowledge includes ethnobiology, ethnobotany, ethnomedicine, ethnomusicology and all other kinds of folk knowledge, in addition to the kinds of things a linguistic and anthropological fieldworker normally observes and documents. Research on some fields of folk knowledge requires the participation of an expert in that area as part of a larger team, although a single fieldworker can make a start.

One gap in most documentation is everyday interactive conversation; archives on endangered languages contain mainly narrative texts. This is a serious issue, as it is difficult to reconstitute authentic conversational phrases and interaction strategies once a language is out of everyday use. Fortunately, nontechnical vocabulary and phrasebook materials by travellers, missionaries and local administrators may sometimes partly fill this gap, as we saw for Kaurna in Chapter 9.

Level of documentation is one of the criteria in some scales of language endangerment discussed in Chapter 2. Although it is obviously true that, from a purely linguistic perspective, a well-documented language does not require additional documentation as urgently as a completely undocumented one, being documented alone is not going to help a language to survive if the various factors identified in Chapters 4–8 are unfavourable; consider Ket (the case study in Chapter 6). Few documentary studies give sufficient attention to the sociolinguistic setting, which is the key to confronting language endangerment.

11.3 SOJOURNERS AND PARACHUTE LINGUISTS

Dorian (2001) calls a linguist who works long-term on a particular endangered language a **sojourner**; they do not do just descriptive linguistic work, but also interact with the community, developing long-term personal relations, and sometimes even living together. We have seen examples of sojourners in the case studies in several chapters: Rob Amery among the Kaurna in Chapter 9, Matthias

Brenzinger with various non-Bantu groups in Southern Africa in Chapter 3 and Nancy Dorian herself, among many others. The other end of the continuum is what we call the parachute linguist – those who drop from the sky unannounced with unfamiliar and enviable equipment, collect their data, go away and are never heard from again, and add to the community tally of troublesome and forgettable nerds (Chapter 3). Most fieldworkers fall somewhere in between: we want to help the community, we try to report back to them and give them something useful from our research, but we also have a life elsewhere.

Clearly there are major ethical problems with parachute linguistics and parachute research of any kind. Communities approached this way can derive no benefit from the research, which could not be done without them, and may understandably be unwilling to accept future fieldworkers. Research done this way is also unlikely to achieve adequate understanding of the society and its language.

11.4 SOME AVAILABLE RESOURCES

In-group members already have their field site; but, for most researchers, there are various practical factors to consider: field access, language of communication, environment and so on; Dixon (2010: 309–30) provides a useful summary. Permission for extended fieldwork can be difficult in many countries; in developed countries, indigenous groups may themselves control access and reject outsiders because of prior bad experiences.

Some communities invite and even employ outsiders to do language description, materials preparation, language maintenance and cultural documentation work. This facilitates field access, but may constrain the work done and restrict its dissemination; it may also be affected by changes in community leadership, desires or outside funding, as when all school-based bilingual education programmes for Aboriginal languages in the Northern Territory in Australia were suddenly shut down by the government in 2008 (Simpson et al., 2009).

There are various places where pre-field training is provided, some fully or partly focused on endangered language fieldwork such as the 3LSS (London/Leiden/Lyons Summer School) in Europe, the InField/CoLang series in the United States, the Linguistic Society of America Summer Institutes and so on. Others provide locally appropriate training, particularly to in-group members, such as the AILDI (American Indigenous Languages Development Institute) with annual training courses in North America since 1978, RNLD (Research Network for Linguistic Diversity) in Australia and many others.

There are two alternative approaches which do not require extended fieldwork. One is for community members to receive advanced training and do the documentation; this has the major advantage that field access and long-term community benefit are assured. The other is based on the fact that many endangered languages are also spoken in displaced locations around the world. Many of these are in urban centres, and research can start there once the speakers are found.

There are various conferences, such as the Foundation for Endangered Languages, yearly since 1997, the Sociolinguistics of Language Endangerment, every two years since 2009, and many others, where current thinking, methodology and results can be observed. Listservs such as www.listserv.linguistlist.org/mailman/listinfo/endangered-languages-l provide a forum for discussion of current issues and dissemination of information about training workshops, conferences and new publications. Online sources attempting to list all the world's endangered languages and rate their degree of endangerment, already discussed in Chapters 2 and 9, include the UNESCO website www.unesco.org/languages-atlas/ and the *Ethnologue*, www.ethnologue.com. Some of the larger digital archives of material in endangered languages are ELAR (Endangered Languages Archive), www.soas.ac.uk/elar/, DoBeS (Dokumetation bedrohter Sprachen [documentation of endangered languages]), www.mpi.nl/DOBES/archive_info/, Pangloss [languages and civilizations with oral tradition]), lacito.vjf.cnrs.fr, and PARADISEC (Pacific and Regional Archive for Digital Sources), www.paradisec.org.au; these are constantly expanding.

Some of the main international funding sources for endangered language work are the Endangered Languages Documentation Program or ELDP, www.endangeredlanguagefund.org, and, for smaller projects, the Foundation for Endangered Languages, www.ogmios.org/grants/index.htm, and the Endangered Language Fund, www.endangeredlanguagefund.org/language_legacies.php. Many of the major national granting bodies also have designated schemes.

The urgent need to document endangered languages, and where possible assist communities to reclaim them, is the major challenge facing linguistics and linguistic anthropology in the twenty-first century. Working for an extended period with a community is not for everyone, but it can be extremely rewarding, both personally and academically – go and try it!

DISCUSSION QUESTIONS

What are the pros and cons of becoming a sojourner within a speech community? What are the characteristics of a good sojourner?

Is it necessary to become a speaker of the language on which one is doing research, and what are some consequences of not learning the language?

How can a fieldworker not trained in the relevant disciplines work effectively on the animals, plants, music, traditional medicine or other areas of folk knowledge? Discuss how to find and use relevant resources and people.

SUGGESTIONS FOR FURTHER READING

Dorian (2001) is an excellent introduction to the fieldwork situation in a community whose language is endangered, by a sojourner, with a frank discussion and many important insights and hints.

Gippert et al. (2006) provide a guide to the various components of a modern linguistic documentation; it is an important supplement to any standard field methods textbook.

Perley (2011) gives an insider perspective on the challenges of language revitalization at the individual and community level in an indigenous group of eastern Canada.

Glossary of Terms

affinal Relationship by marriage; spouses and in-laws. Contrast **consanguineal**.

affix Bound morpheme added to another morpheme to form a new word; an affix like 'pre-' which precedes is a **prefix**; one which follows like '-ed' is a **suffix**.

alphabetic Writing system in which letters or combinations of letters representing individual sounds are combined to write words; contrast **syllabic** and **logographic**. The most widespread alphabetic system is **Romanization**.

anaphoric Something referring back, relating to a previous occurrence, for example, 'he' in 'Yesterday I saw a tall man. He ran out into the street.'

autonym Name used by a group to refer to itself.

alveolar Sound made with the tip of the tongue on the ridge behind the upper teeth; normal for English 't' or 'd', among others.

back Vowel made with the tongue back in the mouth, like English 'u' in most dialects; as opposed to **front** and **central** vowels.

bound Not able to occur alone, like the stem '-flect' in 'reflect'.

case Function of a noun in a sentence: the subject doing the action of the verb, the (direct) object or accusative on which the verb acts, the indirect object or dative (the beneficiary of an action), the possessive or (the noun who possesses another noun), the locative (where the action takes place) and so on. So in 'Mary gives John her book', 'Mary' is the subject, 'John' is the indirect object, 'book' is the direct object and 'her' is the possessor of the book.

central Vowel made with the tongue neither forwards nor backwards in the mouth, like British English 'er' or the short first vowel in English 'about'.

classifier, numeral Extra word which must occur with a numeral, usually selected according to the semantic class of the noun – for example, Thai /ma:^{15} sa:m^{15} tua^{33}/dog three animal classifier 'three dogs'.

click Sounds like the dental click 'tsk tsk' of disapproval, or the lateral click sound made to speed up a horse, and similar sounds; used as consonants in some languages of southern Africa.

cloze Test with words removed from sentences; testees fill the gap. For example, 'The cat sat ___ the mat', correct answer 'on'.

code-switching The use of two (or more) languages alternating in one conversation, where all the participants know both languages.

cognate Historically related words with systematically similar form and meaning reflecting earlier common origin, like English 'foot' and German 'Fuss'; contrast loanwords.

communicative competence The ability to function in an appropriate way within a society; knowledge of social norms and rules for behaviour.

compound Word with two or more parts, where the meaning of the compound is not the sum of its parts; for example, a 'lighthouse' is a tower on a dangerous coast which has a rotating light on top to warn ships.

conjunction Word used to link sentences, parts of sentences or words: 'and', 'or'.

consanguineal Having a relationship by blood, descended from a common ancestor. Contrast **affinal**.

creole Contact language which has become nativized; a language containing elements from two or more languages.

deictic Word which describes the relative position of things; close, medium distance or more distant; in English, 'this', 'that'.

denativization Creation and imposition of a new artificial standard in place of existing spoken varieties.

derivational Morphological element added to change a word from one form class to another, or to make a word of one form class into a different word of the same form class. For example, English '-ness' makes nouns from adjectives: 'happy' + '-ness' > 'happiness'.

devanagari The alphabet now used to write Hindi and a number of other north Indian languages, as well as Sanskrit; contrasted with the use of a modified Persian-Arabic script to write Urdu, the national language of Pakistan.

developmental Related to incomplete acquisition of fully adult fluent speech; non-adult like characteristics of the speech of children.

diacritic Extra mark on a letter, usually to indicate a different pronunciation or sometimes a formerly different pronunciation; this includes the acute accent ´ above a letter and the grave accent ` above a letter, among others.

diglossia Use of two distinct codes in different domains, a formal and especially written High and a primarily spoken Low (adjective diglossic).

diphthong Vowel which has two parts, with the tongue moving from one place to another. English has many diphthongs, as seen in the names of the letters 'A', 'I', 'O' and 'U': 'A' is the diphthong /ei/, 'I' is the diphthong /ai/, 'O' is the diphthong /ou/ and 'U' is the diphthong /ju/. Diphthongs contrast with monophthongs, vowels where the tongue does not move.

discourse marker Short word or phrase used to link an utterance to its social and meaning context: 'well' as in 'Well, he is really clever!'.

distal Deictics which describe the positions of things that are not close; English 'that'; as opposed to nearby or proximal, 'this'.

ELAN Digital annotation software for transcribing and annotating multi-media data including audio and video, developed as part of the DoBeS project (Dokumetation bedrohter Sprachen [documentation of endangered languages]) and available from www.tla.mpi.nl/tools/tla-tools/elan.

etymology Historical origin of a word; source language of loanwords or earlier cognate forms in previous stages of the language and related languages.

exonym Name used by outsiders to refer to a group.

FLEx FieldWorks Language Explorer. Software for organizing sound files and transcriptions, replacement for Toolbox. Available here: www.sil.org/resources/software_fonts/flex.

forced-choice Question with a fixed set of answers to choose between, asking people to indicate only one.

form class Type of grammatical function which a word has: noun, verb, adverb and so on.

fricative Sound made with friction and noise in the mouth, such as English 'f', 's', 'v', 'z' and so on.

front Vowel made with the tongue forwards in the mouth, like English 'e', 'a' and so on; as opposed to **central** and **back** vowels.

glottal stop Sound made by closing the vocal cords, for example, in the middle of the English exclamation of warning 'oh-oh!'; phonetic symbol [ʔ].

homophonous Different words with exactly the same pronunciation, like the English words 'pare', 'pair' and 'pear' in most dialects.

infix Morpheme added inside another morpheme to form a new word, for example, 'fan-bloody-tastic'; cf. **affix**.

inflectional Inflections are affixes added to words or other changes to words marking meaning or grammatical differences: marking of plural with the suffix '-s', as in singular 'cat' versus plural 'cats'.

integrated Use of material from another language, adapted to use the sounds and structure of the borrowing language; phonologically integrated material uses only the phonology of the receiving language, morphologically integrated material uses only the morphology of the receiving language, syntactically integrated material uses only the syntax of the receiving language.

interdental Sound made with the tip of the tongue on or near the upper teeth, as in English 'th' sounds in 'thin' and 'this'.

interference Transfer of linguistic characteristics of the first or dominant language into the second language; for example, replacing English 'th' sounds with 's'/'z', 'f'/'v' or 't'/'d' because the learner's language lacks 'th' sounds.

IPA International Phonetic Alphabet, the standard symbols for representing sounds as used by linguists, including throughout this book.

ISO 639-3 The International Organization for Standardization inventory of the world's languages; each language has a unique three-letter code; see www.ethnologue.com. For the languages cited, these codes are in the index.

Language Nest Translation of Māori term *te Kōhanga Reo*, a preschool staffed by older fluent speakers of an endangered language where children learn background language and culture information.

lexicography Work related to words and dictionaries, including etymology.

Likert scale Scale with an odd number of points including a neutral mid-point, most often five but sometimes seven, with a range from most positive to most negative, asking people to indicate one point on the scale that represents their view about something; for example,

'How important is your mother tongue to you?'

very   fairly   neither important nor unimportant   slightly   not at all
____   ____   ____   ____   ____

lingua franca Existing language learned by others and used for intercultural communication.

logographic Writing system in which a character represents a word, like Chinese; some logographic characters are pictographic (a picture of the word they represent); contrast **syllabic** and **alphabetic**.

lone ranger Fieldworker who is alone in the field, not working in a team; from the leading cowboy character, an anonymous masked do-gooder in a popular American radio serial from 1933. Also known as lone wolf in some linguistic literature.

LWC Language of wider communication: language used for international communication across borders: English, Spanish, French and so on.

master–apprentice Training scheme in which an older fluent speaker teaches a language to a younger interested learner.

matrilineal Tracing relationships and inheritance through the mother's line. Contrast **patrilineal**.

modal Elements associated with the **verb** expressing ability, possibility, obligation, volition and so on (e.g., English: 'can', 'may' or 'must').

morpheme Minimum unit of meaning or grammatical function.

NAATI National Accreditation Authority for Translators and Interpreters, a quango in Australia (www.naati.com.au), testing and accrediting translators and interpreters between sixty languages and English.

nasal Sound made with the back end of the palate lowered and air going through the nose, like English 'm' 'n' and 'ng' in 'sing'; also vowel sounds which are nasalized, as in French *un bon vin*.

neonym New name for a group, often introduced to replace a former name that has become pejorative.

nuclear family Family comprising a mother, a father and their children.

paradigm List of all of the alternative forms of a word used in different grammatical environments; for example, 'sing', 'sings, 'sang', 'sung' or 'singing'.

passive understander Member of a community who can understand but not speak the community's traditional language.

patrilineal Tracing relationships and inheritance through the father's line. Contrast **matrilineal**.

pharyngealized   Produced with creaky voicing, made by holding the vocal cords tight.

phonation   Alternative ways of voicing, normal phonation contrasting with pharyngealized/creaky voicing or breathy voicing as often heard in the 'h' of 'aha' in English.

pidgin   Initial unstable contact language developed where speakers of different languages share no common language, but are in regular and close contact.

pinyin (拼音)   Chinese 'phonetic writing'; alphabetic system used since 1958 to represent the sounds of standard Mandarin.

possessive   The owner of something, the **noun** which possesses another **noun**; also known as genitive in traditional grammar, as in 'John's hat'.

prefix   Morpheme added before another morpheme to form a new word; cf. **affix**.

push-polling   Use of questions which impel people to give a particular answer.

reduplication   Repeating a word or part of a word.

relative clause   Clause which describes or modifies a noun: 'whom I know' in 'the man whom I know'.

renativization   Reintroduction of a language used for limited purposes, such as religion, to wider use as an everyday spoken language.

retroflex   Sound made with the tip of the tongue curled back.

revitalization   Effort to strengthen the use of an endangered language through language maintenance and other projects.

revival   Reintroduction of a language which has been out of use in a community (e.g., Cornish, Kaurna, etc.).

Romanization   Writing system using the letters of the Latin alphabet, 'a', b' and so on; see **alphabetic**.

self-reporting   What someone says that they do or think, often different from what they actually do or think.

semispeaker   Speaker able to function in a language, but with restricted ability and using forms structurally different from those of older fluent speakers.

sojourner   Linguist who becomes a part of the language community, maintaining long-term relationships with community members and helping the community in various ways.

standard deviation   A statistical measure of the amount of internal variation within data.

stem   Core part of the word carrying the main meaning.

stop   Consonant made with complete closure in the mouth, like 'p', 'b', 't', 'd', 'k' and 'g'.

suffix   Morpheme added after another morpheme to form a new word; cf. **affix**.

suppletive   Where the same **morpheme** has irregular forms, not the expected combinations. Standard English 'be' has a number of **suppletive** forms: 'am', 'are', 'is', 'was', 'were' and 'been'.

syllabic Writing system in which a symbol represents a syllable, like Cherokee and the Japanese *kana* system; contrast **logographic** and **alphabetic**.

tense When referring to **verbs**, tense is the expression of time: past tense, present tense and future tense.

tip Abrupt transmission failure: rapid breakdown of transmission of a language to children, leading to language shift within one generation.

tone Phonological contrast based on pitch of the syllable; see Mandarin Chinese *ma* 'mother' with high level tone, 'hemp' with high rising tone, 'horse' with low falling-rising tone, 'curse/abuse' with high falling tone and a yes/no question marker with neutral (usually mid-level) tone.

tone sandhi Changes in the way a tone is pronounced.

toponym Place name: village, town, area, river, mountain compass direction and so on, used to refer to a group who live there.

velar Sound made with the back of the tongue raised to the back of the palate, like English 'k', 'g' and 'ng' (phonetic symbol [ŋ]) in 'sing'.

voiced Sound made with the vocal cords vibrating, like English 'b', 'd', 'g', 'v' and 'z'.

voiceless Sound made with vocal cords open, not vibrating, like English 'p', 't', 'k', 'f' and 's'.

References

Abley, Mark, 2003. *Spoken Here: Travels among Threatened Languages*. Boston: Houghton Mifflin; London: Heinemann.

Agheyisi, Rebecca, & Joshua A. Fishman, 1970. Language attitude studies: a brief survey of methodological approaches. *Anthropological Linguistics* 12(5): 137–57.

American Anthropological Association, 2012. *Statement on Ethics: Principles of Professional Responsibility*, www.aaanet.org/profdev/ethics/, accessed 18 March 2014.

Amery, Rob, 2000. *Warrabarna Kaurna: Reclaiming an Australian Language*. Lisse: Swets and Zeitlinger.

2016. *Warraparna Kaurna! Reclaiming an Australian Language*. Adelaide: University of Adelaide Press.

2018. Revitalization of Kaurna. In Leanne Hinton, Leena Huss & Gerald Roche (eds), *The Routledge Handbook of Language Revitalization*, 330–41. New York: Routledge.

Amery, Rob, & Vincent (Jack) Kanya Buckskin, 2012. Handing on the teaching of Kaurna to Kaurna youth. *Australian Aboriginal Studies* 12(2): 31–41.

Amery, Rob, & Jane Simpson with Kaurna Warra Pintyanthi. 2013. *Kulurdu Marni Ngathaitya! Sounds Good to Me! A Kaurna Learner's Guide*. Kent Town: Wakefield Press.

Anderson, Gregory D. S., 2004. The Languages of Central Siberia: Introduction and Overview. In Edward J. Vajda (ed.) *Languages and Prehistory of Central Siberia*, 1–119. Amsterdam: John Benjamins.

2010. Perspectives on the global language extinction crisis: the Oklahoma and eastern Siberia language hotspots. *Revue Roumane de Linguistique* LV(2): 129–42.

Ansaldo, Umberto, (2017) Creole complexity in sociolinguistic perspective. *Language Sciences* 60: 26–35.

Asher, Ron E., & Christopher Moseley (eds), 2007. *Atlas of the World's Languages*, second edition, with major revision and expansion. New York: Routledge.

Australian Linguistic Society, 1990. *Statement of Ethics for Linguistic Research*, https://als.asn.au/AboutALS/Policies, accessed 20 March 2014.

Avram, Andrei A., 2010. An outline of Romanian pidgin Arabic. *Journal of Language Contact* 3: 20–38.

Bai Bibo & David Bradley (eds), 2011. *Extinction and Retention of Mother Tongues in China* (in Chinese and English). Beijing: Nationalities Press.

Bamo Ayi, Stevan Harrell & Ma Lunzi (eds), 2007. *Fieldwork Connections: The Fabric of Ethnographic Collaboration in China and America*. Seattle: University of Washington Press.

Battin, Tim, Dan Riley & Alan Avery, 2014. The ethics and politics of ethics approval. *Australian Universities Review* 56(1): 4–12.

Baur, Arthur, 1996. *Allegra Genügt Nicht! Rätoromanisch als Herausforderung für die Schweiz*. Chur: Bündnermonatsblatt/Desertina.

Baxter, Alan N., 1988. *A Grammar of Kristang (Malacca Creole Portuguese)*. Canberra: Pacific Linguistics.

2009. O Português em Macau: Contato e assimilação. In Ana M. Carvalho (ed.), *Português em Contato*, 277–312. Madrid: Iberoamericana; Frankfurt: Vervuert.

Baxter, Alan N., & Patrick de Silva, 2004. *A Dictionary of Kristang (Malacca Creole Portuguese) with an English-Kristang Finderlist*. Canberra: Pacific Linguistics.

Becquelin, Aurore Monod, Emmanuel de Vienne & Raquel Guirardello-Damian, 2008. Working Together, the Interface between Researchers and Native People: The Trumai Case. In K. David Harrison, David S. Rood & Arienne M. Dwyer (eds), *Lessons from Documented Endangered Languages*, 43–66. Amsterdam: John Benjamins.

Ben-Yehuda, Eliezer, 1908–59. *Dictionary of Ancient and New Hebrew*, seventeen volumes. Jerusalem: Academy of the Hebrew Language (in Hebrew).

Bentahila, Abdelâli, & Eirlys E. Davies, 1993. Language revival: restoration or transformation. *Journal of Multilingual and Multicultural Development* 14(5): 355–74.

Berkes, Fikret, 2008. *Sacred Ecology*, second edition. New York: Routledge.

Berlin, Brent, & Paul Kay, 1969. *Basic Color Terms: Their Universality and Evolution*. Berkeley: University of California Press.

Berman, Ruth A., 1978. *Modern Hebrew Structure*. Tel Aviv: University Publishing Projects.

Berman, Ruth A., & Dan I. Slobin, 1994. *Relating Events in Narrative: A Crosslinguistic Developmental Study*. Hillsdale, NJ: Lawrence Erlbaum.

Bhruksasri, Wanat, & John McKinnon (eds), 1983. *Highlanders of Thailand*. Kuala Lumpur: Oxford University Press.

Bird, Steven, 2017. Keeping languages strong: technology, pedagogy and design. Talk presented at La Trobe University, 28 November 2017.

2018. Designing Mobile Applications for Endangered Languages. In Kenneth L. Rehg & Lyle Campbell (eds), *Oxford Handbook of Endangered Languages*. Oxford: Oxford University Press.

Bird, Steven, Florian R. Hanke, Oliver Adams & Haejoong Lee, 2014. Aikuma: A Mobile App for Collaborative Language Documentation. *Proceedings of the Workshop on the Use of Computational Methods in the Study of Endangered Languages, Baltimore, MD: Association for Computational Linguistics.*

Birdsong, David, 2005. Interpreting Age Effects in Second Language Acquisition. In Judith F. Kroll & Annette M. B. de Groot (eds), *Handbook of Bilingualism: Psycholinguistic Approaches*, 109–27. New York: Oxford University Press.

Blair, Frank, 1990. *Survey on a Shoestring*. Summer Institute of Linguistics and University of Texas at Arlington Publications in Linguistics 96. Dallas, TX: Summer Institute of Linguistics.

Blake, Barry J., 2002. Reclaiming Languages in Aboriginal Victoria. In David Bradley & Maya Bradley (eds), *Language Endangerment and Language Maintenance*, 156–66. London: RoutledgeCurzon.

Blommaert, Jan, 2007. Sociolinguistic scales. *Intercultural Pragmatics* 4(1): 1–19.

Bowern, Claire, 2008. *Linguistic Fieldwork: A Practical Guide*. Basingstoke: Palgrave Macmillan.

Bradley, David, 1979a. *Proto-Loloish*. London: Curzon Press.

1979b. *Lahu Dialects*. Canberra: Australian National University Press.

1979c. Speech through music: the Sino-Tibetan gourd reed-organ. *Bulletin of the School of Oriental and African Studies* XLII(3): 535–40.

1983. Identity: The Persistence of Minority Groups. In Wanat Bhruksasri & John McKinnon (eds), *Highlanders of Thailand*, 46–55. Kuala Lumpur: Oxford University Press.

1988. Bisu Dialects. In Paul K. Eguchi & Tatsuo Nishida (eds), *Languages and History in East Asia: Festschrift to honour Prof Tatsuo Nishida on His 60th Birthday*, 29–59. Kyoto: Shokado.

1989a. The Disappearance of the Ugong in Thailand. In Nancy C. Dorian (ed.), *Investigating Obsolescence: Studies in Language Contraction and Death*, 33–40. Cambridge: Cambridge University Press.

1989b. Uncles and Aunts: Burmese Kinship and Gender. In Jeremy H. C. S. Davison (ed.), *Festschrift for E. J. A. Henderson*, 147–62. London: School of Oriental and African Studies.

1992a. Chinese as a Pluricentric Language. In Michael G. Clyne (ed.), *Pluricentric Languages: Differing Norms in Different Nations*, 305–24. Berlin: Mouton de Gruyter.

1992b. Tone Alternations in Ugong (Thailand). In Carol J. Compton & John F. Hartmann (eds), *Papers on Tai Languages, Linguistics and Literatures: In Honor of William J. Gedney on his 77th Birthday*, 55–64. DeKalb: Northern Illinois University Center for Southeast Asian Studies.

1994. *A Dictionary of the Northern Dialect of Lisu*. Canberra: Pacific Linguistics.

1996. Kachin. In Stephen A. Wurm, Peter Mühlhäusler & Darrell Tryon (eds), *Atlas of Languages of Intercultural Communication in the*

Pacific, Asia and the Americas, 749–51, Map 90. Berlin: Mouton de Gruyter.

2001. Language Policy for the Yi. In Stevan Harrell (ed.), *Perspectives on the Yi of Southwest China*, 195–214. Berkeley: University of California Press.

2002. Language Attitudes: The Key Factor in Language Maintenance. In David Bradley & Maya Bradley (eds), *Language Endangerment and Language Maintenance*, 1–10. London: RoutledgeCurzon.

2003a. Deictic Patterns in Lisu and Related Southeastern Tibeto-Burman Languages. In David Bradley et al. (eds), *Language Variation: Papers on Variation and Change in the Sinosphere and in the Indosphere in Honour of James A. Matisoff*, 219–36. Canberra: Pacific Linguistics.

2003b. Lisu. In Graham Thurgood & Randy J. LaPolla (eds), *Sino-Tibetan Languages*, 222–35. New York: Routledge.

(ed.), 2005. *Heritage Maintenance for Endangered Languages in Yunnan, China* (in English and Chinese). Bundoora: La Trobe University.

2006. Lisu Orthographies and Email. In Anju Saxena & Lars Borin (eds), *Lesser-Known Languages of South Asia: Status and Policies, Case Studies and Applications of Information Technology*, 125–35. Berlin: Mouton de Gruyter.

2007a. East and Southeast Asia. In Christopher Moseley (ed.), *Encyclopedia of the World's Endangered Languages*, 348–422. New York: Routledge.

2007b. Language Policy and Language Rights. In Osahito Miyaoka, Osamu Sakiyama & Michael E. Krauss (eds), *The Vanishing Languages of the Pacific Rim*, 77–90. Oxford: Oxford University Press.

2007c. What elicitation misses: dominant languages, dominant semantics. *Language Documentation and Description* 4: 136–44.

2007d. Birth-order terms in Lisu: inheritance and contact. *Anthropological Linguistics* 49(1): 54–69.

2009. Language policy for China's minorities: orthography development for the Yi. *Written Languages and Literacy* 12(2): 170–87.

2010. Language endangerment and resilience linguistics: case studies of Gong and Lisu. *Anthropological Linguistics* 52(2): 123–40.

2011a. Resilience Thinking and Language Endangerment. In Bai Bibo & David Bradley (eds), *Extinction and Retention of Mother Tongues in China*, 1–43 (in Chinese and English). Beijing: Nationalities Press.

2011b. Resilience linguistics, orthography and the Gong. *Language and Education* 25(4): 349–60.

2011c. Success and Failure in Yi Orthography Reform. In Joshua A. Fishman & Ofelia García (eds), *Handbook of Language and Ethnicity*, volume 2, 180–91. Oxford: Oxford University Press.

2017. Space in Lisu. *Himalayan Linguistics* 16(1), https://doi.org/10.5070/H916130216, accessed 18 June 2019.

Bradley, David, & Maya Bradley, 1984. *Problems of Asian Students in Australia: Language, Culture, Education*. Canberra: Australian Government Publishing Service.

1999. Standardisation of transnational minority languages: Lisu and Lahu. *Bulletin Suisse de Linguistique Appliquée* 69(1): 75–93.

(eds), 2002. *Language Endangerment and Language Maintenance*. London: RoutledgeCurzon.

Bradley, David, with Bya Beloto & David Fish, 2000. *Lisu Bride Price Song* (in Lisu). Bundoora: Linguistics, La Trobe University.

2008. *Lisu New Year Song* (in Lisu and English). Chiang Mai: Actsco Publishing.

Bradley, David, with Edward R. Hope, Maya Bradley & James Fish, 2006. *Southern Lisu Dictionary*, volume 4. STEDT Monograph Series. Berkeley, CA: Sino-Tibetan Etymological Dictionary and Thesaurus.

Bradley, David, with Paul Lewis, Nerida Jarkey & Christopher Court, 1991. *Thailand Hill Tribes Phrasebook*. Melbourne: Lonely Planet. Second edition 1997, third edition 2008.

Brenzinger, Matthias (ed.), 2007a. *Language Diversity Endangered*. Berlin: Mouton de Gruyter.

2007b. Language Endangerment throughout the World. In Matthias Brenzinger (ed.), *Language Diversity Endangered*, ix–xvii. Berlin: Mouton de Gruyter.

2013. The Twelve Modern Khoisan Languages. In Alena Witzlack-Makarevich & Martina Everett (eds), *Khoisan Languages and Linguistics*, 1–31. Cologne: Rüdiger Köppe.

2014. Classifying the Non-Bantu Click Languages. In Lungisile Ntsebeza & Chris Sanders (eds), *Papers from the Pre-Colonial Catalytic Project*, volume 1, 80–102. Cape Town: University of Cape Town.

Brookshaw, David, 2011a. Politics, patriarchy, progress and postcoloniality: the life in the fiction of Henrique de Senna Fernandes. *Review of Culture* 38: 7–19.

2011b. A cuisine of nostalgia: the role of food in Senna Fernandes's *A Trança Feiticeira*. *Review of Culture* 38: 21–7.

Brown, Susan D., Kirsten A. Unger Hu, Ashley A. Mevi, et al., 2014. The Multigroup Ethnic Identity Measure revised: measurement invariance across racial and ethnic groups. *Journal of Counseling Psychology* 61(1): 154–61.

Buren Buya'er (Xi Murong), 2013. Father's Grassland, Mother's River (song, in Chinese), www.Youtube.com/watch?v=riaP4QhvYi4, accessed 21 June 2013.

Burke Museum of Natural History and Culture, 2016. *Pacific Voices Exhibit*. Seattle, WA: University of Washington.

Busuu.com, 2011. Number 87: Patuá, the sweet language of Macao, http://blog.busuu.com/patua-the-sweet-language-of-macau/, accessed 28 March 2014.

Buszard-Welcher, Laura, 2001. Can the Web Help Save My Language? In Leanne Hinton & Ken Hale (eds), *The Green Book of Language Revitalization in Practice*, 331–45. Cambridge, MA: Academic Press.

Cahill, Michael, & Keren D. Rice (eds), 2014. *Developing Orthographies for Unwritten Languages*. Dallas, TX: SIL International.

Casad, Eugene H., 1974. *Dialect Intelligibility Testing*. Norman, OK: Summer Institute of Linguistics and University of Oklahoma.

1991. State of the Art: Dialect Survey 15 Year Later. In Gloria E. Kindell (ed.), *Proceedings of the SIL International Language Assessment Conference, Horsleys Green, 23–31 May 1989*, 143–53. Dallas, TX: Summer Institute of Linguistics.

Castrén, Mathias Alexander, 1858. *Versuch einer Jennisei-Ostjakischen und Kottischen Spachlehre*. St Petersburg: Kaiserliche Akademie des Wissenschaften.

Chafe, Wallace, 1980. *The Pear Stories: Cognitive, Cultural and Linguistic Aspects of Narrative Production*. Norwood, NJ: Ablex.

Chagnon, Napoleon A., 2013. *Noble Savages: My Life among Two Dangerous Tribes – The Yanomamö and the Anthropologists*. New York: Simon and Schuster.

Chamberlin, J. Edward, & Levi Namaseb, 2001. Stories and Songs across Cultures: Perspective from Africa and the Americas. In Phyllis Franklin (ed.), *Modern Languages Association of America: Profession 2001*, 24–38. New York: Modern Languages Association of America.

Chelliah, Shobhana L., & Willem de Reuse, 2011. *Handbook of Descriptive Linguistic Fieldwork*. New York: Springer.

ChiLin, 1972. *Handbook of Chinese Dialect Vocabulary* (in English and Chinese). Princeton, NJ: Princeton University Chinese Linguistics Project.

Clyne, Michael G., 1967. *Transference and Triggering: Observations on the Language Assimilation of Postwar German-Speaking Migrants in Australia*. The Hague: Martinus Nijhoff.

Collette, Vincent, 2017. Nakhota linguistic assimilation. *Anthropological Linguistics* 59(2): 117–62.

Collins, Chris, & Levi Namaseb, 2011. *A Grammatical Sketch of Nǀuuki with Stories*. Research in Khoisan Studies 25. Cologne: Rüdiger Köppe.

Corson, David, 1985. *The Lexical Bar*. Oxford: Pergamon.

Crippen, James A., & Laura C. Robinson, 2013. In defense of the Lone Wolf: collaboration in language documentation. *Language Documentation and Conservation* 7: 123–135, http://hdl.handle.net/10125/4577, accessed 10 February 2014.

Crystal, David, 2000. *Language Death*. Cambridge: Cambridge University Press.

Cunningham, Denis, David E. Ingram & Kenneth Sumbuk (eds), 2006. *Language Diversity in the Pacific: Endangerment and Survival*. Bristol: Multilingual Matters.

Daubenmier, Judith M., 2008. *The Meskwati and Anthropologists: Action Anthropology Reconsidered*. Lincoln: University of Nebraska Press.

Dawes, Robyn M., 1972. *Fundamentals of Attitude Measurement*. New York: John Wiley & Sons.

Denison, Norman, 1971. Some Observations on Language Variety and Plurilingualism. In Edwin Ardener (ed.), *Social Anthropology and Language*, 157–83. London: Tavistock Publications.

Dentan, Robert K., Kirk Endicott, Alberto G. Gomes & M. Barry Hooker, 1997. *Malaysia and the Original People: A Case Study of the Impact of Development on Indigenous Peoples*. Boston: Allyn & Bacon.

Ding, Hongdi, 2016. *Testing the Competence of First Language(s): A Cross-Generational Study of Ethnic Nuosu in Liangshan, Sichuan*. PhD thesis, University of Hong Kong.

Ding, Picus Sizhi, 2005. Language Modernization of Prinmi: Problems from Promoting Orthography to Language Maintenance. In David Bradley (ed.), *Heritage Maintenance for Endangered Languages in Yunnan, China* (in English and Chinese), 19–26, 67–75. Bundoora: Linguistics Program, La Trobe University.

Dixon, Robert M. W., 1997. *The Rise and Fall of Languages*. Cambridge: Cambridge University Press.

2010. *Basic Linguistic Theory*, volume 1: Methodology. Oxford: Oxford University Press.

Dobrin, Lise, 2008. From linguistic elicitation to eliciting the linguist: lessons in community empowerment. *Language* 84(2): 300–24.

2014. Is Collaboration Really a "Method"? Is "Data" Really the Goal? *Talk Presented at ELAR, School of Oriental and African Studies, University of London, 21 March 2014*.

Dorian, Nancy C., 1977. The problem of the semi-speaker in language death. *International Journal of the Sociology of Language* 12: 23–32.

1978. *Easy Sutherland Gaelic: The Dialect of the Brora, Golspie and Embo Fishing Communities*. Dublin: Dublin Institute of Advanced Studies.

1981. *Language Death: The Life Cycle of a Scottish Gaelic Dialect*. Philadelphia: University of Pennsylvania Press.

(ed.), 1989. *Investigating Obsolescence: Studies in Language Contraction and Death*. Cambridge: Cambridge University Press.

2001. Surprises in Sutherland: Linguistic Variability amidst Social Uniformity. In Paul Newman & Martha Ratliff (eds), *Linguistic Fieldwork*, 133–51. Cambridge: Cambridge University Press.

2010a. The Private and the Public in Language Documentation and Revitalization. In Jose A. Flores Farfán & Fernando F. Ramallo (eds), *New Perspectives on Endangered Languages: Bridging Gaps between Sociolinguistics, Documentation and Language Revitalization*, 29–47. Amsterdam: John Benjamins.

2010b. *Investigating Variation: The Effects of Social Organization and Social Setting*. New York: Oxford University Press.

2011. The Ambiguous Arithmetic of Language Maintenance and Revitalization. In Joshua A. Fishman & Ofelia García (eds), *Handbook of Language and Ethnic Identity: The Success–Failure Continuum in Language and Ethnic Identity Efforts*, volume 2, 461–71. New York: Oxford University Press.

2018. Documentary Fieldwork and Its Web of Responsibilities. In Leanne Hinton, Leena Huss & Gerald Roche (eds), *The Routledge Handbook of Language Revitalization*, 216–24. New York: Routledge.

Dwyer, Arienne M., 2006. Ethics and Practicalities of Cooperative Fieldwork. In Jost Gippert, Nikolaus P. Himmelmann & Ulrike Mosel (eds), *Essentials of Language Documentation*, 31–66. Berlin: Mouton de Gruyter.

Eades, Diana, 2013. *Aboriginal Ways of Using English*. Canberra: Aboriginal Studies Press.

Easton, Catherine, 2007. *Discourses of Orthography Development: Community-Based Practice in Milne Bay (PNG)*. PhD thesis, La Trobe University.

Easton, Catherine, & Diane Wroge, 2012. *Manual for Alphabet Design through Community Interaction for Papua New Guinea Elementary Teacher Trainers*, second edition. Ukarumpa: Summer Institute of Linguistics.

Edwards, John, 1992. Sociopolitical Aspects of Language Maintenance and Loss: Towards a Typology of Minority Language Situations. In Willem Fase, Koen Jaspaert & Sjaak Kroon (eds), *Maintenance and Loss of Minority Languages*, 37–54. Amsterdam: John Benjamins.

Ellen, Roy, 2006. *The Categorical Impulse: Essays in the Anthropology of Classifying Behaviour*. New York: Berghahn Books.

van Engelenhoven, Aone, 2002. Concealment, Maintenance and Renaissance: Language and Ethnicity in the Moluccan Community in the Netherlands. In David Bradley & Maya Bradley (eds), *Language Endangerment and Language Maintenance*, 272–309. London: RoutledgeCurzon.

2003. Language Endangerment in Indonesia; The Incipient Obsolescence and Acute Death of Teun, Nila and Senta (Central and Southwest Maluku). In Mark Janse & Sijmen Tol (eds), *Language Death and Language Maintenance: Theoretical, Practical and Descriptive Approaches*, 49–80. Amsterdam: John Benjamins.

Evans, Nicholas, 2001. The Last Speaker Is Dead – Long Live the Last Speaker! In Paul Newman & Martha Ratliff (eds), *Linguistic Fieldwork*, 250–81. Cambridge: Cambridge University Press.

Ferguson, Charles A., 1959. Diglossia. *Word* 15: 325–40.

1962. The Language Factor in National Development. In Frank A. Rice (ed.), *Study of the Role of Second Language in Africa, Asia and Latin America*, 8–14. Washington, DC: Center for Applied Linguistics.

Fisher, William F., 2011. *Fluid Boundaries: Forming and Transforming Identity in Nepal*. New York: Columbia University Press.

Fishman, Joshua A., 1962. Some Contrasts between Linguistically Homogeneous and Linguistically Heterogeneous Societies. Joshua A. Fishman, Charles A. Ferguson & Jyotirindra Dasgupta (eds) *Language Problems of Developing Nations*, 53–68. New York: Wiley.

1977. Language and Ethnicity. In Howard Giles (ed.), *Language, Ethnicity and Intergroup Relations*, 15–57. Cambridge, MA: Academic Press.

1981. *Never Say Die! A Thousand Years of Yiddish in Jewish Life and Letters*. The Hague: Mouton.

1985. Mother-Tongue Claiming in the United States since 1960: Trends and Correlates. In Joshua A. Fishman (ed.), *The Rise and Fall of the Ethnic Revival: Perspectives on Language and Ethnicity*, 107–94. Berlin: Mouton.

1989. *Language and Ethnicity in Minority Sociolinguistic Perspective*. Bristol: Multilingual Matters.

1991. *Reversing Language Shift: Theoretical and Empirical Foundations of Assistance to Threatened Languages*. Bristol: Multilingual Matters.

(ed.), 2001. *Can Threatened Languages Be Saved? Reversing Language Shift, Revisited: A 21st Century Perspective*. Bristol: Multilingual Matters.

2006. *Do Not Leave Your Language Alone: The Hidden Status Agenda within Corpus Planning in Language Policy*. Mahwah, NJ: Lawrence Erlbaum.

Frawley, William, Kenneth C. Hill & Pamela Munro (eds), 2002. *Making Dictionaries: Preserving Indigenous Languages of the Americas*. Berkeley: University of California Press.

Furer Roverdo, Jean-Jacques, 2005. *Die aktuelle Lage des Romanischen. Eidgenössische Volkszählung 2000*. Neuchâtel: Swiss Federal Statistical Office.

Gardner, Robert C. & Wallace E. Lambert, 1992. *Attitudes and Motivation in Second Language Learning*. Rowley, MA: Newbury House.

Garnier, Roman, Laurent Sagart & Benoît Sagot, 2017. Milk and the Indo-Europeans. In Martine Robbets & Alexander Savelyev (eds), *Language Dispersal Beyond Farming*, 291–311. Amsterdam: John Benjamins.

Garrett, Paul B., 2012. Dying Young: Pidgins, Creoles and Other Contact Languages as Endangered Languages. In Genese M. Sodikoff (ed.), *The Anthropology of Extinction: Essays on Culture and Species Death*, 143–62. Bloomington: University of Indiana Press.

Garrett, Peter, 2010. *Attitudes to Language*. Cambridge: Cambridge University Press.

Georg, Stefan, 2007. *A Descriptive Grammar of Ket, Part I: Introduction, Phonology and Morphology*. Folkestone: Global Oriental.

Gerdts, Donna B. 2010. Beyond Expertise: The Role of the Linguist in Language Revitalization Programs. In Lenore A. Grenoble & Louanna Furbee (eds), *Language Documentation: Practice and Values*, 173–92. Amsterdam: John Benjamins.

Giles, Howard, & Peter F. Powesland, 1975. *Speech Style and Social Evaluation*. Cambridge, MA: Academic Press.

Giles, Howard, Richard Y. Bourhis & Donald M. Taylor, 1977. Towards a Theory of Language in Ethnic Group Relations. In Howard Giles (ed.), *Language, Ethnicity and Intergroup Relations*, 307–48. Cambridge, MA: Academic Press.

Gillon, Carrie, & Nicole Rosen, with Verna Demontigny, 2018. *Nominal Contact in Michif*. Oxford: Oxford University Press.

Gippert, Jost, Nikolaus P. Himmelmann & Ulrike Mosel (eds), 2006. *Essentials of Language Documentation*. Berlin: Mouton de Gruyter.

Gloor, Daniela, Susanne Hohermuth, Hanna Meier & Hans-Peter Maier, 1996. *Fünf Idiome – eine Schriftsprache? Die Frage einer gemeinsamen Schriftsprache im Urteil der romanischen Bevölkerung.* Zürich: Institut Cultur Prospektiv.

Grenoble, Lenore A., 2011. Language Ecology and Endangerment. In Peter K. Austin & Julia Sallabank (eds), *The Cambridge Handbook of Endangered Languages*, 27–44. Cambridge: Cambridge University Press.

Grenoble, Lenore A., & Lindsay J. Whaley, 1998. *Endangered Languages: Current Issues and Future Prospects.* Cambridge: Cambridge University Press. 2006. *Saving Languages: An Introduction to Language Revitalization.* Cambridge: Cambridge University Press.

Gudkynst, William B., & Karen L. Schmidt, 1988. Language and Ethnic Identity: An Overview and Prologue. In William B. Gudkynst (ed.), *Language and Ethnic Identity*, 1–14. Bristol: Multilingual Matters.

Güldemann, Tom, & Rainer Vossen, 2000. Khoisan. In Bernd Heine & Derek Nurse (eds), *African Languages: An Introduction*, 99–122. Cambridge: Cambridge University Press.

Guérin, Valérie, & Sébastien Lacrampe. 2010. Trust me, I am a linguist! Building partnership in the field. *Language Documentation and Conservation* 4: 22–33.

Gumperz, John J., 1982. *Discourse Strategies.* Cambridge: Cambridge University Press.

Gunderson, Lance H., Craig R. Allen & Crawford S. Holling, 2010. *Foundations of Ecological Resilience.* Washington, DC: Island Press.

Hajek, John, 2002. Language Maintenance and Survival in East Timor: All Change Now? Winners and Losers. In David Bradley & Maya Bradley (eds), *Language Endangerment and Language Maintenance*, 182–202. London: RoutledgeCurzon.

Hale, Ken, 1992. On endangered languages and the safeguarding of diversity. *Language* 68(1): 1–3.

Hallett, Holt S., 1890. *A Thousand Miles on an Elephant in the Shan States.* Edinburgh: William Blackwood and Sons.

Hamans, Camiel, 2008. The Charter of Regional and Minority Languages as a Political Factor: Some Facts and Data. *Paper presented at Congrès International des Linguistes XVIII, Seoul, Korea, 21–26 July 2008.*

Harmon, David, & Jonathan Loh, 2010. The Index of Linguistic Diversity: a new quantitative measure of trends in the status of the world's languages. *Language Documentation and Conservation* 4: 97–151.

Harrell, Stevan, 2001. *Ways of Being Ethnic in Southwest China.* Seattle, WA: University of Washington Press.

Haugen, Einar, 1966. *Language Conflict and Language Planning: The Case of Modern Norwegian.* Cambridge, MA: Harvard University Press. 1972. *The Ecology of Language.* Stanford, CA: Stanford University Press.

Hermes, Mary, Phil Cash, Keola Donaghy, Joseph Erb & Susan Penfield, 2016. New Domains for Indigenous Language Acquisition and Use in the USA and Canada. In Serafín M. Coronel-Molina & Teresa L. McCarty (eds), *Indigenous Language Revitalization in the Americas*, 269–91. New York: Routledge.

Hildebrandt, Kristine A., Carmen Jany & Wilson Silva (eds), 2017. *Documenting Variation in Endangered Languages*. Language Documentation and Conservation Special Publications 13. Honolulu: University of Hawai'i Press.

Hill, Kenneth C., 2002. On Publishing the Hopi Dictionary. In William Frawley, Kenneth C. Hill & Pamela Munro (eds), *Making Dictionaries: Preserving Indigenous Languages of the Americas*, 299–311. Berkeley: University of California Press.

Hinton, Leanne, 1994. *Flutes of Fire: Essays on California Indian languages*. Berkeley, CA: Heyday Books.

2001a. Language Planning. In Leanne Hinton & Ken Hale (eds), *The Green Book of Language Revitalization in Practice*, 51–9. Cambridge, MA: Academic Press.

2001b. The Master–Apprentice Language Learning Program. In Leanne Hinton & Ken Hale (eds), *The Green Book of Language Revitalization in Practice*, 217–26. Cambridge, MA: Academic Press.

2002. Commentary: internal and external advocacy. *Journal of Linguistic Anthropology* 12(2): 150–6.

2011. Revitalization of Endangered Languages. In Peter K. Austin & Julia Sallabank (eds), *The Cambridge Handbook of Endangered Languages*, 291–311. Cambridge: Cambridge University Press.

Hinton, Leanne, & Ken Hale (eds), 2001. *The Green Book of Language Revitalization in Practice*. Cambridge, MA: Academic Press.

Hinton, Leanne, Leena Huss & Gerald Roche (eds), 2018. *The Routledge Handbook of Language Revitalization*. New York: Routledge.

Hinton, Leanne, Margaret Florey, Suzanne Gessner & Jacob Manatowa-Bailey, 2018. The Master–Apprentice Language Learning Program. In Leanne Hinton, Leena Huss & Gerald Roche (eds), *The Routledge Handbook of Language Revitalization*, 127–36. New York: Routledge.

Hinton, Leanne, with Matt Vera & Nancy Steele, 2002. *How to Keep Your Language Alive: A Commonsense Approach to One-on-One Language Learning*. Berkeley, CA: Heyday Books.

Hobson, John, Kevin Lowe, Susan Poetsch & Michael Walsh (eds), 2010. *Reawakening Languages: Theory and Practice in the Revitalization of Australia's Indigenous Languages*. Sydney: University of Sydney Press.

Hornberger, Nancy H. (ed.), 2008. *Can Schools Save Indigenous Languages? Policy and Practice on Four Continents*. New York: Palgrave Macmillan.

Hyltenstam, Kenneth, & Åke Viberg (eds), 1993. *Progression and Regression in Language*. Cambridge: Cambridge University Press.

Hymes, Dell, 1964. Introduction: towards ethnographies of communication. *American Anthropologist* 66(6) part 2: 1–35.

1974. *Foundations of Sociolinguistics: An Ethnographic Approach*. Philadelphia: University of Pennsylvania Press.

Johnson, Pat, Howard Giles & Richard Y. Bourhis, 1983. The viability of ethnic vitality: a reply. *Journal of Multilingual and Multicultural Development* 4(4): 255–69.

Jones, Mari C., & Sarah Ogilvie (eds), 2013. *Keeping Languages Alive: Documentation, Pedagogy and Revitalization.* Cambridge: Cambridge University Press.

Katz, Daniel, 1960. The functional approach to the study of attitudes. *Public Opinion Quarterly* 24(2): 163–204.

Kayambazinthu, Edrinnie, 1995. *Patterns of Language Use in Malawi: A Sociolinguistic Investigation into Selected Areas.* PhD thesis, La Trobe University.

Kibrik, Aleksandr E., 1991. The Problem of Endangered Languages in the USSR. In Robert H. Robins & Eugenius M. Uhlenbeck (eds), *Endangered Languages,* 257–73. Oxford: Berg.

King, Jeanette, 2001. Te Kohanga Reo: Maori Language Revitalization. In Leanne Hinton & Ken Hale (eds), *The Green Book of Language Revitalization in Practice,* 119–28. Cambridge, MA: Academic Press.

Kloss, Heinz, 1968. Notes Concerning a Language-Nation Typology. In Joshua A. Fishman, Charles A. Ferguson & Jyotirindra Dasgupta (eds), *Language Problems of Developing Nations,* 69–85. New York: Wiley.

  1969. *Research Possibilities on Group Bilingualism.* Québec: International Center for Research on Bilingualism.

Kotorova, Elizveta G., & Andrey V. Nefedov, 2015. *Comprehensive Dictionary of Ket,* two volumes. Munich: Lincom Europa.

Krauss, Michael E., 1992. The world's languages in crisis. *Language* 68(1): 4–10.

  2000. Preliminary Suggestions for Classification and Terminology for Degrees of Language Endangerment. *Paper presented at the Colloquium Language Endangerment, Research and Documentation – Setting Priorities for the 21st century, Bad Godesberg, Germany, 12–17 February 2000.*

  2007a. Classification and Terminology for Degrees of Language Endangerment. In Matthias Brenzinger (ed.), *Language Diversity Endangered,* 1–8. Berlin: Mouton de Gruyter.

  2007b. Keynote – Mass Language Extinction and Documentation: The Race against Time. In Osahito Miyaoka, Osamu Sakiyama & Michael E. Krauss (eds), *The Vanishing Languages of the Pacific Rim,* 1–24. Oxford: Oxford University Press.

Krigonogov, Viktor P. 2016. Ethnic processes among Kets at the beginning of the XXIst century. *Tomsk State University Journal of History* 6(44): 152–61 (in Russian).

Kulick, Don, 1997. *Language Shift and Social Reproduction: Socialization, Self and Syncretism in a Papua New Guinea Village.* Cambridge: Cambridge University Press.

Labov, William, 1966. *The Social Stratification of English in New York City.* Washington, DC: Center for Applied Linguistics.

1972. *Sociolinguistic Patterns*. Philadelphia: University of Pennsylvania Press.

2001. *Principles of Linguistic Change*, volume 2: Social Factors. Oxford: Blackwell.

Ladefoged, Peter, 1992. Another view of endangered languages. *Language* 68(4): 809–11.

Ladefoged, Peter, with Keith Johnson, 2015. *A Course in Phonetics*, seventh edition. Boston, MA: Cengage.

Lambert, Richard D., & Barbara F. Freed (eds), 1982. *The Loss of Language Skills*. Rowley, MA: NewburyHouse.

Lambert, Wallace E., & G. Richard Tucker, 1969. *Bilingual Education of Children: The St Lambert Experiment*. Rowley, MA: Newbury House.

Lee, Nala Huiying, & John van Way, 2016. Assessing levels of endangerment in the Catalogue of Endangered Languages (ELCat) using the Language Endangerment Index (LEI). *Language in Society* 45: 271–92.

Lenin, Vladimir I., 1961. What Is to Be Done? In *Collected Works*, volume 5, 347–530. Moscow: Progress Publishers, translation of 1902 Russian edition.

Lewis, M. Paul, 2008. Evaluating Endangerment: Proposed Metadata and Implementation. In Kendall A. King, Natalie Schilling-Estes, Lyn Fogle, Jia Jackie Lou & Barbara Southup (eds), *Sustaining Linguistic Diversity: Endangered and Minority Languages and Language Varieties*, 35–49. Washington, DC: Georgetown University Press.

2011. Introduction: The Sustainable Use Model (SUM) for language development. In *American Association for Applied Linguistics, Chicago, 26 March 2011*.

Lewis, M. Paul, & Gary F. Simons, 2010. Assessing endangerment: expanding Fishman's GIDS. *Revue Roumaine de Linguistique* LV(2): 103–20.

(eds), 2014. *Ethnologue, Languages of the World*, seventeenth edition. Dallas, TX: SIL International.

(eds), 2015a. *Ethnologue, Languages of the World*, eighteenth edition. Dallas, TX: SIL International.

2015b. *Sustaining Language Use: Perspectives on Community-Based Language Development*. Dallas, TX: SIL International.

Lewis, M. Paul, Gary F. Simons & Charles D. Fennig (eds), 2016. *Ethnologue*, nineteenth edition. Dallas, TX: SIL International.

Linguistic Society of America, 2009. LSA Ethics Statement, www.linguisticsociety.org/about/who-we-are/committees/ethics-committee, accessed 20 March 2014.

Llamas, Carmen, & Dominic Watt (eds), 2010. *Language and Identities*. Edinburgh: Edinburgh University Press.

Lo Bianco, Joseph, 1987. *National Policy on Languages*. Canberra: Australian Government Publishing Service.

Luo Yan, 2013. *Shilin Sani Spoken Language 400 Sentences* (in Chinese and Sani, with CD and DVD). Beijing: Nationalities Press.

Lüpke, Friedrike, 2011. Orthography Development. In Peter K. Austin & Julia Sallabank (eds), *The Cambridge Handbook of Endangered Languages*, 312–36. Cambridge: Cambridge University Press.

Lynd, Robert S., & Helen M. Lynd, 1929. *Middletown*. New York: Harcourt Brace.

McCarty, Teresa L., 2013. *Language Planning and Policy in Native America: History, Theory, Praxis*. Bristol: Multilingual Matters.

Macri, Martha J., 2010. Language Documentation, Whose Ethics? In Lenore A. Grenoble & Louanna Furbee (eds), *Language Documentation: Practice and Values*, 37–47. Amsterdam: John Benjamins.

Marmion, Doug, Kazuko Obata & Jakelin Troy, 2014. *Community, Identity and Wellbeing: The Report of the Second National Indigenous Languages Survey*. Canberra: Australian Institute of Aboriginal and Torres Strait Islander Studies.

Martí, Fèlix, Paul Ortega, Itziar Idiazabal et al. (eds), 2005. *Words and Worlds: World Languages Review*. Bristol: Multilingual Matters.

Matisoff, James A., 1991. Endangered Languages of Mainland Southeast Asia. In Robert H. Robins & Eugenius M. Uhlenbeck (eds), *Endangered Languages*, 189–228. Oxford: Berg.

Matras, Yaron, 2005. Language contact, language endangerment and the role of the 'salvation linguist'. *Language Documentation and Description* 3: 225–51.

Maung Maung Tun, 2014. *A Sociolinguistic Survey of Selected Bisoid Varieties: Pyen, Laomian and Laopin*. MA thesis, Payap University.

Mayer, Mercer, 1969. *Frog, Where Are You?* New York: Dial Books.

Milroy, Lesley, 1980. *Language and Social Networks*. Oxford: Basil Blackwell.

Moretti, Bruno, Elena Maria Pandolfi & Matteo Casoni (eds), 2011. *Vitaità de una Lingua Minoritaria: Aspetti e proposte metodologiche/Vitality of a Minority Language: Aspects and Methodological Issues*. Ticino: Osservatorio linguistico della Svizzera italiana.

Moseley, Christopher (ed.), 2007. *Encyclopedia of the World's Endangered Languages*. Abingdon: Routledge.

Moser, Rosmarie, 1992. *Sociolinguistic Dynamics of Sango*. MA thesis, La Trobe University.

Moussay, Gérard, 1995. *Dictionnaire Minangkabau–Indonesien–Français*, two volumes. Paris: l'Harmattan.

Murdock, George P., 1949. *Social Structure*. New York: Macmillan.

Nahir, Moshe, 1988. Language Planning and Language Acquisition: The "Great Leap" in the Hebrew Revival. In Christina B. Paulston (ed.), *International Handbook of Bilingualism and Bilingual Education*, 275–95. New York: Greenwood Press.

Narayan, Deepa, with Raj Patel, Kai Schafft, Anne Rademacher & Sarah Koch-Schulte, 2000. *Voices of the Poor: Can Anyone Hear Us?* New York: Oxford University Press for the World Bank.

Nettle, Daniel, 1999. *Linguistic Diversity*. Oxford: Oxford University Press.

Neustupný, Jiří V., & Jiří Nevkapil, 2003. Language management in the Czech Republic. *Current Issues in Language Planning* 4(3–4): 181–366.

Ng, Bee Chin, & Gillian Wigglesworth, 2007. *Bilingualism: An Advanced Resource Book*. New York: Routledge.

Noels, Kimberly A., Hali Kil & Yang Fang, 2014. Ethnolinguistic orientation and language variation: measuring and archiving ethnolinguistic vitality, attitudes and identity. *Language and Linguistics Compass* 8(11): 618–28.

Norman, Arthur M. Z., 1955. Bamboo English: the Japanese influence on American speech. *American Speech* 30(1): 44–8.

O'Leary, Clare F., 1994. The role of recorded text tests in intelligibility assessment and language program decisions. *Notes on Literature in Use and Language Programs*, special issue 3: 48–72.

O'Rourke, Mary J., 2000. *Relatively Nominal: Relativisation in Kathmandu Nepal Bhasa (Newari)*. MA thesis, La Trobe University.

Okell, John A., 1967. Nissaya Burmese. *Journal of the Burma Research Society* 50(1): 95–123.

Okell, John A., & Anna J. Allott, 2001. *Burmese/Myanmar Dictionary of Grammatical Forms*. London: Curzon.

Olthuis, Maria-Liisa, Suvi Kivelä & Tove Skutnabb-Kangas, 2013. *Revitalizing Indigenous Languages: How to Recreate a Lost Generation*. Bristol: Multilingual Matters.

Ong, Walter, 1982. *Orality and Literacy: The Technologizing of the Word*. London: Methuen.

   2002. *Orality and Literacy: The Technologizing of the Word*, second edition. New York: Routledge.

Ostler, Nicholas, 2016. *Passwords to Paradise: How Languages Have Re-invented World Religions*. London: Bloomsbury Press.

Ostler, Nicholas, & Brenda W. Lintinger (eds), 2015. *The Music of Endangered Languages*. In *FEL XIX – Nola: Proceedings of the 19th Fel Conference 19 – Proceedings of the Foundation for Endangered Languages*. Hungerford: Foundation for Endangered Languages.

Palosaari, Naomi, & Lyle Campbell, 2011. Structural Aspects of Language Endangerment. In Peter K. Austin & Julia Sallabank (eds), *The Cambridge Handbook of Endangered Languages*, 100–19. Cambridge: Cambridge University Press.

Pelkey, Jamin, 2011. *Dialectology as Dialectic: Interpreting Phula Variation*. Berlin: Mouton de Gruyter.

Perley, Bernard C., 2011. *Defying Maliseet Language Death*. Lincoln: University of Nebraska Press.

   2012a. Zombie linguistics: experts, endangered languages and the curse of undead voices. *Anthropological Forum* 22(2): 133–9.

   2012b. Last Words, Final Thoughts: Collateral Extinctions in Maliseet Language Death. In Genese M. Sodikoff (ed.), *The Anthropology of*

Extinction: Essays on Culture and Species Death, 127–42. Bloomington: University of Indiana Press.

Person, Kirk R., 2005. Language revitalization or dying gasp? Language preservation efforts among the Bisu of Northern Thailand. *International Journal of the Sociology of Language* 173: 117–41.

2018. Reflections on Two Decades of Bisu Language Revitalization. In Suwilai Premsrirat & David Hirsch (eds), *Language Revitalization: Insights from Thailand*, 155–76. Bern: Peter Lang.

Phinney, Jean S., 1992. The Multigroup Ethnic Identity Measure: a new scale for use with diverse groups. *Journal of Adolescent Research* 7(2): 156–76.

Phinney, Jean S., & Anthony D. Ong, 2007. Conceptualization and measurement of ethnic identity: current status and future directions. *Journal of Counseling Psychology* 54(3): 27–281.

de Pina-Cabral, João, 2002. *Between China and Europe: Person, Culture and Emotion in Macao*. London School of Economics Monographs on Social Anthropology 74. New York: Continuum.

Pinharanda-Nunes, Mário, 2011. *Estudio da Expressão Morfo-Sintáctica das Categorias de Tempo, Modo e Aspecto em Maquista*. PhD thesis, University of Macao.

2012a. Traces of Superstrate Verb Inflection in Makista and Other Asian-Portuguese Creoles. In Hugo C. Cardoso, Alan N. Baxter & Mário Pinharanda-Nunes (eds), *Ibero-Asian Creoles: Comparative Perspectives*, 290–326. Amsterdam: John Benjamins.

2012b. Herança cultural e linguistica dos macaenses: Considerações em torno das suas origens, evolução e continuidade. *Fragmentum* 35: 17–25.

2014. Socio-historical Factors Involved in the Changes of the Creole Matrix of Makista. In Katrine K. Wong & C. X. George Wei (eds), *Macao – Cultural Interpretation and Literary Representations*, 25–41. New York: Routledge.

Podesva, Robert J., & Devyani Sharma (eds), 2013. *Research Methods in Linguistics*. Cambridge: Cambridge University Press.

Posner, Rebecca, 1996. *The Romance Languages*. Cambridge: Cambridge University Press.

Preston, Dennis R. (ed.), 1999. *Handbook of Perceptual Dialectology*, volume 1. Amsterdam: John Benjamins.

2011. Methods in (applied) folk linguistics: getting into the mind of the folk. *AILA Review* 24: 15–39.

Preston, Dennis R., & Daniel Long (eds), 2002. *Handbook of Perceptual Dialectology*, volume 2. Amsterdam: John Benjamins.

Prins, Franz E., 1999. Dissecting diviners: on positivism, trance-formations, and the unreliable informant. *Southern African Humanities* 20(1): 43–62.

Pro Idioms Surselva, 2016. Resoluziun davart il postulat "Allegra" da cussegliera naziunala Silva Semadeni, www.proidioms.ch, accessed 14 March 2019.

Purnell, Herbert C., 1987. Developing practical orthographies for the Iu Mien (Yao), 1932–1986: a case study. *Linguistics of the Tibeto-Burman Area* 10(2): 128–41.

Reed-Danahy, Deborah E., 1997. *Auto/Ethnography: Rewriting the Self and the Social*. Oxford: Berg.

Rice, Keren D., 2009. Must There Be Two Solitudes? Language Activists and Linguists Working Together. In Jon A. Reyhner & Louise Lockard (eds), *Indigenous Language Revitalization: Encouragement, Guidance and Lessons Learned*, 37–59. Flagstaff: Northern Arizona University.

2011. Documentary linguistics and community relations. *Language Documentation and Conservation* 5: 187–207.

Rickford, John R., & Penelope Eckert, 2001. Introduction. In Penelope Eckert & John H. Rickford (eds), *Style and Sociolinguistic Variation*, 1–18. Cambridge: Cambridge University Press.

Robben, Antonius C. G. M., & Jeffrey A. Sluka (eds), 2012. *Ethnographic Fieldwork: An Anthropological Reader*, second edition. Chichester: Wiley-Blackwell.

Robins, Robert H., & Uhlenbeck, Eugenius M. (eds), 1991. *Endangered Languages*, 257–73. Oxford: Berg.

Romaine, Suzanne, 2009. Biodiversity, Linguistic Diversity and Poverty: Some Global Patterns and Missing Links. In Wayne Harbert (ed.), *Language and Poverty*, 127–46. Bristol: Multilingual Matters.

Rubin, Joan, & Björn H. Jernudd, 1971. *Can Language Be Planned? Sociolinguistic Theory and Practice for Developing Nations*. Honolulu: University Press of Hawaii.

Ryan, Ellen B., Miles Hewstone & Howard Giles, 1984. Language and Intergroup Attitudes. In J. Richard Eisler (ed.), *Attitudinal Judgment*, 135–58. New York: Springer.

Russell, Sue, 2001. *Language Shift and Maintenance; A Sociocultural Approach*. PhD thesis, La Trobe University.

Sachs, Geoffrey, 2008. *Common Wealth: Economics for a Crowded Planet*. London: Allen Lane.

Sahlins, Marshall, 1995. *"How Natives Think": About Captain Cook, for Example*. Chicago: University of Chicago Press.

Sallabank, Julia, 2002. Writing in an unwritten language: the case of Guernsey French. *Reading Working Papers in Linguistics* 6: 217–44.

2011. Language Policy for Endangered Languages. In Peter K. Austin & Julia Sallabank (eds), *The Cambridge Handbook of Endangered Languages*, 277–90. Cambridge: Cambridge University Press.

dos Santos Ferreira, José, 1996. *Papiaçâm di Macau*, two volumes. Macao: Fundação Macau.

Schilling, Natalie, 2013. *Sociolinguistic Fieldwork*. Cambridge: Cambridge University Press.

Schmid, Heinrich, 1982. *Richtlinien für die Gestaltung einer gesamtbündnerromanischen Schriftsprache*. Chur: Lia Rumantscha.

Schmid, Monika S., (2011) *Language Attrition*. Cambridge: Cambridge University Press.

Schmidt, Annette, 1985. *Young People's Dyirbal: An Example of Language Death from Australia*. Cambridge: Cambridge University Press.

1990. *The Loss of Australia's Aboriginal Language Heritage*. Canberra: Aboriginal Studies Press.

Schumpeter, Joseph A., 1976. *Capitalism, Socialism and Democracy*, fifth edition. Crows Nest: George Allen & Unwin.

Scott, James C., 2009. *The Art of Not Being Governed: An Anarchist History of Upland Southeast Asia*. New Haven, CT: Yale University Press.

Scott, James G., & John P. Hardiman, 1900. *Gazetteer of Upper Burma and the Shan States*. Rangoon: Superintendent of Government Printing.

Selfart, Frank, 2006. Orthography Development. In Jost Gippert, Nikolaus P. Himmelmann & Ulrike Mosel (eds), *Essentials of Language Documentation*, 275–300. Berlin: Mouton de Gruyter.

Seliger, Herbert W., & Robert M. Vago (eds), 1991. *First Language Attrition*. Cambridge: Cambridge University Press.

Senna Fernandes, Miguel, & Alan N. Baxter, 2001. *Maquista Chapado: Vocabulário e expressões do crioulo português de Macau*. Macau: Instituto Internacional de Macau.

2004. *Maquista Chapado: Vocabulary and Expressions of Macao's Portuguese Creole*. Macau: University of Macau.

Shah, Sheena, & Matthias Brenzinger, 2016. *Ouma Geelmeid ke kx'u ǀxaǀxa Nǀuu ◊ Ouma Geelmeid gee Nǀuu ◊ Ouma Geelmeid teaches Nǀuu*. Cape Town: CALDi, University of Cape Town, https://open.uct.ac.za/handle/11427/17432, accessed 14 March 2019.

2017. Writing for Speaking: The Nǀuu Orthography. In Mari Jones & Damien Mooney (eds), *Creating Orthographies for Endangered Languages*, 109–25. Cambridge: Cambridge University Press.

Simons, Gary F., & Charles D. Fennig (eds), 2017. *Ethnologue, Languages of the World*, twentieth edition. Dallas, TX: SIL International.

(eds), 2018. *Ethnologue, Languages of the World*, twenty-first edition. Dallas, TX: SIL International.

Simpson, Jane, Jo Caffery & Patrick McConvell. 2009. *Gaps in Australia's Indigenous Language Policy: Dismantling Bilingual Education in the Northern Territory*. AIATSIS Discussion Paper 24. Canberra: Australian Institute of Aboriginal and Torres Strait Islander Studies.

Smolicz, Jerzy J., 1981. Core values and cultural identity. *Ethnic and Racial Studies* 4: 75–90.

Spiro, Melford E., 1977. *Kinship and Marriage in Burma: A Cultural and Psychodynamic Approach*. Berkeley: University of California Press.

Spolsky, Bernard, & Robert L. Cooper, 1991. *The Languages of Jerusalem*. Oxford: Oxford University Press.

Stanford, James N., & Dennis R. Preston (eds), 2009. *Variation in Indigenous Minority Languages*. Amsterdam: John Benjamins.

Stapp, Darby C. (ed.), 2012. *Action Anthropology and Sol Tax in 2012: The Final Word?* Richland, WA: Northwest Anthropology.

Stary, Giovanni, 2003. Sibe: An Endangered Language. In Mark Janse & Sijmen Tol (eds), *Language Death and Language Maintenance: Theoretical, Practical and Descriptive Approaches*, 81–8. Amsterdam: John Benjamins.

Stebbins, Tonya, 2003. *Fighting Language Endangerment: Community Directed Research on Sm'algyax (Coast Tsimshian)*, A2–026. Tokyo: Endangered Languages of the Pacific Rim.

Strehlow, Theodors G. H., 1947. *Aranda Traditions*. Melbourne: University of Melbourne Press.

1971. *Songs of Central Australia*. Sydney: Angus & Robertson.

Suastra, I. Made, 1995. *Speech Levels and Social Change: A Sociolinguistic Study in the Urban Balinese Setting*. PhD thesis, La Trobe University.

Sun Hongkai & Huang Xing, 2005. Language Diversity in China. In Fèlix Martí, Paul Ortega, Itziar Idiazabal et al. (eds), *Words and Worlds: World Languages Review*, 235–7. Bristol: Multilingual Matters.

Swadesh, Morris, 1948. Sociologic notes on obsolescent languages. *International Journal of American Linguistics* 14(4): 226–35.

Svensén, Bo, 2009. *Handbook of Lexicography*. Cambridge: Cambridge University Press.

Tajfel, Henri, 1978. *Differentiation between Social Groups: Studies in the Social Psychology of Intergroup Relations*. Cambridge, MA: Academic Press.

1981. *Human Groups and Social Categories: Studies in Social Psychology*. Cambridge: Cambridge University Press.

Tamsang, Kamal Prasad, 1980. *The Lepcha–English Encyclopedic Dictionary*. Kalimpong: Shiva Mani Pradhan Mani Press.

Tessarolo, Mariselda, & Gian Peder Pedrotti, 2009. Languages in the canton of Grisons. *International Journal of the Sociology of Language* 199: 63–88.

Thamrin, Temmy, 2015. *Minangkabau Language Use and Attitudes*. PhD thesis, La Trobe University.

Thieberger, Nicholas, 2002. Extinction in Whose Terms? Which Parts of a Language Constitute a Target for Language Maintenance Programmes? In David Bradley & Maya Bradley (eds), *Language Endangerment and Language Maintenance*, 310–28. London: RoutledgeCurzon.

Thomason, Sarah Grey, & Terrence Kaufman, 1988. *Language Contact, Creolization and Genetic Linguistics*. Berkeley: University of California Press.

Tierney, Patrick, 2000. *Darkness in El Dorado: How Scientists and Journalists Devastated the Amazon*. New York: Norton.

Timonima, Ljudmila G., 2004. On Distinguishing Loanwords from the Original Proto-Yeniseic Lexicon. In Edward J. Vajda (ed.), *Languages and Prehistory of Central Siberia*, 135–42. Amsterdam: John Benjamins.

Todd, Brett. 2015. *Linguistic Reparative Justice for Indigenous Peoples: The Case of Language Policy in Colombia*. PhD thesis, University of New South Wales.

Tollefson, James W. (ed.), 1991. *Planning Language, Planning Inequality: Language Policy in the Community*. Harlow: Longman.

(ed.), 1995. *Power and Inequality in Language Education*. Cambridge: Cambridge University Press.

Traill, Anthony, 1996. !Khwa-Ka Hhouiten Hhouiten "The Rush of the Storm": The Linguistic Death of the |Xam. In Pippa Skotnes (ed.), *Miscast: Negotiating the Presence of the Bushmen*, 161–83. Cape Town: University of Cape Town Press.

1999. *Extinct: South African Khoisan Languages*. CD and booklet. Johannesburg: University of the Witwatersrand.

Triandis, Harry C., 1971. *Attitude and Attitude Change*. New York: John Wiley & Sons.

Trudgill, Peter, 2002. *Sociolinguistic Variation and Change*. Washington, DC: Georgetown University Press.

Tsunoda, Tasaku, 2006. *Language Endangerment and Language Revitalization: An Introduction*. Berlin: Mouton de Gruyter.

UNESCO, 2003a. *Language Vitality and Endangerment*. Document prepared for the Intangible Cultural Heritage Unit of UNESCO by the Ad Hoc Expert Group on Endangered Languages, Akira Yamamoto & Matthias Brenzinger, co-chairs. Adopted at the International Expert Meeting on the UNESCO Programme Safeguarding Languages, 12 March 2003.

2003b. *Education in a Multilingual World*. Paris: UNESCO.

2009. *Atlas of Languages in Danger*. Paris: UNESCO.

2015. *Consultative Expert Meeting: Revision of UNESCO Language Vitality Index*. Paris: UNESCO Knowledge and Societies Division, Communication and Information Sector.

Unger, John, 2005. Cherokee Language and Literacy. In David Bradley (ed.), *Heritage Maintenance for Endangered Languages in Yunnan, China* (in English and Chinese), 37–46, 85–93. Bundoora: La Trobe University.

Unseth, Peter, 2008. The sociolinguistics of script choice: an introduction. *International Journal of the Sociology of Language* (192): 1–4.

Vajda, Edward J., 2001. *Yeniseian Peoples and Languages: A History of Yeniseian Studies with an Annotated Bibliography and a Source Guide*. Richmond: Curzon.

2004. *Ket*. Munich: Lincom Europa.

Valdes, Guadalupe, & Richard A. Figueroa, 1994. *Bilingualism and Testing: A Special Case of Bias*. Norwood, NJ: Ablex.

Vovin, Alexander, 2000. Did the Xiongnu speak a Yeniseian language? *Central Asian Journal* 44(1): 87–104.

Vovin, Alexander, Edward J. Vajda & Étienne de la Vaissière, 2016. Who were the Kjet and what language did they speak? *Journal Asiatique* 304(1): 125–44.

de Vries, John, 1992. Language Maintenance and Shift: Problems of Measurement. In Willem Fase, Koen Jaspaert & Sjaak Kroon (eds), *Maintenance and Loss of Minority Languages*, 211–22. Amsterdam: John Benjamins.

Walker, Anthony R., 2003. *Merit and the Millennium: Routine and Crisis in the Ritual Lives of the Lahu People.* New Delhi: Hindustan Publishing.

Walker, Brian, & David Salt, 2006. *Resilience Thinking: Sustaining Ecosystems and People in a Changing World.* Washington, DC: Island Press.

2012. *Resilience Practice: Building Capacity to Absorb Disturbance and Maintain Function.* Washington, DC: Island Press.

Walsh, Michael, 2009. The Rise and Fall of GIDS in Accounts of Language Endangerment. In Hakim Elnazarov & Nicholas Ostler (eds), *Endangered Languages and History. Proceedings of the Thirteenth FEL Conference, 24–26 September 2009, Khorog, Tajikistan*, 134–41. Bath: Foundation for Endangered Languages.

2010. Why Language Revitalization Sometimes Works. In John Hobson, Kevin Lowe, Susan Poetsch & Michael Walsh (eds), *Re-awakening Languages: Theory and Practice in the Revitalization of Australia's Indigenous Languages*, 22–36. Sydney: University of Sydney Press.

2018. "Language Is Like Food. . ." Links between Language Revitalization and Health and Well-Being. In Leanne Hinton, Leena Huss & Gerald Roche (eds), *The Routledge Handbook of Language Revitalization*, 5–12. New York: Routledge.

Weinreich, Uriel, 1951. *Languages in Contact: French, German and Romansch in Twentieth-Century Switzerland.* PhD thesis, Columbia University. Published in 2011 with an introduction by Ronald I. Kim & William Labov. Amsterdam: John Benjamins.

1953. *Languages in Contact: Findings and Problems.* New York: Linguistic Circle of New York.

Werner, Heinrich, 1997. *Das Jugische (Sym-Kettische).* Wiesbaden: Otto Harrassowitz.

Whorf, Benjamin L. 1956. *Language, Thought and Reality: Selected Writings of Benjamin Lee Whorf.* Cambridge, MA: MIT Press.

Wild, Ron A., 1974. *Bradstow: A Study of Status, Class and Power in a Small Australian Town.* Sydney: Angus & Robertson.

Winnington, Alan, 1959. *The Slaves of the Cool Mountains.* London: Lawrence & Wishart.

Wolfensohn, James D., with Jill Margo, 2010. *A Global Life: My Journey among Rich and Poor, from Sydney to Wall Street to the World Bank.* New York: PublicAffairs.

World Conference on Linguistic Rights, 1996. *Universal Declaration of Linguistic Rights*, Barcelona, 6–9 June 1996, https://unesdoc.unesco.org/images/0010/001042/1042673.pdf, accessed 14 March 2019.

Wurm, Stephen A., 1991. Language Death and Disappearance: Causes and Circumstances. In Robert H. Robins & Eugenius M. Uhlenbeck (eds), *Endangered Languages*, 1–18. Oxford: Berg.

(ed.), 1996. *Atlas of the World's Languages in Danger of Disappearing.* Paris: UNESCO.

1998. Methods of Language Maintenance and Revival, with Selected Cases of Language Endangerment in the World. In Kazuto Matsumura (ed.), *Studies in Endangered Languages: Papers from the International Symposium on Endangered Languages, Tokyo, 18–20 November 1995*, 191–211. Tokyo: Hituzi Syobo.

(ed.), 2001. *Atlas of the World's Languages in Danger of Disappearing*, second edition, revised and expanded. Paris: UNESCO.

2002. Strategies for Language Maintenance and Revival. In David Bradley & Maya Bradley (eds), *Language Endangerment and Language Maintenance*, 11–23. London: RoutledgeCurzon.

Wurm, Stephen A., Benjamin K. T'sou & David Bradley (eds), 1987/1991. *Language Atlas of China*. Hong Kong: Longmans; Beijing: Chinese Academy of Social Sciences (in Chinese), two fascicles.

Wurm, Stephen A., Peter Mühlhäusler & Darrell Tryon (eds), 1996. *Atlas of Languages of Intercultural Communication in the Pacific, Asia and the Americas*. Berlin: Mouton de Gruyter.

Wurm, Stephen A., & Shiro Hattori (eds), 1981/1983. *Language Atlas – Pacific Area*. Canberra: Pacific Linguistics.

Wyman, Leisy Thornton, 2013. *Youth Culture, Language Endangerment and Linguistic Survivance*. Bristol: Multilingual Matters.

Xu Shixuan, 2001. *The Bisu Language,* translated by Cecilia Brassett. Munich: Lincom Europa.

2005. Survey of the current situation of Laomian and Laopin in China. *International Journal of the Sociology of Language* 173: 99–115.

Xu Xianming (ed.), 2007. *Records and Transmission of Ethnic Groups: Second Symposium on Heritage Maintenance for Endangered Languages in Yunnan, China* (in Chinese). Bundoora: La Trobe University.

Yamamoto, Akira, 1994. When a Language Dies, Does a Culture Die, Too? *University of Arizona 1994 Distinguished Lecturer/Multicultural Series and Special Summer Speaker on Native American Bilingual Multicultural Education (in conjunction with the 15th Annual American Indian Language Development Institute), University of Arizona, Tucson, Arizona, 21 June 1994.*

1996. Endangered languages data summary. *Kansas Working Papers in Linguistics* 21: 159–229.

Yamane, Linda, 2001. New Life for a Lost Language. In Leanne Hinton & Ken Hale (eds), *The Green Book of Language Revitalization in Practice*, 429–32. Cambridge, MA: Academic Press.

Yang, Cathryn, 2009. Nisu dialect geography. *Summer Institute of Linguistics Electronic Survey Reports* 7.

2010. *Lalo Regional Varieties: Phylogeny, Dialectometry and Sociolinguistics*. PhD thesis, La Trobe University.

Yuan Yichuan, 2005. *Attitude and Motivation of English Learning of Ethnic Minority Students in China*. PhD thesis, La Trobe University.

Zepeda, Ofelia, 2008. *Where Clouds Are Formed*. Tucson: University of Arizona Press.

Index